New Perspectives in History

America and the Origins of World War II, 1933–1941

Edited by

ARNOLD A. OFFNER
Boston University

Houghton Mifflin Company • **Boston**

New York • *Atlanta* • *Geneva, Illinois* • *Dallas* • *Palo Alto*

Printed in the U.S.A.

Library of Congress Catalog Card Number: 72-130655

ISBN: 0-395-11240-0

Contents

Introduction

For thirty years scholars (and politicians and diplomats) have sought to explain how and why the United States became involved in the Second World War in 1941. For a variety of reasons the "debate" during the first decade and a half tended to be highly partisan and frequently acrimonious. Many of the first people to write about American entry into the war had reached political maturity during the 1920's and 1930's and brought strong personal as well as intellectual predispositions to assessments of the foreign and domestic policies of the New Deal administration of Franklin D. Roosevelt. In many cases, people's attitudes toward Roosevelt's domestic policies shaped their responses to his foreign policies. Later, many people who had accepted American entry into the war as inevitable, if undesirable, became disappointed with the political results of the war and grew upset over the intensifying Cold War between the two most powerful former "Allies," the United States and the Soviet Union. They then began to wonder whether Americans had been led to war between 1939 and 1941 through an unwise, if not altogether sinister, policy of abandoning the nation's strict neutrality laws and supplying the British and the Russians with military aid. Still others wondered whether political machinations were responsible for the vulnerability of the American naval forces at Pearl Harbor. All of these factors contributed to asking questions, and writing answers in the form of history, that too often resembled the prosecuting or defense attorney approaches then recently on display at the "war crimes" trials of German and Japanese officials in Nuremberg and Tokyo.

Equally important in shaping the writing about American entry into the Second World War was the nature and amount of material available to scholars. For example, while the United States government quickly published a few documentary accounts of its relations with other governments prior to 1941, and the evidence gathered by a congressional investigation of the Pearl Harbor episode, the most comprehensive and significant bodies of material relating to United States foreign policy and the origins of the Second World War were not available until at least a decade or more after the war had ended. The most important collection of diplomatic dispatches that the American government publishes is its *Foreign Relations of the United States,* and it was not until 1956 that all the volumes for the calendar year 1941 were published.[1] Nor was it until the middle and later 1950's that the vast stores of material in the Department of State archives and the extensive diplomatic materials in the collections of personal papers (deposited in various libraries) of President Roosevelt and many of his key advisers and diplomats were opened for study. Thus, the earliest writings about American foreign policy in the 1930's frequently rested on thin or circumstantial evidence, which was not always conducive to drawing the soundest conclusions.

The lack of publication and archival availability of the diplomatic records of other governments has also hampered scholarship. The American, British, and French governments hoped to publish quickly the German record in *Documents on German Foreign Policy, 1919-1945* (five series, Washington, D. C., 1949——), but not until 1964 did they complete the thirteen-volume Series D covering the calendar years 1937-1941, and only between 1957 and 1966 were five of a projected six volumes of Series C for the calendar years 1933-1937 published. It will be many years before the volumes covering the 1920's (Series A and B) and 1940's (Series E) are completed, and even then tens of thousands of significant documents remain unpublished and untranslated, and scholars must painstakingly work through vast archival collections or pore over thousands of reels of microfilmed documents. Similarly, the government of Great Britain has published only a small part of its diplomatic record in its *Documents on British Foreign Policy, 1919-1939* (three series, London, 1946——), and only as late as 1970 has it opened its archives for the period through the calendar year 1939. The French government has only recently begun to publish part of its diplomatic record, *Documents Diplomatiques Français,* 1932-1939 (three series, Paris, 1963——) and its archives, as well as those of the Soviet Union, are still closed to scholars.

For barely more than a decade, then, have scholars had real opportunity, freed from the immediacy and partisanship of events,

---

[1]For thoughtful comments on the political and financial problems surrounding the publication and use of the Department of State records, see Richard W. Leopold, "The *Foreign Relations* Series: A Centennial Estimate," *Mississippi Valley Historical Review,* XLIX (March 1963), 595-612.

to begin to put together the complex story of how a *world* war began. The recently available rich supply of source materials has allowed researchers to explore events in great detail, and to ask and try to answer many questions that had been ignored or not posed before. For example, the United States did relatively little to stop the aggressive moves of Japan in Asia and Germany in Europe between 1933 and 1941. But precisely to what extent did American diplomats foresee or take part in the fateful developments of those years? To what extent did American diplomats act alone or in concert with diplomats of other nations? Were government officials all of one mind, or were there internal controversies and debates? And why did one view prevail over the others? Appeasement once was considered an honorable process whereby adversary nations used adjudication and compromise to preclude the use of force in settling disputes and became a term of opprobrium only after it had failed as a policy in the 1930's. What were the real causes of appeasement in the 1930's—a "failure of nerve" or misreading and misunderstanding of current problems? What of America's increasing belligerency during 1939-1941? Did Roosevelt insist in the presidential campaign of 1940 that he would never send American boys to fight on foreign shores knowing that he intended to do otherwise, or did he really believe that he was speaking the truth and that he could keep America out of war even while aiding the British? To what extent did he commit the United States to England? Were the Anglo-American naval talks, and even Roosevelt's meeting with Winston Churchill in 1941, intended as preparations for partnership in war or efforts toward preserving peace? Did the United States genuinely seek accommodation with Japan during the tedious negotiations in 1941, and if the American bargaining position was not wholly consistent, how and why did changes come about?

The increasing availability of foreign sources has had an equally profound impact upon writing about American entry into the Second World War. Again, it has been possible to ask a wide range of new questions. To what extent and why did Hitler discount American power in the 1930's? Might the United States have done anything, at any time, to have caused Hitler to withdraw his support for General Francisco Franco in the first months of the Spanish Civil war during the summer of 1936? Was there anything that the United States might have done, or did do, that affected the fate of Czechoslovakia in the summer of 1938? Did all German diplomatic and military officials agree upon what the United States would do if war came to

Europe, and did they agree on what policy Germany should follow with regard to American interests once war did come? What were Hitler's precise intentions when he formed the Tripartite Alliance with Italy and Japan in September 1940? Was it an offensive or defensive pact? To what extent did Germany encourage Japan to increasing belligerency in the Far East, and did the Germans in fact achieve what they intended? Were they complicit in any way in the attack on Pearl Harbor? And why did Hitler declare war on the United States when he was under no political or treaty obligation to do so?

Japanese sources have revealed crucial information about the nation's ultimate conflict with the United States. Did the Japanese really understand what the Americans were proposing by way of long- or short-range agreement in Asia in 1941, or might there have been some language or communication problems that led to critical misinterpretations or misunderstandings? Who controlled Japan's foreign policy, the civilian or military authorities, and might the latter have been more reckless than the former? Why did the Japanese attack Pearl Harbor? What were the political and military calculations that led them to involve their most potentially powerful opponent when they could have limited their attack to British and Dutch territories and achieved the same immediate success and been in a stronger position than ever to bargain for a favorable political and economic settlement?

These are some of the questions that a wealth of materials, enterprise on the part of many scholars, and the passage of time, have permitted us to ask, and these are the questions to which the readings that follow address themselves. No one book, and no one set of readings, can hope to answer all the pertinent questions finitely, if indeed there are finite answers. But it is my hope that these selections will afford interested readers a modest overview of a problem whose roots and causes were surely multidimensional and multinational.

A. A. O.
Boston, Massachusetts

I The Old Historical Debate

Even before the Second World War had ended many persons (and governments) had begun to prepare and publish their accounts of how it all began. By the middle of the 1950's American historians, political scientists, politicians, and diplomats had published literally hundreds of works—historical and documentary accounts, memoirs, diaries—seeking to answer how and why the United States became involved in a world war in December 1941. The first selection, Wayne S. Cole's article, "American Entry into World War II: A Historiographical Appraisal," surveys the literature written *before* 1957. Cole's major purpose is to point out the nature and limits of the arguments between the pre- and post-Pearl Harbor "non-interventionists" and "internationalists," and "revisionists" and "court historians." He discusses the political and intellectual climates which shaped the views men held and the positions they took before and after the war, and he shrewdly suggests that as more records become available, and as times change, future writers will ask different questions and reach new conclusions. Cole's survey serves as a convenient bibliographical and intellectual point of departure for the readings which follow and the new problems which they explore.

WAYNE S. COLE

American Entry into World War II:
A Historiographical Appraisal

Wayne S. Cole (born 1922) is Professor of History at the University of Maryland. He is the author of *America First: The Battle Against Intervention, 1940-1941* (1953) and *Senator Gerald P. Nye and American Foreign Relations* (1962).

THE AGGRESSIVE EXPANSION of the Axis powers in Europe and Asia in the 1930's aroused an impassioned debate on American foreign policy. "Isolationists" contended with "interventionists" over the policies adopted by the Roosevelt administration. Though few, if any, of the so-called isolationists wanted literally to isolate the United States from the rest of the world, they joined in opposition to what seemed the major trend in foreign affairs under President Roosevelt. A second phase in the dispute over policy was inaugurated by the attack on Pearl Harbor on December 7, 1941, for with that event the old quarrels became academic. But the policies of the Roosevelt administration continued as the core of dispute between two schools of historians who launched their own war of words over the background of America's entry into war. In the years after 1941 the "internationalist" writers were met by the "revisionists"—the latter term now used almost universally to describe the historians who have written critically of Roosevelt's pre-Pearl Harbor foreign policies and of American entry into World War II.[1] Since the controversy is a continuing one, and because the

---

[1] The terms commonly used on this subject are somewhat less than satisfactory. The term "isolationist" was widely used to describe the opponents of Roosevelt's foreign policies before Pearl Harbor, but the term "non-interventionist," though used much less frequently before Pearl Harbor, is a more accurate description of opponents of Roosevelt's foreign policies.

The term "internationalist" was a satisfactory description of many defenders of Roosevelt's foreign policies before Pearl Harbor. It was perhaps inappropriate, however, for many others who supported his foreign policies by 1941, such as the American Legion. The term "interventionist" likewise has inaccurate connotations. It is acceptable only if defined to include those who wished the United States to limit its "intervention" to methods short of war, as well as those who wanted full military

---

Reprinted by permission from *The Mississippi Valley Historical Review*, XLIII (March 1957), pp. 595-617.

books and articles on the subject have grown to confusing proportions, some orientation is necessary both for the reader who must work his way through the published historical materials and for those attracted to the problem as a field for further research and writing.

Histories of American entry into World War II published during the war defended the pre-Pearl Harbor policies of the Roosevelt administration. Forrest Davis and Ernest K. Lindley had close ties with the administration which enabled them to obtain important data for their volume, *How War Came.*[2] Walter Johnson's book, *The Battle against Isolation*,[3] published in 1944, was a study of the most powerful interventionist pressure groups before Pearl Harbor. Johnson, unlike some later writers, based his study upon previously unused manuscripts—principally the William Allen White papers. In the same year Dexter Perkins provided a concise survey in *America and Two Wars*.[4] The authors of these books shared and endorsed most of the assumptions and convictions of the interventionists and the Roosevelt administration on foreign affairs. The emotional atmosphere of the war years, the necessity for unity in the prosecution of the war, and the inadequacy of available source materials combined to prevent any serious challenge to the pro-Roosevelt interpretation during the war. Pamphlets by John T. Flynn, published in 1944 and 1945, advanced the revisionist point of view, but they received relatively little attention.[5]

During and since World War II growing quantities of raw materials for historical research and interpretation on the subject have been published and made available to scholars. The United

---

intervention. The term "court historian," used by Harry Elmer Barnes and Charles C. Tansill to describe pro-Roosevelt writers, is, like the term "isolationist," unsatisfactory on two counts: (1) It is not literally accurate. (2) It carries such a high emotional content that it interferes with dispassionate thought on the subject. The term "internationalist" is reasonably satisfactory for most historians who have defended Roosevelt's prewar foreign policies. The use of this term for pro-Roosevelt writers implies, however, that revisionists are not "internationalists." This implication may be valid for some; but other historians who believe the United States should not have entered World War II are in fact "internationalists."

[2] *How War Came: An American White Paper, from the Fall of France to Pearl Harbor* (New York, 1942).

[3] (Chicago, 1944).

[4] (Boston, 1944).

[5] *The Truth about Pearl Harbor* (New York, [1944]); *The Final Secret of Pearl Harbor* (New York, [1945]).

States government published special sets of documents related to American entry into the war, beginning with the publication in 1943 of *Peace and War: United States Foreign Policy, 1931-1941*.[6] In addition, the regular *Foreign Relations* series is now being brought close to Pearl Harbor.[7] Military leaders and civilians associated with the Roosevelt administration published personal accounts. Among Americans whose memoirs or letters have been published in full or in part are Raymond Moley, William E. Dodd, Joseph E. Davies, Sumner Welles, Frances Perkins, John G. Winant, Henry Morgenthau, Jr., Henry L. Stimson, Cordell Hull, James A. Farley, Sherman Miles, Eleanor Roosevelt, William D. Leahy, Samuel I. Rosenman, Joseph C. Grew, Ernest J. King, Harold L. Ickes, Husband E. Kimmel, and Jay P. Moffat.[8] Several key figures thus far have not published memoirs—including George C. Marshall, Harold R. Stark,

[6]Department of State, *Papers Relating to the Foreign Relations of the United States: Japan, 1931-1941* (2 vols., Washington, 1943); Department of State, *Peace and War: United States Foreign Policy, 1931-1941* (Washington, 1943); Department of State, *Nazi-Soviet Relations, 1939-1941* (Washington, 1948); *Foreign Relations of the United States: Diplomatic Papers; The Soviet Union, 1933-1939* (Washington, 1952). See also, Office of Naval Intelligence, *Fuehrer Conferences on Matters Dealing with the German Navy, 1939-1941* (5 vols., Washington, 1947).

[7]Department of State, *Foreign Relations of the United States: Diplomatic Papers, 1861-1941* (Washington, 1861-1956). The series has been completed through the year 1938. Three of the five volumes for 1939, one of the five for 1940, and one for 1941 have also been published.

[8]In the order of publication: Raymond Moley, *After Seven Years* (New York, 1939); William E. Dodd, Jr., and Martha Dodd (eds.), *Ambassador Dodd's Diary, 1933-1938* (New York, 1941); Joseph E. Davies, *Mission to Moscow . . .* (New York, 1941); Joseph C. Grew, *Ten Years in Japan* (New York, 1944); Sumner Welles, *The Time for Decision* (New York, 1944); Frances Perkins, *The Roosevelt I Knew* (New York, 1946); John G. Winant, *Letter from Grosvenor Square: An Account of a Stewardship* (Boston, 1947); Henry Morgenthau, Jr., "The Morgenthau Diaries," *Collier's* (New York), October 4, 11, 18, 25, 1947; Henry L. Stimson and McGeorge Bundy, *On Active Service in Peace and War* (New York, 1948); *The Memoirs of Cordell Hull* (2 vols., New York, 1948); James A. Farley, *Jim Farley's Story: The Roosevelt Years* (New York, 1948); Sherman Miles, "Pearl Harbor in Retrospect," *Atlantic Monthly* (Boston), CLXXXII (July, 1948), 65-72; Eleanor Roosevelt, *This I Remember* (New York, 1949); William D. Leahy, *I Was There: The Personal Story of the Chief of Staff to Presidents Roosevelt and Truman* (New York, 1950); Samuel I. Rosenman, *Working with Roosevelt* (New York, 1952); Joseph C. Grew, *Turbulent Era: A Diplomatic Record of Forty Years, 1904-1945* (2 vols., Boston, 1952); Ernest J. King and Walter M. Whitehill, *Fleet Admiral King: A Naval Record* (New York, 1952); Harold L. Ickes, *The Secret Diary of Harold L. Ickes* (3 vols., New York, 1953-1954); Husband E. Kimmel, *Admiral Kimmel's Story* (Chicago, 1955); Nancy H. Hooker (ed.), *The Moffat Papers: Selections from the Diplomatic Journals of Jay Pierrepont Moffat, 1919-1943* (Cambridge, 1956).

Walter C. Short, Frank Knox, and President Roosevelt. Edited volumes of Roosevelt's speeches, press conferences, and personal letters, however, have been published.[9] Documents, testimony, and reports of the several Pearl Harbor investigations were made available with the publication in 1946 of a total of forty volumes covering the work of the Joint Congressional Committee on the Investigation of the Pearl Harbor Attack.[10] The war crimes trials in Nuremberg and the Far East added pertinent documents and testimony.[11] Documents on British and German foreign policy before the war have been published.[12] Memoirs of leaders of European states were printed, containing much information of value for an understanding and analysis of American policies. The volumes by Winston Churchill and Count Ciano's diaries are two important examples.[13] And gradually in recent years historians have obtained increased opportunities for research in unpublished manuscripts.

Most of the histories published from 1947 to 1950 on American entry into World War II were based almost exclusively on published sources—particularly on the volumes growing out of the Pearl Harbor investigations and on the memoirs of Hull, Stimson, and others. Most of these early books followed the lead of either the

[9]Samuel I. Rosenman (ed.), *The Public Papers and Addresses of Franklin D. Roosevelt* (13 vols., New York, 1938-1950); Elliott Roosevelt (ed.), *F. D. R.: His Personal Letters* (4 vols., New York, 1947-1950).

[10]*Hearings before the Joint Committee on the Investigation of the Pearl Harbor Attack,* 79 Cong., 2 Sess. (39 parts, with exhibits; Washington, 1946); *Report of the Joint Committee on the Investigation of the Pearl Harbor Attack,* 79 Cong., 2 Sess. (Washington, 1946).

[11]International Military Tribunal, *Trial of the Major War Criminals before the International Military Tribunal, Nuremberg* (42 vols., Nuremberg, 1947-1949); Office of the United States Chief Counsel for Prosecution of Axis Criminality, *Nazi Conspiracy and Aggression* (11 vols., Washington, 1946-1948); International Military Tribunal for the Far East, *Record of Proceedings* (Washington, 1946).

[12]*Documents on British Foreign Policy, 1919-1939* (Third Series, 9 vols., London, 1949-1955); and *Documents on German Foreign Policy, 1918-1945: From the Archives of the German Foreign Ministry* (Series D, 9 vols. to date, Washington, 1949-   ). The British series, now complete, covers the period from March 9, 1938, to September 5, 1939. The German documents in this series begin in 1936 and have now been brought to June 22, 1940. In addition, several European governments published sets of selected documents in 1939 and 1940 around the time of the outbreak of the war.

[13]Winston S. Churchill, *The Second World War* (6 vols., Boston, 1948-1953); Hugh Gibson (ed.), *The Ciano Diaries, 1939-1943: The Complete Unabridged Diaries of Count Galeazzo Ciano, Italian Minister for Foreign Affairs* (Garden City, 1946). See also Togo Shigenori, *The Cause of Japan* (New York, 1956).

majority (pro-Roosevelt) or the minority (anti-Roosevelt) report of the congressional investigation committee. Among the volumes of this sort defending Roosevelt's foreign policies were *This Is Pearl,* by Walter Millis,[14] and *Roosevelt, from Munich to Pearl Harbor,* by Basil Rauch.[15] Revisionist volumes, based largely on published sources, included *Pearl Harbor,* by George Morgenstern;[16] *President Roosevelt and the Coming of the War, 1941,* by Charles A. Beard;[17] *America's Second Crusade,* by William Henry Chamberlin;[18] *Design for War,* by Frederic R. Sanborn, published in 1951;[19] and *The Final Secret of Pearl Harbor,* by Robert A. Theobald, published in 1954.[20]

Gradually in the late 1940's and early 1950's scholars began to expand into new frontiers by research in unpublished manuscripts. Most of this group wrote from points of view sympathetic with the policies followed by the American government before Pearl Harbor. Robert E. Sherwood used the files of Harry Hopkins as the basis for his Pulitzer-prize-winning *Roosevelt and Hopkins,* published in 1948.[21] *The Battle of the Atlantic* and *The Rising Sun in the Pacific,*[22] by Samuel Eliot Morison, traced the naval side of the background of American entry into the war. *Chief of Staff: Prewar Plans and Preparations,* by Mark S. Watson, analyzed the role of the Army.[23] Herbert Feis's study of American relations with Japan, entitled *The Road to Pearl Harbor,* was based on more extensive research than earlier volumes on that subject.[24] The culmination of the internationalist interpretation came with the publication in 1952 and 1953 of the two-volume work by William L. Langer and S.

[14]*This Is Pearl! The United States and Japan—1941* (New York, 1947).

[15]*Roosevelt, from Munich to Pearl Harbor: A Study in the Creation of a Foreign Policy* (New York, 1950).

[16]*Pearl Harbor: The Story of the Secret War* (New York, 1947).

[17]*President Roosevelt and the Coming of the War, 1941: A Study in Appearances and Realities* (New Haven, 1948). See also Charles A. Beard, *American Foreign Policy in the Making, 1932-1940: A Study in Responsibilities* (New Haven, 1946).

[18](Chicago, 1950).

[19]*Design for War: A Study of Secret Power Politics, 1937-1941* (New York, 1951).

[20]*The Final Secret of Pearl Harbor: The Washington Contribution to the Japanese Attack* (New York, 1954).

[21]*Roosevelt and Hopkins: An Intimate History* (New York, 1948).

[22]These are Volumes I (1947) and III (1948) of Morison, *History of the United States Naval Operations in World War II* (10 vols. to date, Boston, 1947-   ).

[23](Washington, 1950). This is a volume in the series entitled *United States Army in World War II,* being prepared by the Office of the Chief of Military History, Department of the Army.

[24]*The Road to Pearl Harbor: The Coming of the War between the United States and Japan* (Princeton, 1950).

Everett Gleason under the general title of *The World Crisis and American Foreign Policy.*[25] This massive study, covering the years from 1937 to 1941, was sponsored and financed by the Council on Foreign Relations and the Rockefeller Foundation. These volumes were based not only on published materials but also on extensive research in the records of the Department of State and in the material at the Franklin D. Roosevelt Library at Hyde Park. Since the publication of the Langer-Gleason work, the most recent book written from this same general point of view is *The Passing of American Neutrality, 1937-1941,* by Donald F. Drummond, published in 1955.[26] On the revisionist side, Charles Callan Tansill, after research comparable to that of Langer and Gleason, published his *Back Door to War* in 1952.[27] Harry Elmer Barnes, who had published several pamphlets on the subject earlier, edited a volume called *Perpetual War for Perpetual Peace* that included essays written by most major revisionists.[28] Richard N. Current's critical study, *Secretary Stimson,* was published in 1954.[29] In addition, other books and numerous articles have appeared, particularly since 1950, on specialized aspects of the subject.[30]

The interpretative controversies among historians concerning

[25] *The Challenge to Isolation, 1937-1940* (New York, 1952); and *The Undeclared War, 1940-1941* (New York, 1953).

[26] (Ann Arbor, 1955).

[27] *Back Door to War: The Roosevelt Foreign Policy, 1933-1941* (Chicago, 1952).

[28] *Perpetual War for Perpetual Peace: A Critical Examination of the Foreign Policy of Franklin Delano Roosevelt and Its Aftermath* (Caldwell, Idaho, 1953).

[29] *Secretary Stimson: A Study in Statecraft* (New Brunswick, 1954).

[30] For examples in addition to items cited elsewhere in this article, see: Hans L. Trefousse, *Germany and American Neutrality, 1939-1941* (New York, 1951); William L. Langer, *Our Vichy Gamble* (New York, 1947); Edgar E. Robinson, *The Roosevelt Leadership, 1933-1945* (Philadelphia, 1955); Fillmore H. Sanford, "Public Orientation to Roosevelt," *Public Opinion Quarterly* (Princeton), XV (Summer, 1951),189-216; Immanuel C. Y. Hsu, "Kurusu's Mission to the United States and the Abortive *Modus Vivendi,*" *Journal of Modern History* (Chicago), XXIV (September, 1952), 301-307; Norman L. Hill, "Was There an Ultimatum before Pearl Harbor?" *American Journal of International Law* (Washington), XLII (April, 1948), 355-67; Richard N. Current, "How Stimson Meant to 'Maneuver' the Japanese," *Mississippi Valley Historical Review* (Cedar Rapids), XL (June, 1953), 67-74; William L. Neumann, "Franklin D. Roosevelt and Japan, 1913-1933," *Pacific Historical Review* (Berkeley), XXII (May, 1953), 143-53; Tracy B. Kittredge, "The Muddle before Pearl Harbor," *United States News and World Report* (Washington), XXXVII (December 3, 1954), 52-63, 110-39; Joseph W. Ballantine, "Mukden to Pearl Harbor: The Foreign Policies of Japan," *Foreign Affairs* (New York), XXVII (July, 1949), 651-64; Herbert Feis "War Came at Pearl Harbor: Suspicions Considered," *Yale Review* (New Haven), XLV (Spring, 1956), 378-90.

American entry into World War II are in part a direct extension of the pre-Pearl Harbor debate between interventionists and non-interventionists. Writers of history have not only dealt with the same basic subject and issues, but have also used the same arguments, made the same fundamental assumptions and advanced similar hypotheses. For most major hypotheses advanced by post-war historians, counterparts could be found in the writings and speeches of prewar interventionists and non-interventionists. Furthermore, the debate among historians aroused some of the same emotional heat, the same ideological dogmatism, the same intolerance of conflicting views, and the same black-and-white portraits—on both sides—as were aroused in the "Great Debate" before Pearl Harbor. There are exceptions, of course, but there were also exceptions before Pearl Harbor.

In many instances the individuals who have written scholarly histories on the subject were involved directly (sometimes prominently) in the pre-Pearl Harbor foreign policy debate—and on the same side that they are now defending in their histories. There is no evidence that any of these writers was persuaded to change his basic point of view as the result of historical research after the war. It is true, of course, that Walter Millis' *Road to War,* published in 1935, was a major revisionist interpretation of American entry into World War I. Millis, however, was on the editorial staff of the interventionist New York *Herald Tribune,* and by 1939 he publicly endorsed the interventionist position. In June, 1940, he signed a petition urging an American declaration of war on Nazi Germany. In 1941 he was a sponsor of the Fight for Freedom Committee—a major pressure group advocating full United States participation in the war against the Axis.[31] Robert E. Sherwood's Pulitzer-prize-winning play, *Idiot's Delight,* with its arraignment of war and war passions, undoubtedly aroused pacifist and non-interventionist emotions. By 1939-1941, however, Sherwood was an interventionist. He actively and prominently supported William Allen White's Committee to Defend America by Aiding the Allies. Harry Hopkins assured himself of the vigor of Sherwood's interventionist views before he added the playwright to President Roosevelt's speech-writing staff in 1940.[32]

---

[31]Walter Millis, "1939 Is Not 1914," *Life* (New York), VII (November 6, 1939), 69-75, 94-98; Johnson, *Battle against Isolation,* 114-15, 247, 251-52.

[32]Johnson, *Battle against Isolation,* 43, 70 n, 85-88, 94 n, 116 n, 152-53, 206; Sherwood, *Roosevelt and Hopkins,* 49-50, 167, 303.

Barnes and Tansill refer to the internationalist writers as "Court Historians." One need not endorse the sinister implications of this sobriquet. Many internationalist writers, however, did have sympathetic personal ties and friendships with key figures in the events they described in their histories. Several of them have held important government positions in the administration whose foreign policies they were analyzing and evaluating. Ernest K. Lindley's personal friendship with President Roosevelt and other key administration figures enabled him to obtain special interviews and inside information for the preparation of his sympathetic volume.[33] Robert E. Sherwood assisted President Roosevelt with the writing of his speeches from 1940 until the President's death in 1945.[34] Herbert Feis was an economic adviser in the Department of State from 1931 to 1943 and was special consultant to the Secretary of War from 1944 to 1946. William L. Langer from 1941 to 1946 held various positions in the Office of Coordinator of Information, the Office of Strategic Services, and the Department of State. He served the Central Intelligence Agency in 1950-1951. S. Everett Gleason was with the Office of Strategic Services from 1943 to 1945 and the Department of State in 1945. He has served as deputy executive secretary to the National Security Council since 1950. Samuel Eliot Morison was commissioned in the naval reserve with the sole duty of preparing the history of United States naval operations in World War II. He rose to the rank of rear admiral by the time he retired in 1951. Mark S. Watson's book is a part of the official history of the Army in World War II. None of the major revisionist writers, on the contrary, held important administrative positions under either President Roosevelt or President Truman.[35]

All revisionists for whom specific evidence is available adhered to the non-interventionist position before Pearl Harbor. Charles A. Beard's prewar "Continentalism" as expressed in such books as *The Open Door at Home*[36] and *A Foreign Policy for America*[37] is well known. He publicly endorsed (but did not join) the America First

---

[33]Davis and Lindley, *How War Came*, vii-viii; Beard, *President Roosevelt and the Coming of the War*, 243 n.

[34]Sherwood, *Roosevelt and Hopkins*, 183-84.

[35]Biographical data in this and the following paragraph were obtained largely from *Who's Who in America* and from the contents and jackets of the various books written by these men.

[36]*The Open Door at Home: A Trial Philosophy of National Interest* (New York, 1934).

[37](New York, 1940).

Committee, the leading non-interventionist pressure group before Pearl Harbor.[38] He also testified against Lend-Lease before the Senate Foreign Relations Committee.[39] Harry Elmer Barnes, one of the leading and more uncompromising revisionists regarding the origins of World War I, spoke at meetings of the America First Committee in 1941.[40] Charles C. Tansill in 1938 published the best of the revisionist studies of American entry into World War I.[41] George Morgenstern joined the editorial staff of the non-interventionist Chicago *Tribune* in 1941. For revisionist as well as internationalist it is possible to discern a continuity in viewpoint, extending from the pre- to the post-Pearl Harbor period.

Any brief summaries of the revisionist and internationalist interpretations of American entry into World War II can at best be no more than simplified versions of detailed and complicated accounts. It is necessary in presenting such a summary to pass over countless important details and individual variations in interpretation. There is, nevertheless, a wide area of agreement among writers on each side of the interpretative controversy.

Internationalist writers, looking back to the days before Pearl Harbor, view the Axis powers as extremely serious threats to American security and interests. They point to the strength and speed of the Axis forces which by the middle of 1940 had rolled over Austria, Czechoslovakia, Poland, Denmark, Norway, the Netherlands, Luxemburg, Belgium, and France. Britain alone was successfully resisting Nazi assaults on her home islands. By May, 1941, Hitler was in control of the Balkan Peninsula and was threatening the Middle East. Most authorities at the time expected the Soviet Union to fall quickly after Hitler's *Blitzkrieg* was turned against Russia on June 22, 1941. Axis successes in North Africa raised fears that control of that continent might prove a stepping-stone to the Western Hemisphere. In the meantime Japan took advantage of the European crises to step up her aggressive campaigns in Asia.

According to the internationalist interpretation, President Roosevelt believed the United States could most effectively in-

---

[38] *New York Times,* September 9, 1940; Wayne S. Cole, *America First: The Battle against Intervention, 1940-1941* (Madison, 1953), 75.

[39] *Hearings before the Committee on Foreign Relations* [on S. 275], *United States Senate,* 77 Cong., 1 Sess. (Washington, 1941), 307-13.

[40] Harry Elmer Barnes, *The Genesis of the World War: An Introduction to the Problem of War Guilt* (New York, 1926); Cole, *America First,* 45, 76, 79.

[41] *America Goes to War* (Boston, 1938).

crease the possibility of peace in the 1930's by using its power to discourage potential aggressors from provoking war. In this aim, however, he was handicapped by the "isolationist" attitude of the American people and particularly by the powerful opposition in Congress. After war began in Asia and in Europe, according to this interpretation, the President hoped to prevent the United States from becoming involved in the hostilities—providing that could be accomplished without sacrificing American security, vital interests, and principles.

President Roosevelt and his major advisers believed that aggression by Germany and Italy in Europe constituted a more serious threat to American security than did Japanese actions in the Far East. In general, internationalist writers follow the administration view that the defeat of Nazi Germany and Fascist Italy was essential to American peace and security. Like the Roosevelt administration, most of these writers tend to rule out a negotiated peace as a possible acceptable alternative in Europe—particularly after the fall of France. President Roosevelt hoped that his policy of extending aid short of war to the victims of Axis aggression in Europe would prevent the defeat of Great Britain, contribute to the essential defeat of the Axis powers, and thereby enable the United States to maintain both its peace and its security. Among the many steps taken by the Roosevelt administration to aid the victims of aggression in Europe were repeal of the arms embargo, the destroyer deal, Lend-Lease, the Atlantic patrol system, occupation of Iceland, the shoot-on-sight policy, arming of American merchant ships, and permitting the use of those ships to transport goods directly to England.

According to the internationalist interpretation, Roosevelt and Hull wanted to prevent war between the United States and Japan—in part because such a war would interfere with the main task of defeating Hitler. They believed that the best way to preserve American peace and security in the Pacific was to take steps short of war to check Japanese aggression. Among American actions of this sort were the "moral embargo," the termination of the commercial treaty with Japan, various forms of aid to Chiang Kai-shek, keeping the American fleet at Pearl Harbor, and freezing Japanese assets in the United States. The United States was eager to seek a peaceful settlement with Japan—providing such a settlement would not jeopardize American security and principles, and providing it would not require the United States to abandon China, Britain, France, and the Netherlands in the Pacific. As it became increasingly apparent that compromise was impossible on terms acceptable to both countries, the Roosevelt administration tried to delay war to gain time for military preparations.

With regard to the European theater as well as the Pacific, there were distinct variations in the views of administration leaders before Pearl Harbor about implementing American policies and presenting them to the American people. Cordell Hull, hoping to avoid war and fearful of non-interventionist opposition, generally advised caution. He favored limiting action to steps short of war and he explained each step in terms of peace, security, and international morality. Henry L. Stimson, Frank Knox, Henry Morgenthau, Jr., and others were critical of this indirect and step-at-a-time approach. They early came to believe that aid short of war would not be sufficient to insure the defeat of the Axis and they urged the President to take more vigorous action against the aggressors. Stimson believed the American people would support the President in a declaration of war even before Pearl Harbor. Of a different temperament, President Roosevelt, like Hull, was fearful of arousing effective public opposition to his policies and adhered to the step-at-a-time, short-of-war approach.[42]

Internationalist interpretations tend to reflect these variations in attitudes among prewar interventionists. Feis treats Hull with considerable respect. Rauch's interpretation is similar to that advanced by Hull, though the hero in Rauch's book is definitely President Roosevelt. A number of writers, like Davis, Lindley, Millis, and Sherwood, generally feel that in view of conditions then existing President Roosevelt's decisions and methods on foreign policy matters were wise and sound at most crucial points before Pearl Harbor. Dexter Perkins has emphasized that Roosevelt's actions to check the Axis in Europe short of war reflected and expressed the desires of the majority of the American people. Langer and Gleason are sympathetic with the more direct and vigorous approach urged by Stimson—particularly as applied to the European theater. They believe that Roosevelt overestimated the strength of the opposition to his policies among the American people.[43]

[42]For example, see Stimson and Bundy, *On Active Service,* 365-76; Sherwood, *Roosevelt and Hopkins,* 132-35; Langer and Gleason, *Challenge to Isolation,* 5-9; Langer and Gleason, *Undeclared War,* 457-58.

[43]Davis and Lindley, *How War Came,* 23-29, 332; Millis, *This Is Pearl,* x-xi; Rauch, *Roosevelt, from Munich to Pearl Harbor,* 3-6, 22-23, 495-96; Sherwood, *Roosevelt and Hopkins,* 133, 151; Dexter Perkins, "Was Roosevelt Wrong?" *Virginia*

Writers of the internationalist school find the fundamental causes for American involvement in the war in developments in other parts of the world—beyond the American power to control by 1941. They do not find the explanation within the United States—except in so far as non-interventionist opposition inhibited administration actions that might have prevented the war from beginning or from reaching such a critical stage. Nearly all internationalist histories are highly critical of the opponents of Roosevelt's foreign policies. Needless to say, they all deny that President Roosevelt wanted to get the United States into war. They are convinced that the Japanese attack on Pearl Harbor was a genuine surprise to the members of the Roosevelt administration. These leaders knew that Japanese armed forces were under way and that war was imminent, but they expected the blows to fall in the southwest Pacific. In that event, administration leaders believed the United States would have to fight—though they were worried about the reaction of the American people to a declaration of war on Japan if American territory were not attacked. In so far as there was any American responsibility for the disaster at Pearl Harbor most internationalist writers blame the military commanders in Hawaii—Admiral Husband E. Kimmel and General Walter C. Short. None of them believe that there were any alternatives available to President Roosevelt by 1940-1941 which could have prevented American involvement in World War II without sacrificing American security and principles.[44]

Revisionists have formed an entirely different estimate of Roosevelt's role and policies. Most of the revisionist interpretation can be summarized under four major headings. First, revisionists believe the Axis powers did not (or, need not—if the United States had followed wiser policies) constitute a serious threat to American security and vital interests. Second, they contend that President Roosevelt followed policies that he knew (or should have known) would lead to war in Asia and Europe and would involve the United States in those wars. Third, while leading the nation to war, the President deceived the American people by telling them he was working for peace. And fourth, revisionists maintain that American

---

Quarterly Review (Charlottesville), XXX (Summer, 1954), 359-64; Langer and Gleason, *Challenge to Isolation*, 5-6; Langer and Gleason, *Undeclared War*, 195-97, 441-44.

[44]For example, see Millis, *This Is Pearl*, x-xi; Morison, *Rising Sun in the Pacific*, 127-42; Langer and Gleason, *Undeclared War*, 936-37; Rauch, *Roosevelt, from Munich to Pearl Harbor*, 467-93; Watson, *Chief of Staff*, 498-520.

policies before and during World War II contributed to the rise of a much more serious threat to peace and security—Communist Russia and her satellites.

In striking contrast to the internationalist interpretation, the revisionists minimize or reject the idea that the Axis powers constituted a threat to American security. They point out that Hitler had no concrete plans for attacking the Western Hemisphere. They portray the Japanese attack on Pearl Harbor as an action provoked by American restrictions that threatened Japanese security and vital interests. In so far as revisionists concede the reality of an Axis threat to the United States, they believe it was caused largely by American shortsighted and provocative policies. Like non-interventionists before Pearl Harbor, the revisionists maintain that the issue was not primarily security but instead was war or peace. And revisionists hold that the United States government had the power to choose for itself whether it would or would not enter the war. Thus, in contrast to internationalists, the revisionists find the explanation for American entry into World War II primarily within the United States rather than in the actions of nations in other parts of the world. In seeking the explanation within the United States, they focus their attention almost exclusively upon administration and military leaders—and particularly upon President Roosevelt.

Some revisionist historians believe that the Roosevelt foreign policies helped to provoke and prolong war in Asia and Europe.[45] They interpret Roosevelt's steps to aid Britain short of war as actually steps *to* war. Opinions of revisionists vary on the question of whether Roosevelt deliberately meant these as steps to war. In any event, they contend, these actions did not provoke Hitler into war against the United States; and the shooting incidents that

[45]Tansill contends (and Barnes concurs) that "There would seem to be only one logical explanation for Roosevelt's insistence on peace at the time of Munich and his pressure for an Anglo-French-Polish stand which he knew meant war in 1939, namely, that he did not want any war to start in Europe which might terminate so rapidly that the United States could not enter it. In September, 1938, the French, British, Russian, and Czech armies could have faced Hitler and might have defeated him rather rapidly. By summer, 1939, the situation had drastically changed. Russia became aligned with Germany and the Czech Army had been immobilized. War, in 1939, might stretch on indefinitely and afford Roosevelt ample time to involve the United States." Barnes (ed.), *Perpetual War for Perpetual Peace,* 171, 201-202 n. See also Chamberlin, *America's Second Crusade,* 59-60. Most revisionists do not take such an extreme position.

occurred in the Atlantic did not arouse American enthusiasm for entering the European war.

Instead, according to most revisionist writers, the Roosevelt administration got the United States into war through the Asiatic "back door" by provoking the Japanese attack on Pearl Harbor.[46] This was accomplished by increasing pressures on Japan while refusing any compromise that the Japanese could accept. The decisive economic pressure in 1941 was exerted through the curtailment of oil shipments, and the key issue on which compromise proved impossible was China. The freezing of Japanese assets in the United States on July 26, 1941, accompanied by parallel action by the British and Dutch, virtually terminated American trade with Japan. This was particularly serious in cutting Japan off from her essential oil supplies. On August 17, 1941, at the suggestion of Churchill, President Roosevelt presented a formal and vigorous warning to the Japanese against further expansion. The President then rejected Premier Konoye's proposal for a personal meeting between the two leaders. Then, Secretary of State Hull, after objections from China and Britain, abandoned the idea of proposing a *modus vivendi*. Instead, on November 26, Hull (though aware that time was running out) submitted a ten-point program to Japan— including the demand that the Japanese withdraw from China and Indo-China. This proposal (which revisionists generally call an "ultimatum") was so extreme that Hull knew in advance that Japan would not accept it. According to most revisionists these and other actions by the Roosevelt administration (out of either design or blunder) provoked war with Japan. The United States confronted Japan with the alternatives of backing down or fighting. With oil reserves falling dangerously low, and believing that their vital interests and security were at stake, the Japanese chose to fight.[47]

Through all of this, according to the revisionists, President Roosevelt deceived the American people concerning his policies and objectives in foreign affairs. Revisionists maintain that Roosevelt publicly committed his administration to a policy of peace while secretly leading the nation to war—a war that these writers consider contrary to national interests and contrary to the desires of 80 per

---

[46]Morgenstern, *Pearl Harbor*, 283-84; Beard, *President Roosevelt and the Coming of the War*, 564-66; Tansill, *Back Door to War*, 615-16; Barnes (ed.), *Perpetual War for Perpetual Peace*, 220-21.

[47]For example, see Barnes (ed.), *Perpetual War for Perpetual Peace*, 299-307, 327-86.

cent of the American people. The most famous expression of this thesis is in Beard's last book and particularly in his final chapter.[48]

Most revisionists maintain that administration and military leaders in Washington gave inadequate, ambiguous, and belated warnings to the commanders in Hawaii and withheld essential information from them. According to their contention, officials in Washington had sufficient information—including that obtained by breaking the Japanese secret diplomatic code—to anticipate an early Japanese attack. Furthermore, most of the revisionists believe that data at the disposal of leaders in Washington were sufficient (if properly analyzed) to have warned of a possible attack on Pearl Harbor. After Pearl Harbor, they say, the administration attempted unjustly to make General Short and Admiral Kimmel, the commanders in Hawaii, scapegoats for the tragedy. Instead of blaming the commanders in Hawaii, the revisionists place the main responsibility upon civilian and military leaders in Washington—including Marshall, Stark, Stimson, Knox, and particularly President Roosevelt. Tansill phrased the idea of Washington responsibility for the war most starkly when he wrote: "It seems quite possible that the Far Eastern Military Tribunal brought to trial the wrong persons. It might have been better if the tribunal had held its sessions in Washington."[49] On this, as on other phases of the subject, some revisionists, including Beard, Current, and William L. Neumann, write in more restrained and qualified terms than either Tansill or Barnes.

Finally, the revisionists insist that the Roosevelt foreign policies failed to serve American national interests. If, as Roosevelt and Hull contended, American aid to the victims of aggression was designed to keep America out of war, these policies obviously failed. If the Roosevelt policies were designed to protect American security, they were, according to revisionists, of questionable success. By helping to crush Germany and Japan the United States removed two major barriers to Soviet expansion and created power vacuums and chaos which contributed to the rise of the Soviet Union to world power and to the resultant explosive Cold War situation. China, which was considered too vital to compromise in 1941, is now in Communist hands—in part, some revisionists say, because of Roosevelt's policies before and during World War II. Revisionists maintain in

[48]Beard, *President Roosevelt and the Coming of the War*, 573-91.
[49]Tansill, *Back Door to War*, 629.

general that American involvement left the United States less secure, more burdened by debts and taxes, more laden with the necessity of maintaining huge armed forces than ever before in American history. Some revisionists predict that unless the United States returns to a policy of "continentalism" the nation may be headed for the nightmare described by George Orwell in *Nineteen Eighty-Four,* and toward World War III.[50]

It is probable that the reception accorded the revisionist or the internationalist interpretation has been affected as much by the climate of thought and the international developments since Pearl Harbor as by the specific evidence and reasoning relied upon by historians. Emotional, ideological, political, economic, and military conditions from 1942 to 1950 contributed to a widespread acceptance of the internationalist interpretation. The historian who conformed to prevailing modes of thought in the profession did not seriously question the pro-Roosevelt interpretation of American entry into World War II. Revisionist hypotheses were viewed for the most part as biased and unsound. Critical references to the Beard group were in vogue.

With the breakdown of bipartisanship around 1950, the beginning of a new "Great Debate," the development of neo-isolationism of the Hoover-Taft-Knowland variety, and the Republican campaign of 1952, revisionist interpretations found a somewhat more receptive environment. The Cold War tensions and insecurity encouraged the conviction that American entry into World War II had some aftereffects dangerous to American security. These developments were supplemented by a growth of political, economic, and intellectual conservatism that encouraged a more critical attitude toward Roosevelt's prewar domestic policies as well as his actions in foreign affairs. Revisionist volumes and articles were published in increasing numbers. Although most historians continued to express themselves sympathetically toward Roosevelt's foreign policies before Pearl Harbor, there was a more widespread inclination to question specific features of the internationalist interpretation. Internationalist historians, such as Feis, or Langer and Gleason, phrased their accounts in moderate, restrained, and qualified terms. At the same time some revisionist historians became less defensive and more positive in their phrasing. But the neo-isolationism of the early 1950's did not win the dominant position in popular thought or

[50]Barnes (ed.), *Perpetual War for Perpetual Peace,* viii-ix, 69, 502-42.

national policies. And revisionist interpretations still failed to gain a really large following among American historians.[51] It well may be that the future attitudes of many historians and of the American people toward American entry into World War II will be shaped as much by the future course of the United States as by the evidence uncovered by historical research.

Historians need not speak disparagingly, however, of the results of their inquiries during a period of only fifteen years on the subject of American entry into World War II. A prodigious amount of research has been accomplished. The diplomatic and military phases have been examined with striking thoroughness within the limits of available sources. Important beginnings have been made in the study of other aspects of the subject. Both revisionist and internationalist writers have advanced provocative and stimulating interpretations and have buttressed them with impressive documentation.

Despite these major accomplishments, there are important deficiencies and much work remains. Individuals will vary widely in their evaluations of what has been done and what remains to be done, but many of the criticisms of existing studies (criticisms which suggest possible directions for future efforts) may be analyzed under two major headings. In the first place, the narrow focus of most publications has left major areas almost untouched by serious historical research. Secondly—though the problem is probably incapable of final solution—there is need for a serious reexamination of the role and limitations of historical interpretation.

When measured by the standards of the "actualities" of pre-Pearl Harbor events, the scope and depth of available publications on American entry into World War II have been quite narrow in terms of time covered, subject matter, and source materials. Only a few books dealing specifically with this subject put it in the time context of the two World Wars. The volumes by Perkins, Chamberlin, Tansill, and Barnes all have this merit. Most studies of American entry into World War II, however, begin with 1940 or 1937. This point of departure is defensible if the scholar remains sensitively aware that he is examining only a tiny segment of the path that led to Pearl Harbor. Many historians, however, write

---

[51]The analysis in this paragraph is not meant to suggest that all revisionists are "neo-isolationists" or conservative. But the growth of "neo-isolationism" and conservatism did provide a more receptive environment for their interpretations.

almost as though the years from 1937 through 1941 were separated from and uninfluenced by earlier developments. For example, from a study of most available volumes a reader would not learn that these years were preceded by a devastating world depression with jolting economic, social, ideological, emotional, political, and power consequences that influenced the course of nations to December 7, 1941. Despite many important volumes and articles now available, there is much need for substantial research on foreign affairs in the years from 1921 to 1937. And a more meaningful perspective might be obtained if the subject were put in the broader context of the long-term but changing power relationships, industrialization of the world, the rise of the common man, and the development of secular ideologies designed to explain the mysteries of social, economic, and political changes whose ultimate form can only be dimly and imperfectly perceived.

Most published volumes are concerned largely with diplomatic, military, and some political aspects of the subject. The authors trace in intricate detail the policy planning, the minutiae of diplomatic exchanges, and the reactions of statesmen to the developments abroad. These phases are of major importance. They do not, however, constitute the whole story nor necessarily the most meaningful part. Economic, social, psychological, ethnic, religious, and political conditions that help to give direction and meaning to the diplomacy have been inadequately and imprecisely studied.

Political influences have been given much attention. Even the political analyses, however, often leave much to be desired when the subject is American entry into World War II. A good many historians on both sides have followed the almost standard procedure of charging individuals whose foreign policy views they do not like with partisan political motives. Writers on both sides often seem blind to political influences among those with whom they sympathize.[52] Political analysts also have directed their attention largely to the top administration, military, and diplomatic officials. There has been relatively little serious study of the influence of individual congressmen and of state political organizations on the nation's foreign policies before Pearl Harbor. Furthermore, most references to political figures—even the prominent administration leaders—are of a two-dimensional variety. There is need for

---

[52]For examples, see Morgenstern, *Pearl Harbor,* 327; Tansill, *Back Door to War,* 476-77; Langer and Gleason, *Undeclared War,* 574; Sherwood, *Roosevelt and Hopkins,* 367-68.

thorough biographies of scores of individuals. Frank Freidel's excellent biography of Franklin D. Roosevelt, now being published, suggests the sort of work needed on countless other figures in the story.[53] Some important beginnings have been made, too, in studying sectional variations, but this subject has by no means been exhausted.[54]

One need not be an economic determinist to be disturbed by the neglect of economic influences in existing histories of American entry into World War II. How did foreign policies affect those groups of persons who shared a particular economic interest? How did such effects influence the attitude of those groups toward foreign policy? What influence did those groups exert on policy making? Articles by John W. Masland and Roland N. Stromberg provide important beginnings on this phase of the subject, but much more remains to be done.[55]

Samuel Lubell and John Norman have published studies on the foreign policy attitudes of German-Americans and Italian-Americans.[56] There is need, however, for additional research on the role of numerous ethnic and religious groups in the history of American foreign affairs before Pearl Harbor. Volumes have been published on such pressure groups as the Committee to Defend America by Aiding the Allies, the Fight for Freedom Committee, the America First Committee, and the American Legion.[57] But studies

[53]Frank Freidel, *Franklin D. Roosevelt* (3 vols. to date, Boston, 1952-   ).

[54]George L. Grassmuck, *Sectional Biases in Congress on Foreign Policy* (Baltimore, 1951); Ralph H. Smuckler, "The Region of Isolationism," *American Political Science Review* (Menasha, Wis.), XLVII (June, 1953), 386-401; Jeannette P. Nichols, "The Middle West and the Coming of World War II," *Ohio State Archaeological and Historical Quarterly* (Columbus), LXII (April, 1953), 122-45; Wayne S. Cole, "America First and the South, 1940-1941," *Journal of Southern History* (Lexington, Ky.), XXII (February, 1956), 36-47.

[55]John W. Masland, "Commercial Influence upon American Far Eastern Policy, 1937-1941," *Pacific Historical Review*, XI (October, 1942), 281-99; Roland N. Stromberg, "American Business and the Approach of War, 1935-1941," *Journal of Economic History* (New York), XIII (Winter, 1953), 58-78.

[56]Samuel Lubell, "Who Votes Isolationist and Why," *Harper's Magazine* (New York), CCII (April, 1951), 29-36; John Norman, "Influence of Pro-Fascist Propaganda on American Neutrality, 1935-1936," in Dwight E. Lee and George E. McReynolds (eds.), *Essays in History and International Relations in Honor of George Hubbard Blakeslee* (Worcester, 1949), 193-214.

[57]Johnson, *Battle against Isolation;* Cole, *America First;* Roscoe Baker, *The American Legion and American Foreign Policy* (New York, 1954). See also Robert Edwin Bowers, "The American Peace Movement, 1933-1941," (Ph.D. dissertation, University of Wisconsin, 1949).

are needed on the attitudes and influence of countless other organized pressure groups of all sorts on American foreign policies
before Pearl Harbor. Several books and articles have analyzed the
non-interventionists and interventionists—but neither of these
groups has by any means been exhausted as a field for constructive
historical research.[58]

There has been almost no serious research on the influence of
psychological and emotional factors. Both revisionists and internationalists write almost as though the actions of the key figures
could all be explained in intellectual and rational terms. It is
conceivable that historians could learn as much about American
entry into World War II by studying the psychological and
emotional make-up of the individuals involved, as by studying the
phrasing of the diplomatic dispatches and state papers. Ralph K.
White, Harold Lavine, and James Wechsler have published suggestive studies on the role of propaganda in pre-Pearl Harbor
developments,[59] but for the most part the role of psychological
influences on the attitudes of the American people and of American
statesmen has scarcely been touched.

Results of the limited research on these non-diplomatic influences
have seldom been integrated into the major works. Thomas A.
Bailey's interpretative survey, *The Man in the Street,* contains more
data on these phases of the subject than do any of the major
volumes on American entry into World War II.[60] But his study is
suggestive rather than definitive.

In addition to the narrowness of approach with regard to time
span and subject matter, there has been a narrowness in terms of the
source materials used. If the focus of the subject matter is to be
broadened as suggested in this article, historians will have to
demonstrate a high degree of ingenuity in tapping additional source

[58]Johnson, *Battle against Isolation;* Cole, *America First;* Smuckler, "Region of
Isolationism," *American Political Science Review,* XLVII (June, 1953), 386-401;
Lubell, "Who Votes Isolationist and Why," *Harper's,* CCII (April, 1951), 29-36; John
C. Donovan, "Congressional Isolationists and the Roosevelt Foreign Policy," *World
Politics* (New Haven), III (April, 1951), 299-316; William Appleman Williams, "The
Legend of Isolationism in the 1920's," *Science and Society* (New York), XVIII
(Winter, 1954), 1-20.

[59]Ralph K. White, "Hitler, Roosevelt, and the Nature of War Propaganda," *Journal
of Abnormal and Social Psychology* (Albany), XLIV (April, 1949), 157-74; Harold
Lavine and James Wechsler, *War Propaganda and the United States* (New Haven,
1940).

[60]*The Man in the Street: The Impact of American Public Opinion on Foreign Policy*
(New York, 1948).

materials—including manuscripts in private hands. This appeal for greater breadth and depth is not meant to disparage the work thus far completed. But much of great importance remains to be done by scholars on the subject of American involvement in the war.

Montaigne's assertion that "nothing is so firmly believed as what we least know" suggests a second deficiency in most major volumes on American entry into World War II. The most heated controversies among historians do not center on those matters for which the facts and truth can be determined with greatest certainty. The interpretative controversies, on the contrary, rage over questions about which the historian is least able to determine truth. Despite the thousands of documents and tons of manuscripts, the written record and the physical remains constitute only a tiny fraction of the reality of America's course toward World War II—and these remains do not necessarily represent the "truth."

With the relatively inexact methods and incomplete data at his command, even the finest historian can often make only semi-informed guesses concerning motives, causes, and wisdom of pre-Pearl Harbor decisions. As Herbert Butterfield phrased it, the historian "can never quite carry his enquiries to that innermost region where the final play of motive and the point of responsibility can be decided. . . . He does not study human nature, therefore, in the way that an omniscient deity might observe it, with an eye that pierces our unspoken intentions, our thick folds of insincerity and the motives that we hardly avow to ourselves."[61] The historian can determine that certain events preceded American entry into World War II and he may find circumstantial evidence suggesting possible causal relationships. But he cannot conduct controlled experiments to measure with any degree of certainty the causal significance of antecedent developments and incidents. Furthermore, these various interpretations of individual historians are based upon different opinions concerning the widsom of possible pre-Pearl Harbor policies as judged in terms of certain criteria, such as world peace and security, American peace and security, economic order and prosperity, and freedom and democracy. As Sumner Welles phrased it, "The wisdom of any foreign policy can generally be determined only by its results."[62] But in order to measure this wisdom, the results of policies that were actually followed would have to be

[61]Herbert Butterfield, *History and Human Relations* (New York, 1951), 116-17.
[62]Welles, *Time for Decision*, 288.

compared with the results of possible alternative policies that were not followed. It is, of course, impossible to run controlled experiments to determine what would have happened if alternative policies had been followed. Furthermore, the possible alternatives were not necessarily of the simple "either/or" variety. The path to Pearl Harbor was filled with millions of decisions, great and small, each based upon other decisions which preceded it. There were countless forks in the road that led to Pearl Harbor. And no historian can know for certain what lay at the end of the paths that were not followed.

Writers on both sides, of course, are conscious of limitations inherent in historical interpretation. All of them qualify their generalizations with references to the inadequacy of their sources. But they recognize the limitations more clearly when referring to interpretations with which they do not agree. Sanborn, a revisionist, wrote that the internationalists' "first line of defense has always rested and still rests upon a foundation blended of faith, emotion, and hypothesis."[63] Dexter Perkins, on the other side, has written that revisionism is "shot through with passion and prejudice. . . . It also rests upon hypotheses which . . . cannot be demonstrated."[64] To a certain extent both Sanborn and Perkins are correct. But their generalizations apply in varying degree to books on *both* sides in the interpretative controversy.

Probably no one would want the historian to refrain from interpreting the course of events simply because he cannot scientifically prove the truth of his interpretations. The historian could not avoid some degree of interpretation even if he tried. Inadequate though his analyses may be, who is better qualified to perform the function? Both revisionist and internationalist historians have a responsibility to attempt to explain American entry into World War II as they understand it.

Nevertheless, considering the incompleteness and inexactness of their knowledge and understanding, historians do not seem justified in the cavalier, dogmatic tone that they so frequently use. They base their interpretations in part on a personal faith in the wisdom of the policies they support. Like devout believers in less secular faiths, writers on both sides tend to be intolerant of conflicting beliefs. This

[63] Barnes (ed.), *Perpetual War for Perpetual Peace,* 190.
[64] Perkins, "Was Roosevelt Wrong?" *Virginia Quarterly Review,* XXX (Summer, 1954), 372.

may not be true of all writers on the subject, but it does apply in varying degree to many on both sides. Historians need to emphasize the limits of their knowledge as well as the expansiveness of it. There is need for more awareness of the tentative nature of human inquiry, for self-criticism and the humility of an Albert Einstein, rather than the positive, dogmatic, self-righteousness of the propagandist. Perhaps in the furious twentieth-century struggle for men's minds there can be no real place for moderation and restraint—even in historical interpretation. Numerous critics, however, both here and abroad, are fearful of the immaturity of American attitudes toward international affairs. If the historian is sensitive to the many-sided complexities of issues and demonstrates intellectual humility and ideological tolerance, perhaps others, influenced by his example, may be less inclined to grasp at simplified, crusading,. utopian theories regarding contemporary international affairs.

II The Consensus on Appeasement, 1933-1938

Historians of the era of Franklin D. Roosevelt usually have focused first on the New Deal domestic reforms of 1933-1938 and then on foreign policy developments between the outbreak of war in Europe in 1939 and the Japanese attack on Pearl Harbor in 1941. But as shown in Part II in the excerpts from Dorothy Borg's *The United States and the Far Eastern Crisis of 1933-1938* (1964) and Arnold A. Offner's *American Appeasement: United States Foreign Policy and Germany, 1933-1938* (1969), American diplomats were deeply involved in world affairs between 1933 and 1938. Borg explains in her summary chapter, "The Trend of American Foreign Policy," how the Roosevelt government tried to cope with Japan's increasing demands on China for political and economic concession, and how American policy shifted from supporting peace to avoiding conflict with Japan. The United States, Borg explains, would not consider any cooperative undertaking to end the Sino-Japanese war, limited itself to a policy of moral suasion (which it thought bold), and in the end was reduced to searching for an almost "magic solution" to the problems it faced. Offner discusses the American role in the quest for peace in Europe through the appeasement of Germany, focusing in this chapter, "To Munich and War," on the German-Czech crisis of 1938 which led to the Munich Conference, and then recapitulating American policy during the previous six years. Although Borg's and Offner's works were done independently of each other, they agree on the genuine efforts made at appeasement, the shortcomings and ultimate failure of American diplomacy, and the way in which problems in the Far East and Europe were gradually merged, and perceived to be merging by American diplomats, into a larger context which would lead to world war with the so-called Axis powers. The two works provide a complementary analysis of American foreign policy in this crucial period.

DOROTHY BORG

The United States and the Far Eastern
Crisis of 1933-1938

Dorothy Borg (born 1902) is Senior Research Associate andLecturer at the East Asian Institute of Columbia University. She has written *American Policy and the Chinese Revolution, 1925-1928* (1947), as well as numerous articles.

THIS VOLUME has dealt intensively with American policy in the Far East during the period that started with the Tangku Truce[1] and ended in January 1938, when the first phase of the undeclared war in China was terminated by the severance of relations between the Japanese and Chinese governments. The following is presented as a brief review of the broad trend of our diplomacy during these years.

The events of the Manchurian crisis[2] had, it is felt, a significant influence upon the United States government's subsequent policy. Stimson's initial objective in respect to the crisis was to strengthen the movement for the establishment of universal order that had developed since the World War. His concern with that movement was readily understandable within the context of the time. Before the World War the creation of an organization like the League of Nations had seemed little more than a vague and highly idealistic goal. Yet immediately following the war, the League had come into existence and in many respects had achieved remarkable results during the 1920's. It had moreover been supplemented by the conclusion of various multilateral agreements designed to provide solutions to the problem of war. Many people therefore felt that a system for the establishment and maintenance of peace had been created which for the first time in history offered some promise that the world might achieve international order. As a result they

[1]Tangku Truce—agreement of May 31, 1933, between China and Japan establishing a cease-fire and demilitarized zone between Chinese and Japanese forces in North China. [Editor's note.]

[2]Manchurian crisis—the period beginning with the outbreak of hostilities between Japan and China in Manchuria in September 1931. [Editor's note.]

Reprinted by permission of the publishers from Dorothy Borg, *The United States and the Far Eastern Crisis of 1933-1938: From the Manchurian Incident Through the Initial Stage of the Undeclared Sino-Japanese War,* Cambridge, Mass.: Harvard University Press, Copyright, 1964, by the President and Fellows of Harvard College.

regarded Japan's invasion of Manchuria as primarily significant *is threat* because it constituted the first great attack upon the peace system *to League* that had evolved in the postwar years; further, they believed that *system* the way in which other nations responded to Japan's action would go far to determine whether that system would be progressively strengthened or gradually destroyed.

Stimson's efforts during the early months of the Manchurian crisis were to a large extent directed toward supporting the League. Although he failed at times to supply the League with all the assistance that it wanted, he certainly had no intention of weakening its stand. Rather, he was concerned with warding off what he regarded as the attempts of the League when engaged in any joint undertaking with the United States to shift the burden of responsibility upon this country, thereby forcing it into a position of leadership. Moreover, in some respects his views differed from those of the League, notably in that he placed more emphasis upon the necessity of exhibiting tolerance toward the Japanese in the hope that, with outside support, the moderates in the Japanese government would be able to control the extremists.

After the fall from power of the moderates in Japan, Stimson felt *Konoye* that the situation in the Far East had taken a radical turn for the worse. His objective remained the strengthening of the peace system but it seemed evident that this aim could not be achieved by the tactics he had used to date. At the same time the Secretary recognized that few lines of action were open to him if for no other reason than that President Hoover was opposed to the use of any measures stronger than moral sanctions. Faced with new and increasingly serious evidence that Japan was determined to continue its invasion of Manchuria in defiance of the whole world, he however believed that some quick move was necessary to indicate that the "peace loving nations" were willing to adopt a definite stand against Japan's efforts to undermine the peace structure. He consequently decided to take unilateral action immediately, which meant assuming the initiative he had hitherto left to the League, and issued his note of January 7, 1932,[3] in the hope that other countries

---

[3]Note of January 7, 1932—a note by Stimson to the governments of both China and Japan declaring the United States would not recognize the legality of any *de facto* situation in China or any agreement which impaired the treaty rights of United States citizens in China, "including those which relate to the sovereignty, the independence, or the territorial and administrative integrity of the Republic of China." [Editor's note.]

would follow suit thereby refusing to recognize any gains Japan might achieve in violation of the Paris Pact[4] as an expression of their disapproval of Japan's acts of aggression. Soon after it became apparent that other countries were not going to fall in line as he desired, Stimson began to consider making a second statement which would be similar to his note of January 7. However, this statement, which ultimately became his letter to Senator Borah, was to emphasize the Nine Power Treaty over and above the Paris Pact in order to implement another major aspect of Stimson's policy which was his desire to maintain the strong ties that he felt existed between the United States and China. Convinced that, primarily as a result of the American missionary movement, Americans had a deep and idealistic attachment to China which was not to be found among other peoples, he wished to reaffirm the faith of the United States in the principles of the Nine Power Treaty[5] at a moment when the Chinese, subjected to defeat and humiliation, were in great need of encouragement. In its final form the letter to Senator Borah also contained the suggestion that the treaties concluded at the Washington Conference were indivisible, which was intended as a warning to the Japanese that the United States might feel free to disregard the restrictions imposed upon her naval power by the Washington Conference agreements if Japan continued to disregard the provisions of the Nine Power Treaty.

In the last phase of the Manchurian crisis, Stimson devoted himself to persuading the League to adopt a firm position on the basis of the Lytton report.[6] He attempted, however, to remain in the background, insisting that the League must not revert to its tendency to transfer its responsibilities to the United States. When the League finally censured Japan and agreed to apply the nonrecognition doctrine to Manchukuo, the Secretary felt that a "momentous

[4]Paris Pact—or The Kellogg-Briand Pact of August 27, 1928, by which the signatories agreed to renounce war as an instrument of national policy and to solve all disputes by peaceful means. [Editor's note.]

[5]Nine Power Treaty—signed at Washington, D.C., on February 6, 1922, by the United States, Great Britain, France, Italy, Japan, China, Belgium, Portugal, and the Netherlands, and guaranteeing China's territorial integrity and independence, and equal commercial opportunity for all nations. [Editor's note.]

[6]Lytton report—drawn up by a League of Nations Commission under Lord Lytton and made public in October 1932 and adopted by the League of Nations in February 1933. The report blamed Japan for hostilities in Manchuria and Shanghai and recommended the evacuation of Japanese troops from the territory they had seized in Manchuria. Japan thereupon withdrew from the League of Nations. [Editor's note.]

event" had occurred which represented a "great step forward" in the postwar effort to abandon the "jungle law of international diplomacy" that had existed before 1914.

It is doubtful whether many members of the American government shared Stimson's optimistic estimate of the League's action. In general, as the Roosevelt administration took office most American officials connected with the making of our Far Eastern policy seem to have been in agreement on three main points concerning the Manchurian crisis. First, contrary to Stimson, they did not believe that the Manchurian crisis had resulted in strengthening the postwar movement to establish world order; in fact, some officials were convinced that that movement had been totally discredited. Secondly, they felt that the Manchurian crisis had left the United States in a very precarious position in relation to Japan. [In their estimation the conquest of Manchuria and the ousting from power of the moderates in Tokyo meant that the Japanese were determined to fulfill their expansionist ambitions at almost any cost.] Granted a bellicose Japan, they thought that there not only existed the possibility of an ultimate clash between Japan and the United States but that such a possibility had been made substantially more real by the increase in anti-American feeling among the Japanese which had resulted from the Manchurian crisis. Thirdly American officials appear almost uniformly to have concluded that the Manchurian crisis had demonstrated the dangers of the United States' engaging in action against Japan either unilaterally or in cooperation with other nations. They had in particular been impressed by the precautions which the American government had repeatedly felt compelled to take during the Manchurian crisis to avoid being pushed into a position of leadership which entailed risks that it did not want to incur.

2 reasons for Jap expansion

The views of American officials relative to the Manchurian crisis commenced to have an effect upon the trend of our policy in the Far East at the very outset of the Roosevelt administration. The initial stage of the struggle for North China, ending in the Tangku Truce, marked a transition period for the United States in which ideas that had governed our diplomacy during the Stimson era began to give way to a new set of concepts that were to predominate throughout the next years. In particular, the emphasis which had been placed upon the necessity of supporting the peace system began to be shifted to another objective: the avoidance of a conflict between the United States and Japan. In keeping with this objective, it was

New ideas of Amer. for policy (after Stimson)

decided that if any joint measures were adopted by outside powers to arrest Japan's penetration of North China, the United States should leave the initiative to others and participate only in a relatively inconspicuous role; even more importantly, it was felt that it would be in the best interests of America to take no action whatever.

The aspects of American policy that began to emerge at the time of the Tangku Truce became progressively evident during the incident involving the Amau declaration.[7] The views of policy-making officials in Washington relative to the whole problem with which the Amau doctrine was concerned—the establishment of a strong China—were on the whole well defined. They continued to believe in the theory underlying the Nine Power Treaty that the soundest way of attaining peace in the Pacific area was to create a strong China capable of maintaining a balance of power in the Far East. At the same time they thought that the transformation of China into a strong state could not be accomplished by the Chinese without substantial outside assistance. They were in favor of the kind of technical aid that the League was providing for China but basically were convinced that no country still on the threshold of industrialization could hope to modernize unless it obtained large-scale financial help from abroad.

On the question of whether the Kuomintang[8] was capable of achieving the reconstruction of China the opinions of officials in Washington differed from those of the leading American Foreign Service officers in China. Men such as Nelson Johnson had become increasingly disappointed at what they regarded as the failure of the Nationalist regime to fulfill much of the promise of the political tutelage period. As a result, by 1934 their dispatches to Washington reflected an almost unrelieved sense of discouragement. The main burden of their criticism was that the leadership of the Kuomintang had deteriorated so that it was unable to carry out the task of unifying the country and that the party as a whole had lost the revolutionary fervor necessary to effect the reforms essential for the rehabilitation of China. Officials in Washington on the other hand tended to judge the Kuomintang less severely. They were disturbed

[7]Amau declaration—statement by Japanese foreign office official, Eiji Amau, of April 17, 1934, that Japan opposed any foreign aid for China; the Japanese government subsequently disavowed the declaration. [Editor's note.]

[8]Kuomintang—National People's Government of China headed by Chiang Kai-shek. [Editor's note.]

by the constant military and political conflicts among its leaders which they felt inevitably jeopardized any effort at national reconstruction. But they nevertheless believed that the Kuomintang had made decided progress in the political tutelage period, especially in light of the magnitude of the problems with which it was confronted, and that although China's future might still be uncertain it was by no means devoid of promise.

The views maintained by officials in Washington contrasted sharply with the actions taken by the United States government following the Amau declaration. The most important moves made by the State Department initially consisted of: the Department's assertion to the British that if any cooperative measures were undertaken in protest against the Amau declaration the United States might participate but that it did not want to be thrust into a position of leadership; Hull's *aide-mémoire*[9] which was sent to the Japanese on April 29 and which he himself subsequently described to the Japanese ambassador as a message issued in a "respectful and friendly spirit"; and the Secretary's comments on his *aide-mémoire* to the press, which amounted to an appeal to try to promote better relations between the United States and Japan. But an even more significant step was taken by the State Department after the agitation over the Amau declaration had to a large extent subsided when Hull asked the Far Eastern Division to re-examine our policy on aid to China to see if any changes should be made in view of the objections which the Japanese had raised. For, as a consequence, the Department arrived at the conclusion that at least for the present the United States government should refrain from giving the Chinese any financial assistance in no matter what form. It reached this conclusion for various reasons, among them being that the Chinese already owed substantial sums to the United States government and its nationals which they were making no apparent effort to repay. But it was largely influenced by a determination to avoid taking any action that might lead to the development of further friction between the United States and Japan. Moreover, the State Department subsequently decided that if, at some time in the future, the United States did furnish the Chinese with financial assistance, it

---

[9]Hull *aide-memoire* of April 29 [1934]—a note to the Japanese government in intentionally nonprovocative language reasserting the United States' intention to respect the rights, obligations, and legitimate interests of all other sovereign nations. [Editor's note.]

would have to do so in cooperation with other powers including Japan. It therefore requested the American group of the Consortium,[10] which was on the verge of dissolution, to remain intact so that, should the opportunity ultimately present itself, the various Consortium groups would be able to collaborate in helping China.

In sum, the main views entertained by officials in Washington were that the internal development of China was a matter of high importance; that China had entered upon a new period in its history in which, after years of turmoil, it had a chance of attaining national reconstruction; but that no country could expect to become a strong state in the modern world unless it obtained extensive foreign support. All of these ideas pointed in the direction of the United States' aiding China. But the Amau declaration led the State Department to advocate a contrary course based—as has already been indicated—upon the concepts which had been tentatively suggested at the time of the Tangku Truce, namely, that within the foreseeable future the primary aim of our Far Eastern policy should be to avert trouble with Japan and that the best means of achieving this objective was for the most part to adhere to a strategy of inaction.

The naval talks of 1934 seemed to American officials both in the State Department in Washington and the embassy in Tokyo, to provide a further indication of the possibility of war between the United States and Japan. The fear of such a war was most strikingly expressed in the letter that Ambassador Grew sent to the Secretary of State on December 27, 1934, in which he asserted in substance that the Japanese, driven by a fierce and blind chauvinism, would probably attempt to gain control over most of the western part of the Pacific area and might even suddenly try to seize some of the island possessions of the United States, such as Guam. The ambassador's comments had a marked influence in Washington, if only because they set forth ideas which had prevailed in the State Department for some time but had not as yet been stated in so definite or com-

---

[10]Consortium—an international banking group organized in 1920 and made up of the United States, Great Britain, France, and Japan which was intended to assist the Chinese to finance long-range reconstruction programs, but which was largely ineffective and disliked even by the Chinese, who feared foreign control of their financial operations. [Editor's note.]

prehensive a manner. The net result was that, after the failure of the naval conferences, the Department attached considerably more significance to the development of naval power. It felt primarily that the United States should be prepared to defend itself in case an attack by Japan eventuated but, in addition, it hoped that the mere existence of a strong American navy would deter the Japanese from ever launching such an attack.

In the year 1934, the moral aspect of the State Department's policy in the Far East was also demonstrated. Because of the manner in which he approached Hull, Ambassador Saito's proposal that America and Japan should issue a joint statement of policy seemed part of a scene from an *opéra bouffe.* Yet the Secretary's response was very significant. Hull objected to the ambassador's proposal for two reasons: One was that in his opinion for the United States government to sign a statement containing the provisions outlined by Ambassador Saito would have been tantamount to an outright declaration that America was willing to sanction Japan's efforts to attain what the Secretary frequently referred to as the "overlordship of the Orient." The other was that any bilateral agreement between Japan and the United States suggested a tie of intimacy between the two countries which carried with it the connotation that America approved Japan's purposes and policies. The Secretary's position was therefore basically that the United States did not have the moral right to engage in any action that either directly or indirectly appeared to endorse Japanese aggression. The moral stand taken by Hull became part of the State Department's policy. However, in considering the moral aspect of American diplomacy, it is important to recognize that the State Department drew a sharp distinction between endorsing Japanese aggression and accepting it without opposition. This distinction was defined by Hornbeck, who had devoted considerable thought to the matter, in the memorandum of April 1935, in which he pointed out that to "acquiesce" passively in Japan's encroachments on China was different from actively giving "assent" and indicated that the former was morally justifiable while the latter was not.

Thus by 1934 the objective of preventing a clash with Japan, a strategy which emphasized on the one hand refraining from action in the face of Japan's current involvement in China and on the other the strengthening of our naval power, and the moral considerations which have just been noted characterized the trend of American policy in the Far East. But before discussing the events which took place after 1934, a word should be added about certain aspects of the naval talks conducted in that year which further suggested the general direction in which American policy was moving. As has already been related in some detail, the position taken by the United States at the naval meetings was squarely based on the thesis that the principles of the Washington Naval Treaty should be maintained because they provided the United States and Japan with equality of security by limiting the fleet of each nation so that it could operate only on its own side of the Pacific Ocean. In adopting this stand, the United States demonstrated a willingness to retain restrictions on its naval power which went far to curtail its ability to support the Nine Power Treaty by forceful measures and, indeed, seemed to indicate that it had little intention of doing so. At the same time Secretary Hull reaffirmed that he would not, even by implication, endorse Japan's efforts to destroy the Nine Power Treaty through his refusal to negotiate with the Japanese under conditions which he believed suggested a participation by the United States in their denunciation of all the Washington Conference agreements.

In 1935 the United States was confronted with two major developments in the Far East: the deterioration of the economic situation in China as a result of our silver policy and a dramatic resurgence of Japan's efforts to get control of China. By the end of 1934, it will be recalled, it had become evident that the impact of our silver policy on China was having disastrous consequences. The Chinese currency system seemed on the verge of collapse—a collapse which, it was predicted, might bring with it not only economic chaos but the political ruin of the Nanking regime. Anti-American feeling was rising and was likely to increase progressively as conditions in China worsened. According to the statements of leading Chinese officials, the Japanese were trying to capitalize on the situation with the result that the Nanking government might soon have to choose between cooperation with—which meant complete submission to—Japan or the extension of Japanese control over a large part of China.

Under these circumstances it was apparent that the United States would have to take some kind of action. The controversy that developed between the Treasury and State Departments was over the form which that action should assume. The State Department at the outset argued vigorously for a radical change in our silver policy[11] and against the procedure recommended by the Treasury, which was to provide China with financial assistance. Its attitude no doubt stemmed in part from the antipathy which existed within the Department to the silver legislation in general. But the Far Eastern specialists in the Department were especially concerned over the fact that, in their opinion, the Nanking government did not have the capacity to carry out a reorganization of its currency and that, consequently, if the United States supplied the Chinese with funds to engage in monetary reforms, it would soon find itself deeply involved in China's domestic affairs. Beyond that, Secretary Hull and his advisers on the Far East wished to adhere to the policy that they had decided upon at the time of the Amau declaration, which decreed that in view of the opposition of the Japanese the United States should not by itself undertake to furnish China with financial help. When it became evident that the President and Morgenthau would not make any significant change in our silver policy, the State Department suggested that the United States should consider assisting China in cooperation with other nations including Japan. This suggestion was followed to the extent of the United States government's expressing a willingness to support the initiative and leadership of the British, who wished to explore the possibility of aiding the Chinese in conjunction with the United States, France, and Japan. Secretary Morgenthau, however, objected to collaborating with the British. He feared that a situation would develop in which the representatives of other countries would embarrass the administration in Washington by advancing proposals for drastic alterations in our silver policy which, for domestic political reasons, it would be compelled to reject. But even more fundamentally, Morgenthau believed that the entire trend of the policy which the United States government was pursuing in the Far East should be reconsidered. The United States, he insisted, should cease to concentrate upon trying to avoid a conflict with Japan, and acting on its own should embark upon a vigorous effort to strengthen China

[11]Silver policy—The American policy, established by the Silver Purchase Act of June 1934, authorized the Secretary of the Treasury to buy silver until it constituted one fourth of the total United States monetary stocks of silver and gold. The law, brought about by the silver-producing states of the West to raise the price of silver, thus encouraged the export of Chinese silver to the United States, and this helped to drain silver from China and to undermine its currency, which was supposed to be backed by a silver reserve. [Editor's note.]

irrespective of the effect upon our relations with the Japanese. As the State Department held to its position, it looked for a while as though an impasse had been reached. After the Chinese issued their currency decree of November 1935,[12] however, the United States Treasury concluded the first of a series of agreements involving the purchase of Chinese silver. Secretary Morgenthau thereby instituted what he himself called his "monetary diplomacy," which, in the long run, was undoubtedly of great service to the Chinese and which he came to regard as one of the most important contributions he made during his years in office. The State Department, while attempting to keep a careful watch on Morgenthau's "monetary diplomacy" agreed to it because it was limited to a particular kind of financial transaction to which the Japanese raised no objections. The State Department felt, therefore, that Morgenthau's efforts did not interfere with the mainstream of the policy which it had been following and from which it did not want to depart.

Both in 1935 and 1936 that policy was put to a severe test by the renewal of Japanese aggression in China. Despite all the details contained in the large number of reports written by American Foreign Service officers on the Sino-Japanese struggle during those years, one overriding conclusion emerged, namely, that Japan was inexorably advancing toward its aim of securing control of China. There were presumed to be differences between the military faction, which represented the extremists in Japan, and the Foreign Office, which represented the moderates. The military were seen as attempting to take over China by a process of territorial partition starting with the alienation of the northern provinces. As long as they appeared to have a chance of dividing China by such methods as the establishment of puppet regimes, the Japanese armies would not, it was thought, resort to force. Moreover, it was hoped that the Japanese civilians still retained the will and the power to prevent an outright military invasion of China. The Japanese Foreign Office was regarded as determined to negotiate with the Nanking government on the basis of Hirota's three-point program.[13] However, this program, in the opinion of American Foreign Service officers, was

[12]Chinese . . . currency decree of November 1935—a decree which nationalized silver in China, forcing private holders, who had been selling it to the United States for dollars, to exchange their silver for Chinese legal tender notes only. [Editor's note.]

[13]Hirota's three-point program— program suggested by Japan's Foreign Minister, Koki Hirota, calling for China to (1) ally with Japan to suppress Communism in Asia;

far from being as innocuous as its vague phraseology might suggest. It was felt that, on the contrary, the realization of Hirota's "three principles" would gradually have the effect of transforming China into a colony, economically, politically, and militarily dependent upon Japan and devoid of all connection with other powers. Whether the blatantly aggressive tactics of the Japanese military or the ostensibly restrained procedures of the Japanese Foreign Office prevailed, the final outcome, if the Japanese were successful, would therefore be the same: the subjugation of China. By the end of 1935 the situation between Japan and China had reached the point where both our embassies in Peiping and in Tokyo were inclined to assume that this outcome was, in fact, all but inevitable—a position which they did not modify until the autumn of the following year.

American policy toward the Sino-Japanese struggle during 1935 and 1936 was first discussed in the interchange which occurred at the outset (January 1935) involving Hornbeck and Hull, and, finally, the President. Although the decisions reached were regarded as tentative, one need only bring them back to mind to recognize that the rules of conduct they embraced continued to serve as a guide for the administration during the next two years. The United States, it was agreed, should watch the situation developing between the Chinese and Japanese closely and, whenever necessary, ask for information from both sides; for the rest, it should refrain from action and as far as possible from comment without, however, creating an impression of indifference.

Subsequently the American government showed itself very reluctant to engage in any move regarding the various crises that arose, whether in connection with Japan's encroachments on North China or negotiations such as were conducted by General Chang Chun and Ambassador Kawagoe relative to Hirota's three points. Perhaps the United States would have elected to remain entirely silent if it had not been for the British. However, when the British undertook to register quite vigorous protests with the Japanese government, the United States was inclined to make some corresponding gesture if only to preserve the tradition of an Anglo-American parallel policy in the Far East, which it regarded as an important instrument of our diplomacy. At any rate, American officials held a number of

---

(2) abandon the policy of playing off one foreign nation against another; and (3) establish economic cooperation between China, Japan, and Manchukuo (Manchuria). [Editor's note.]

conversations with Japanese officials in Washington and Tokyo. But every effort was made, as the State Department itself explained on several occasions, to handle these conversations as tactfully as possible. For the most part the American officials involved, in accordance with the precepts laid down initially, avoided commenting upon developments and limited themselves to requesting information and indicating that the United States was not lacking in interest in what was taking place. The only time an exceptional note was injected into these talks was when Secretary Hull, in his interview with Yoshida in June 1936, expressed the opinion that to all appearances Japan was trying to attain exclusive economic domination first of China and then of other countries, which would eventually entail political and military domination as well. Hull's remarks as a whole, however, constituted another step in his general endeavor to meet the growing threat of aggression in Europe and Asia by educating both individual statesmen and the general public to an understanding and acceptance of the fundamentals of peace. In his comments to Yoshida, the Secretary emphasized that one of the avenues to peace lay in international cooperation of the kind he was attempting to promote through his reciprocal trade agreements. In addition to remarks made by American officials to Japanese officials in private, the Secretary issued his public statement of December 1935. Even more than his assertions to Yoshida, this pronouncement was intended as an appeal for greater comprehension and support of the cause of peace. The Japanese themselves apparently thought that Hull spoke in such general terms that his words provided no occasion for resentment in contrast to the specific and sometimes sharp representations made by the British.

The current of American policy, therefore, continued to flow in channels which by this time were well established. The United States government interfered in the Sino-Japanese controversy to only a minor degree and on the whole maintained a position which was at times described within the confines of the State Department as "playing no favorites" between the disputants. The main reason for not altering American policy itself remained unchanged, being clearly the desire of the administration to stabilize our relations with Japan. However, since despite an official attitude of impartiality there existed a large reservoir of sympathy for the Chinese within the administration, much thought was given to the effect of our policy on China. It was often contended that if the United States took a definite position against Japan and exercised nonmilitary pressures (coercion admittedly being out of the question) the consequences might actually be harmful to the Chinese. The anger generated by Stimson's diplomacy would almost inevitably be revived with the result that the Japanese people and especially their military leaders might well become even more chauvinistic and belligerent. It was also argued that under any circumstances it was useless for the United States to engage in measures short of war as the only means of stopping the Japanese was through military action. But in the case of many internationalists, both in and out of the administration, this argument seems to have been at least partially a rationalization. For they became strong advocates of the use of measures short of war against Japan when, after the Marco Polo Bridge incident,[14] the paramount issue was once again the establishment and maintenance of world order.

From the viewpoint of the United States, the most important conclusion to be drawn from the events of 1935 and 1936 was that the trend of our policy was in fact so fixed that, as has been suggested in previous chapters, it was not likely to be changed unless some new and vitally important element was introduced into the situation. The MacMurray memorandum[15] and the pertinent dispatches written in the winter of 1935-1936 by Ambassadors Grew and Johnson show that American officials were already accepting as a possibility, if not a probability, that the struggle between Japan and China would continue in its present form and result in the Japanese achieving all they wanted in the near future. The question raised among American officials was not, however, whether the United States could forestall this eventuality but rather whether it should subsequently enter into some agreement or agreements with the Japanese which might, hopefully, render its position *vis-à-vis* Japan less dangerous.

Yet the events which dominated the closing months of the year 1936 unexpectedly challenged the view that the subjugation of

[14]Marco Polo Bridge incident—the clash between Japanese and Chinese troops outside of Peiping on July 7, 1937, that marked the beginning of Japan's war against China. [Editor's note.]

[15]MacMurray memorandum—a note by John Von Antwerp MacMurray, formerly United States Minister to China 1925-1929, to Secretary Hull in November 1935, which said that in the long run Japan would dominate China and that America ought to maintain its diplomatic principles but do nothing in fact that would antagonize Japan. [Editor's note.]

China by Japan was both inevitable and imminent. The reports of American Foreign Service officers, which had for so long been devoid of any note of optimism in regard to China, suddenly adopted a new tone. Beginning with the Suiyuan campaign,[16] they were filled with descriptions of the success being achieved by the Chinese people in attaining unity, the growth of the popular determination to resist Japan, and the transition from defeatism to hope through which the country was passing. Nevertheless, American officials seem frequently to have been unaware of even the major developments that were contributing to the ferment in China. A case in point is the interpretation by officials, both in China and in Washington, of the Sian incident as a play for personal aggrandizement on the part of Chang Hsueh-liang comparable to the act of an old-fashioned warlord or an ordinary "gangster." Even admitting that various aspects of the Sian incident[17] are still obscure, there was certainly enough evidence available to the United States government at the time to indicate that the capture of the Generalissimo involved the most important issues facing the nation and could not reasonably be regarded as a venture undertaken by the Young Marshall merely for selfish gains.

Moreover, the favorable reaction of American Foreign Service officers to developments in China was not matched by any practical support from the United States of the kind which the Chinese were seeking—economic assistance. The American government, the American banking group in the Consortium, and the American industrial community, each for its own reasons, remained reluctant to participate in China's reconstruction as other governments and nationals were doing. The first sign of a possible change of major significance in the American position came when in July 1937 the Export-Import Bank indicated its willingness to consider the extension of substantial credits to China. By then, however, the situation in the Far East was in the process of being radically transformed and the administration soon arrived at the decision to postpone all action indefinitely.

[16]Suiyuan campaign—Japanese military campaign in this northern China province in the summer of 1935 which failed to secure desired political and/or economic concessions. [Editor's note.]

[17]Sian incident—In December 1936, Chang Hsueh-liang, warlord of Manchuria whose forces had been driven out by Japan, kidnapped Chiang Kai-shek in an effort to get him to declare war on Japan. Chinese public support for Chiang, however, was so great that Chang Hsueh-liang had to release him shortly and was himself imprisoned. [Editor's note.]

The confusion concerning the Chinese Communists that existed among American officials in the early and mid-1930's has been discussed at some length in chapter VII, partly because of its current interest. The examination of the documents which formed the basis of this chapter seemed repeatedly to suggest that the confusion was caused by a particular set of circumstances. With few exceptions American Foreign Service officers in China had little more than a superficial knowledge of the Chinese Communist movement owing primarily to the many obstacles which either hampered or prevented the ferreting out of information and owing also to their own lack of enterprise. The specialists on China within the State Department at home were unable to make up for the deficiencies of the officers in the field for the simple reason that as human beings they were influenced by the intellectual atmosphere in the United States at a time when few people as yet saw the need for any genuine understanding of communism. In turn, the inadequacies of the China specialists were not rectified by the experts on the Soviet Union in the State Department whether because of a lack of coordination or an inclination to view communism in China as a peripheral subject. Whatever the causes of the confusion, the immediate consequence was that American officials were ill-prepared first to recognize and then to interpret the extension to China of the united front policy promulgated in Moscow. As, following the Sian incident, there was more and more talk of a "reconciliation" between the Communists and the Kuomintang, our embassy in China saw the action of the Chinese Communists as another example of the "tremendous growth" of the "ideal of national unity" affecting all Chinese political factions.

The spring of 1937 was also marked by the discussion which arose within the administration over the problem of fortifying the Pacific islands. This discussion, together with the manner in which the administration handled the entire fortifications issue, assumes particular significance in retrospect. The President's plan for the neutralization of the Pacific islands had important implications. Admittedly, Roosevelt in all likelihood did not expect his neutralization scheme to be incorporated in a treaty in precisely the form in which he initially conceived it. Nevertheless the mere fact that he advanced such a proposal shows that as late as the eve of the Sino-Japanese war he was still thinking in terms of solving the problems of the Pacific area not by the exercise of pressure against Japan but by negotiating a multilateral agreement to which it would be a party. Moreover, the agreement which Roosevelt envisaged was bound to be regarded not only as a friendly gesture toward the Japanese but an exceedingly friendly gesture. For it required the Western powers to disarm most of their territories in the Pacific in return for a pledge from Japan that it would do likewise. Since, as critics of Roosevelt's neutralization idea pointed out, experience had demonstrated that Japan was not likely to observe its pledges, the chances were that the President's scheme would operate overwhelmingly in its favor.

In any event, Roosevelt's plan elicited little support within either the American or British governments and was gradually set aside. In addition, no agreement on the fortifications issue was concluded with the Japanese. On the other hand, no steps were taken in respect to the construction of defenses in the Pacific area that could reasonably lead to dissension between the United States and Japan. Thus, even in relation to a matter of great military significance, the administration held to the passive position which it had been maintaining in the Far East.

Shortly after the President had advanced his neutralization plan, Neville Chamberlain suggested that the United States and Great Britain might reach some sort of an understanding with Japan which would help to prevent the outbreak of a general war in the Pacific area. In connection with these developments, the State Department indicated on several occasions that it was in favor of awaiting the time when it would be possible to conclude another comprehensive settlement comparable to that achieved at the Washington Conference. What the Department evidently had in mind was an agreement that would both reaffirm the general principles embodied in the Nine Power Treaty and deal with specific problems like those with which the Washington Naval Treaty had been concerned. Before the summer of 1937, Department officials seem to have entertained little hope of being able to negotiate such a settlement with Japan for a long time, perhaps even within the next decade. But by June 1937 they were more optimistic about the possibility of Japan's cooperating with other powers in the interests of peace.

All optimism was, however, quickly dispelled. In July 1937 the phase of the struggle between Japan and China that had been marked by an absence of extensive fighting came to an end. The outbreak of a major armed conflict in the Far East created a situation analogous to that which had prevailed during the Manchurian crisis. As a consequence, the American government was again confronted with the question of whether to adopt the isolationist view that the United States should not intervene in disputes between other nations or whether to take the internationalist position that an act of aggression anywhere should be dealt with by all the "law-abiding" members of the community of nations for the sake of preserving world peace. It was evident, however, that if the adminstration chose the second of these alternatives it would have to contend with even greater difficulties than those which beset Stimson. The international machinery for the maintenance of peace, created after the World War, had progressively deteriorated since the Manchurian crisis and within the United States itself isolationism had become more widespread. At the same time the whole problem of suppressing aggression had assumed a far greater urgency owing to the possibility of war in Europe which might be joined with the struggle in Asia.

In the first months of the Sino-Japanese conflict, Hull emerges as the most conspicuous figure in the conduct of our diplomacy. The Secretary showed at once that he intended to adopt a policy that, like Stimson's, would have as its primary purpose the furtherance of the internationalist cause which would also serve to counter the spread of war in Europe. The most important step that Hull took initially was the issuance of his statements of July 16 and August 23. These statements were intended, first, to lay down the thesis that any war was essentially the concern not only of the parties to the dispute but of all countries interested in the maintenance of world peace and, secondly, to declare that this thesis applied specifically to the situation in the Far East. Hull deliberately refrained from stating which party was the aggressor in the conflict in the Far East and insisted that he was adhering to a policy of "strict impartiality." Nevertheless, he undoubtedly felt that he was making quite a drastic move in proclaiming a doctrine which ran counter to the basic tenet of isolationism and which established a theoretic foundation for action by the United States in respect of the disputes of others.

Hull also revealed, perhaps more clearly than was recognized at the time, the nature of the action that he intended to take for the present, which was essentially one of moral suasion. In his statement of July 16, the Secretary enumerated the principles which, in his opinion, had to be respected if universal peace was to be preserved. In a passage, which he himself repeated verbatim on a number of important occasions thereafter, he listed such precepts as "abstinence by all nations from the use of force," "adjustment of problems in international relations by process of peaceful negotiation," "respect by all nations for the rights of others," and observance of the "sanctity of treaties." The Secretary sent his July 16 statement to all of the governments of the world requesting an expression of their views. By doing so he sought to prod other statesmen into arousing their peoples to express disapproval of the breach of the peace that had occurred in the Far East which meant, at least by implication, of Japanese aggression. World public opinion, he believed, would operate as a moral sanction toward dissuading the Japanese from continuing their attack upon China. In addition, Hull hoped to achieve certain long-term results. Consonant with his faith in the efficacy of moral education, he thought that by engaging in a prolonged and persistent campaign of reiterating the "principles upon which peace alone can exist" he could gradually awaken the conscience of peoples everywhere to the point of supporting vigorous action against any nation that violated those principles. In particular, he felt that through such a process of enlightenment—and perhaps only through such a process—he could lead the American people themselves away from isolationism. Hull also believed that, if an awareness of the importance of moral values became more widespread, the rulers who entertained false nationalistic ambitions for their countries might resist the temptation to resort to aggression or, failing this, might be prevented from embarking upon military adventures by the opposition of their own people. Long-term as these results might be, the Secretary apparently trusted that he could make sufficient progress toward their attainment to avert the catastrophe of a war in Europe.

Hull's activities during the late summer of 1937 constituted an effort to carry forward the policy initiated in his statements of July 16 and August 23. In this connection, it is of interest to remember the entries in Pierrepont Moffat's diary, which relate that the Secretary wished to issue still a third moral pronouncement in September and only relinquished the idea with considerable reluctance upon the earnest counsel of his advisers. Certainly the Secretary's behind-the-scenes activities during the debates on the Sino-Japanese case at the League were almost exclusively directed toward getting the states represented at Geneva to make a declaration which would have amounted to a restatement of the principles which he had already enunciated and a renewed expression of disapproval of any country that transgressed them. At first Hull wanted the League to adhere to the "strict impartiality" which he had continued to observe, and refrain from explicitly putting the blame for the breach of the peace in the Far East upon Japan; but as the proceedings at Geneva progressed he seems to have changed his mind on this point. In the end the League did censure the Japanese, though for its own reasons it based its disapprobation on Japan's violation of the Kellogg-Briand Pact and the Nine Power Treaty rather than the general moral precepts which the Secretary thought should be made the focus of attention. Hull immediately endorsed the League's action but also doggedly held to his own brand of moral denunciation by seizing the opportunity to repeat the principles, which he had been proclaiming, and to assert that the Japanese had ignored these fundamental rules of conduct as well as the terms of the specific agreements cited by the League.

Hull thus consistently adhered to his strategy of moral suasion. At the same time he made every effort to avoid any situation which might result in the United States government's having to take a stronger stand against Japan. In the period before the League considered the Sino-Japanese dispute, the British approached the State Department with as many as half a dozen different proposals for attempting to terminate the fighting in China through some form of Anglo-American cooperation. Hull rejected the British plans for a variety of reasons but foremost among them was certainly the fear that they might entail the exercise of considerable pressure against the Japanese. After the League took official cognizance of the Sino-Japanese conflict, the Secretary adamantly refused to associate himself with the proceedings at Geneva in any but the most perfunctory way. Evidently haunted by memories of the Manchurian crisis, he was determined not to be drawn into a discussion in which other powers might seek to make the United States assume the leadership of a movement directed against the Japanese. Again, at the beginning of October, Hull turned aside the British suggestion for an exploration of the possible use of a boycott against Japan and all but stated that the American government would not resort to economic sanctions. Indeed, a few days later the Secretary frankly told the Japanese ambassador that while he had felt fully justified in supporting the censure of Japan, voted by more than fifty nations at the League, he was not considering any departure from the policy which he had been pursuing since the outbreak of hostilities in the Far East.

If Hull was the central figure in the conduct of our policy in the first months of the Sino-Japanese war, he was dramatically supplanted by the President in early October when Roosevelt delivered his "quarantine" speech at Chicago. The President's own statements leave no doubt that, like Hull, his main aim in dealing with the Sino-Japanese conflict was to strengthen the internationalist movement and to forestall the advent of an armed clash in Europe which might merge with that in Asia. The question of the President's strategy, however, requires closer scrutiny and takes us back to the story of Roosevelt's search for a peace plan.

The main elements of the story which were emphasized in detail in the discussion presented earlier, can be briefly summarized. The President embarked upon his effort to find a peace plan well before the commencement of the fighting in China. From early 1936 to his enthusiastic espousal of the Welles plan immediately following his Chicago address, Roosevelt considered a whole series of schemes that contained certain fundamental differences. Some had as their goal the establishment of a "lasting peace," others the elimination of the immediate threat of war on either a world-wide or regional basis, while still others were designed to fulfill both these objectives. Even more importantly, they relied upon a wide variety of methods to attain their ends.

In general, however, the plans which sought to meet the immediate situation provided for the use of conciliatory measures. As in the case of the President's proposal for the neutralization of the Pacific islands, they tended to call for the conclusion of a multilateral agreement which would remove some of the problems leading to the existing international tension. But in the summer of 1937 Roosevelt also spoke on a number of occasions of the idea of quarantining an aggressor, which he incorporated in his Chicago address. To all appearances, the President was looking for an answer to the much discussed problem of how to develop a better method of collective action against an aggressor than that provided for in the Covenant of the League which, it was felt, was likely to result in a general war. More specifically, the President hoped to find a method of international organization which would enable the "peace-loving" members of the international community to oppose an aggressor without resorting to military sanctions or otherwise involving themselves in hostilities. For the reasons previously indicated, Roosevelt seems to have thought that his concept of quarantining or isolating an aggressor was a step in the right direction. But the President's concept was so rudimentary that he may well have advanced it more as a suggestion that in his opinion held considerable promise than one which he himself regarded as furnishing a practical basis for action. In any event, Roosevelt never decided upon any plan for applying his "quarantine" idea. At times, he indicated that it might be incorporated in a treaty to be signed by all the countries of the world which would lay the foundations of a "lasting peace," presumably by discouraging would-be aggressors. At other times, he mentioned the possibility of excluding Germany, Italy, and Japan from such an agreement as a warning to them not to engage in acts of international violence. In the latter connection the President stated, however, that he was thinking in terms of deterring the "three bandit nations" in the future rather than of stopping Japan's current assault upon China, since what had been done could not be undone. All in all, Roosevelt advanced one proposal after another with bewildering rapidity. Moreover, he never stopped considering plans which were based upon the kind of conciliatory approach he had favored from the outset. In the end he settled upon the program suggested by Sumner Welles which involved the negotiation of a multilateral agreement dealing with relatively noncontroversial issues such as certain rules of international law. The main purpose of this program was to secure the participation of Hitler and Mussolini in an undertaking that might improve their relations with the democracies and thereby lead to a subsequent effort to solve some of the major causes of friction. In the case of the Far East, it was thought that if it proved possible to reduce the tensions in Europe, Germany and Italy might withhold their support of Japan at least to the extent of forcing that country to conclude a peace with China on terms that did not violate the principles of the Nine Power Treaty. However, the Welles plan was also soon to be laid aside although it was revived in the following year in the brief but famous episode that included its rejection by Prime Mininster Chamberlain.

The story of Roosevelt's search for a peace plan consequently points to the conclusion that up to the beginning of October 1937 the President did not have any definite strategy for dealing with the international situation in general, much less the Sino-Japanese conflict in particular. While at times he may have hoped to discover a magic solution and been impatient with the slow methods adopted by his Secretary of State, the fact of the matter seems to be that he had not devised any alternative course and, in regard to the crisis in the Far East, was prepared to support the policy Hull was following.

At the beginning of October censure of Japan was therefore to all appearances as far as either the President or the Secretary intended presently to go. Among the many factors influencing their attitude, public opinion has been emphasized in this study because of its apparent importance. Like the administration, the American people as a whole ostensibly felt that for the United States the main issue involved in the struggle in Asia was whether to follow an isolationist or an internationalist course. The problems which proved to be most controversial were the protection of our nationals in China, the possible application of the Neutrality Act[18] to the hostilities in the Far East, and the President's "quarantine" speech. The groups that expressed themselves with the greatest vigor consisted of congressmen, sections of the press, and representatives of organizations that largely belonged to the peace movement.

Throughout the discussion of the questions of protection and neutrality, there was sufficient division of opinion among both the isolationists and internationalists to allow the administration considerable latitude to act as it chose. As a consequence, additional troops were sent to China to provide adequate safeguards for American citizens and the Neutrality Act was not invoked. However, at such times as vigorous opposition to the measures undertaken by the government developed on the isolationist side, especially in the wing of the peace movement that was currently advocating many isolationist tenets, the extreme sensitivity of the administration to adverse criticism became strikingly evident. While by no means fully retreating, both the President and Hull made substantial concessions.

The administration was similarly responsive to the outcries of isolationists following the President's "quarantine" speech. Hull has testified to his own great distress at what he regarded as the widespread violent denunciation of the address and, according to others, Roosevelt was scarcely less disturbed. The effect of their concern upon our subsequent policy toward the Far Eastern crisis is essentially an imponderable factor. But certainly as the Brussels Conference approached the administration seemed, if anything, more determined than ever to avoid making any move that might invite an isolationist attack. The memorandum that Roosevelt dictated before the opening of the conference to guide Norman Davis in his relations with the British was nothing if not a powerful

---

[18]Neutrality Act—of May 1937 which forbade shipment of war materials to all belligerent powers, but allowed shipment of goods other than munitions on a "cash and carry" basis. [Editor's note.]

injunction to remain within the bounds prescribed by isolationist sentiment with its anti-British bias. Moreover, in his instructions regarding our policy as a whole at Brussels, Roosevelt went far toward stating that he did not want to take any strong action against the Japanese unless and until isolationist opinion in the United States altered radically. Further, it is apparent from the dispatches sent to Davis that throughout the Brussels Conference both the President and Hull paid the closest attention to the isolationist criticism to which the administration as a whole and Davis in particular was subjected. In chapter XI, which deals with public opinion, the question has been raised of whether, in their desire to avoid a political struggle, the President, Hull, and the administration in general did not pay undue attention to all signs of isolationist opposition while overlooking important manifestations of inter-nationalist support (a case in point being their evaluation of the country's reaction to the "quarantine" speech). This is a question which does not lie within our province in reviewing the trend of American policy. It is, however, one that needs further exploration, as historians of the Roosevelt era fully recognize.

The test of whether the administration would or would not go beyond the policy that it had been pursuing since the start of the war in China came at the Brussels Conference. The preparatory stage of the conference was dominated by the President's instructions to Norman Davis. In retrospect, these instructions are primarily important because they indicate that Roosevelt's position remained the same in that he had no means of dealing with the conflict in the Far East beyond the use of the kind of moral suasion that Hull favored. The President's directions to Davis were clear in so far as they stated that at the outset of the conference every effort must be made to bring about a settlement of the conflict between Japan and China and that the pressure of world public opinion must be brought to bear on the Japanese to assist in the attainment of this end. But when it came to the question of what should be done, if the attempt to secure a settlement failed, Roosevelt had no definite proposals. While he spoke of possible punitive action against Japan and mentioned that the conference might consider a general attempt to "ostracize" the Japanese, he never amplified these points. Moreover, he hedged by laying down conditions that there was virtually no hope of fulfilling. Any action, he said in substance, that was decided upon by the conference must represent the almost unanimous opinion of the people in the "overwhelming majority" of the nations of the world. There can be no doubt that Davis understood the President to mean that if it proved impossible to persuade Japan to come to terms with China he was prepared to join with the other powers at Brussels in adopting a program of sanctions. But one may surmise that owing to the confused nature of the President's remarks Davis read into them more than was there. This likelihood is even greater since Davis himself was convinced that, if the Japanese remained intransigent, it was imperative for the conference to demonstrate that the "law-abiding" nations of the world were determined to put an end to aggression, if necessary even at the cost of fighting a war.

The Brussels Conference would in any event have been a challenge to the administration to determine whether it would exceed its present policy. For the other large powers represented at Brussels went much further than had been anticipated in Washington in urging a consideration of the use of coercive measures against Japan. But the real challenge came from Davis himself when he asked Washington to submit a resolution to the conference which included provisions for the application of the nonrecognition doctrine and of financial sanctions against Japan, and to recommend to Congress the suspension or repeal of the Neutrality Act. The situation was not entirely lacking in irony since Davis must have thought that his proposals not only lay within the boundaries of his instructions but were very modest compared to the President's idea that it might be possible to "ostracize" Japan. In any event, there followed the administration's rejection of Davis's suggestions, Davis's appeal for a reconsideration of his plan, and finally Hull's assertion that the United States government would not go beyond the policy which it had been pursuing since the beginning of the trouble in the Far East.

The intensity of feeling on the administration's side was demonstrated by the unusual bitterness that the State Department injected into its exchange with Davis. The main points were that the Department insisted that a consideration of coercive measures did not fall within the scope of the conference which had been called for the sole purpose of negotiating an agreement between Japan and China. Davis countered by saying that none of the other interested governments shared this view. The Department then declared that the question of punitive measures had been debated by the members of the League in September and decided in the negative; it therefore had no place in the present discussions. Further, the Department charged that the other countries represented at Brussels were attempting largely through inspired stories in the press, to place the blame upon the United States for the failure of the conference to impose sanctions upon Japan when the blame was really theirs, since they had already demonstrated their unwillingness to entertain the idea of taking any action. Davis replied in effect that the Department's claims did not conform to the realities of the situation. The issue of sanctions, he said, had purposely been left open by the members of the League when they met at Geneva; moreover, since the beginning of the proceedings at Brussels most of the other nations had consistently maintained the position that they would resort to "pressure methods" against Japan if the United States would cooperate. The Department, however, held to its opinions and even threatened to issue a public statement proving its contentions.

The net result of the Brussels Conference was that the administration not only repudiated any thought of altering its course but Hull reasserted his belief that much could be accomplished by adhering to his policy of reiterating the principles which must govern international relationships if peace was to prevail. Throughout the latter part of the conference the Secretary persistently urged the delegates at Brussels to issue a declaration comparable to his statements of July 16 and August 23 and eventually succeeded in having a reaffirmation of some of the principles he had enunciated earlier incorporated in the final pronouncement of the conference.

Another fundamental aspect of the administration's policy was put to the test by the efforts of the Japanese to reach an agreement with China outside the framework of the Brussels Conference or any organized group of nations operating on the basis of the right of collective intervention in international disputes. It is evident from the material made available since the war that for a variety of reasons the government at Tokyo genuinely wanted to negotiate a settlement with Nanking and to use the good offices of other nations—especially Great Britain, the United States, and Germany—for that purpose. Although the chances that Japan and China would have come to terms are small, the possibility cannot be discounted. It has been suggested that the likelihood of a settlement might have been increased by a well-timed move on the part of Great Britain and the United States to serve as intermediaries. If so, the position adopted by the United States becomes all the more significant. At any rate, that position was that the administration in

Washington would not undertake to convey peace proposals between China and Japan unless assured by the Japanese in advance that the terms they would offer would conform to the principles of the Nine Power Treaty. To lay down any such condition, however, went far toward precluding action since little hope was entertained that the Japanese would accept it. The American attitude differed sharply from that of the British, who contended that the important factor was to get the negotiations under way after which various influences might conspire to bring about a satisfactory outcome; furthermore, that the American and British governments could safeguard their own integrity by announcing that they were merely trying to facilitate an exchange of views between the belligerents but were not responsible for whatever proposals were advanced. But officials in Washington did not modify their stand nor is there any reason to suppose they would have done so even if circumstances had not changed. For the administration was evidently convinced that to associate itself in any way with negotiations which might terminate in an agreement that was incompatible with the principles of the Nine Power Treaty would be to grant the Japanese a measure of the moral support for their aggression in China which it had long been determined to withhold.

With the sinking of the gunboat *Panay* in December 1937, the possibility arose that the American government might completely reverse the current of its policy in the Far East and engage in vigorous, retaliatory measures which would result in war with Japan. But such a possibility appears to have remained remote. The attack upon the *Panay* was an extraordinary affront to the United States and therefore inevitably a great shock to the country as a whole. Some high officials, primarily naval officials, advocated an immediate showdown with the Japanese on the grounds that it was only a matter of time before a clash would occur between the United States and Japan and that there was more to lose than to gain by postponing it. However, as far as could be judged the American people, whether internationalist or isolationist minded, did not regard the *Panay* incident as a justifiable cause for war as there was no proof that the Japanese government had been directly implicated. At the outset the President explored many different ways of dealing with the situation, some of which were very drastic, such as the possible seizure of Japanese assets, the feasibility of which he asked Morgenthau to investigate. But in discussing the *Panay* crisis at the cabinet meeting, which was held when matters were at their worst, Roosevelt indicated that he neither wanted to go to war with Japan nor to adopt measures that ran the risk of precipitating a war and—at least in the writer's judgment—he probably never departed far from this position. Certainly the measures which were put into practice were exceedingly moderate. The most important of these was the dispatch of Captain Ingersoll to England on the mission on which he engaged in staff talks with the British. As we now know, however, the talks were conceived from the first as a modest undertaking and produced relatively insignificant results.

The main feature of the days following the *Panay* crisis was the fact that while the administration's concern over the possibility of a general war between the democracies and the dictatorships increased, no real change was effected in American policy. A search for a fresh solution of the international situation was renewed. But the plans which were discussed continued to be temperate, the underlying idea being for the most part to make a further effort to bring the European powers together and to undertake some limited naval move in the Pacific which would be designed as a display of Anglo-American cooperation *vis-à-vis* Japan. In the end, for a variety of reasons, little of consequence was achieved.

Meanwhile, Japan and China were absorbed in the acute controversy which terminated in the severance of relations between their governments in mid-January, bringing to a close the first stage of the Sino-Japanese conflict. American officials watched events approach their denouement with a heavy sense of foreboding that the Chinese were heading into disaster as their armies appeared on the verge of collapse while conditions had reached a point where a settlement with the Japanese was obviously impossible except on terms of abject surrender. The only move which the administration seems to have seriously contemplated, however, was a last-minute appeal to the Japanese government to modify its actions. A message to this effect, it will be remembered, was actually drafted by the State Department but was not submitted to the authorities in Tokyo on the advice of Ambassador Grew.

It is apparent that there were differences between the policy of the Roosevelt administration in the period preceding and following the Marco Polo Bridge incident. Before July 1937 our relations with the countries of East Asia were mainly influenced by the views of members of the Far Eastern Division of the State Department and certain Foreign Service officers. Subsequently, policy was formed on the highest level of the United States government. In advance of the outbreak of fighting in the Far East, the administration dealt with the struggle between China and Japan as though it was in large measure confined to those two countries although admittedly it had serious implications for the security of the United States in the long run. But after the development of a full-scale war in the Far East, the President and Secretary of State themselves were convinced that the Sino-Japanese conflict involved broader issues which were intimately connected with the welfare of all nations; and furthermore, that Japan's attack upon China might precipitate a concerted effort on the part of the Axis powers to overwhelm the European democracies. As a consequence of their assumption that the character of the Far Eastern crisis had changed, the aims of American policy shifted automatically. Nevertheless the administration's method of procedure remained to a remarkable extent the same. In the making of specific decisions, officials in Washington returned again and again to the conclusion that they should avoid any action or should hold action to a minimum. The degree of passivity which the United States government maintained is the feature of our record in the Far East in the mid-1930's that is most likely to seem astonishing in retrospect. For with the benefit of hindsight it is evident that the events which culminated in the second World War were closing in upon peoples everywhere with a terrible rapidity.

ARNOLD A. OFFNER

American Appeasement, 1933-1938

Arnold A. Offner (born 1937) is Associate Professor of History at Boston University. He has written several articles as well as the book from which this selection is taken.

FROM SPRING to autumn 1938 the developing crisis between Germany and Czechoslovakia absorbed European energies. American diplomats abroad seemed to fear most that England and France would oppose Hitler's demands and thus precipitate world

Reprinted by permission of the publishers from *American Appeasement: United States Foreign Policy and Germany, 1933-1938,* Cambridge, Mass.: The Belknap Press of Harvard University Press, Copyright, 1969, by the President and Fellows of Harvard College.

war. Ambassador Wilson, sympathetic toward German aspirations, confessed limited admiration for Czechoslovakia's "gallant impulse" to resist, but doubted its wisdom if it jeopardized peace. He also suspected, as he confided to his equally suspicious colleague in Berlin, Nevile Henderson, that the Czechs were counting on French and Soviet, and eventually British, support and therefore intended to provoke a showdown with Germany rather than await negotiations.[1] Ambassador Bullitt, once the champion of the Soviet Union but after three disillusioning years in Moscow now its bitter critic, believed that the best way to thwart Soviet designs would be to encourage reconciliation between France and Germany.[2] He seemed relieved when in May French Premier Edouard Daladier snapped "With what?" when he asked if France would fight if Germany attacked Czechoslovakia.[3] Ambassador Kennedy thought that almost no price was too high to pay to avert war and that, above all, if war came the United States must stay out. In August he worriedly told Foreign Secretary Halifax that if Hitler seized Czechoslovakia "it will be hell," and that if France went in, so must Great Britain, with the United States following shortly. Perhaps, then, if Germany were allowed to control southeastern Europe, economic developments would either paralyze or pacify Germany politically.[4] Kennedy's unabashed favoring of German economic expansion and closer Anglo-German relations, and his desire to say publicly, "I can't for the life of me understand why anybody would want to go to war to save the Czechs"—the State Department struck this from the text of an address in September—implied too much for his superiors in Washington. Roosevelt concluded to Morgenthau that Kennedy "needs his wrists slapped rather hard."[5] But the

[1]Wilson to Hull, Apr. 28, 1938, U.S. Department of State, *Foreign Relations of the United States, 1938,* 5 vols. (Washington, D. C., 1955), I, 490; Henderson to Halifax, May 13, 1938, E. L. Woodward and Rohan Butler (eds.), *Documents on British Foreign Policy, 1919-1939,* three series, 32 vols., (London, 1946——), 3d ser., I, 290-291.

[2]William W. Kaufmann, "Two American Ambassadors: Bullitt and Kennedy," in Gordon A. Craig and Felix Gilbert, eds., *The Diplomats: 1919-1939* (Princeton, 1953), 656-657; Beatrice Farnsworth, *William C. Bullitt and the Soviet Union* (Bloomington, Ind., and London, 1967), 158-159.

[3]Bullitt to Hull, May 9, 1938, *FR 1938,* I, 493-494.

[4]Halifax to Lindsay, Sept. 2, 1938, *DBFP,* 3d ser., II, 212-213. See also Kaufmann, "Two Ambassadors," in Craig and Gilbert, eds., *The Diplomats,* 658-659.

[5]Morgenthau Diary, as cited in John Morton Blum, *From the Morgenthau Diaries: Years of Crisis, 1928-1938* (Boston, 1959), 518.

American attitude toward European developments and the position the United States might take in event of a crisis, or war, remained ambiguous at best, on the side of misguided appeasement at worst.

* * *

During the summer of 1938 diplomats in Washington watched European events through worried eyes. Reports from overseas led them to conclude that Hitler would wage war over the Sudetenland but might be dissuaded by firm statements. As Bullitt put it, clearly overoptimistically, fear of what the United States might do was a "large factor in Hitler's hesitation to start war."[6] The State Department, helping to draft a speech for Roosevelt, hoped that was the case. As Assistant Secretary Adolf A. Berle wrote, Europe was on the verge of a "blow-up" and the purpose of the speech would be "to create a certain amount of doubt as to what our intentions may be," and thus have "a moderating effect."[7]

At Queens University in Kingston, Ontario, on August 18 Roosevelt declared that the United States would not sit idly by if another empire tried to dominate Canada, and that the day had passed when controversies beyond the seas did not interest or harm the people of the Americas.[8] This meant, of course, that the United States would defend Canada, not European nations, and Roosevelt admitted privately that an American president could have made the identical statement fifty years before; he had made it then because it seemed "to fit in with the Hitler situation," and perhaps would have "some small effect in Berlin."[9]

Hitler paid no attention, at least to judge from his military preparations and dismissal of Beck's[10] warnings. The German press ridiculed assertions, which the French were attempting to give rise to, that Roosevelt's remarks had extended the guarantee for Canada

[6]Bullitt to Roosevelt, Aug. 17, 1938, Franklin D. Roosevelt papers, President's Secretary's File, France: William Bullitt, Franklin D. Roosevelt Library, Hyde Park, N.Y.

[7]Berle Memorandum for Roosevelt, Aug. 15, 1938, Roosevelt papers, PSF, State Department Files: Adolf A. Berle.

[8]Text in Samuel I. Rosenman, comp., *The Public Papers and Addresses of Franklin D. Roosevelt,* 13 vols. (New York, 1938-50), VII, 491-494.

[9]Roosevelt to Lord Tweedsmuir, Aug. 31, 1938, Roosevelt papers, President's Personal File, 3396.

[10]General Ludwig Beck, Chief of the General Staff of the German Army, who opposed going to war over Czechoslovakia and warned that the United States would aid England and France. Beck resigned his post on August 18, 1938. [Editor's note.]

to the whole British empire and France.[11] The British, or at least Halifax, approved the address; on August 24 he told the chargé in London, Herschel Johnson, that they feared German military action in the near future, and he said that perhaps another similar statement might help to restrain Hitler.[12] Halifax also saw Kennedy a week later and apparently asked him to inquire what position the United States would assume if Germany marched but England did not.[13] Kennedy meanwhile conferred with Chamberlain on August 30. Chamberlain made a veiled reference to the secret talks on August 18-19 between the chief diplomatic adviser for the Foreign Office, Sir Robert Vansittart, and Churchill, and the emissary who had been sent to London by the German military, Ewald von Kleist. Kleist had emphatically warned that Hitler intended war at a specific date, that the military opposed the plan, and that Hitler might be restrained if a leading British statesman warned that a German attack would lead to a "general catastrophe."[14] According to Halifax's report to Ambassador Lindsay in Washington, Chamberlain on August 30 told Kennedy that the British had heard from various sources that Hitler intended to invade Czechoslovakia and that only a firm British declaration could force him to abandon the idea. But, Chamberlain said, the British were in no position to stop Hitler, and threats would be unwise. Kennedy agreed, and added that "it will be hell" if Germany attacked Czechoslovakia, and that if France went in, and the British had to, the United States would probably follow before long. Both men concluded that repetition of Roosevelt's warning would be "bad" and Kennedy said that Roosevelt had "decided to go in with Chamberlain; whatever course

[11]Boris Celovsky, *Das Münchener Abkommen von 1938* (Stuttgart, 1958), 250; Joseph Engelbert Heindl, *Die diplomatischen Beziehungen zwischen Deutschland und den Vereinigten Staaten von Amerika, von 1933 bis 1939* (Ph.D. dissertation, University of Wurzburg, 1963 [privately printed, 1964?]), 123-124.

[12]Johnson to Hull, Aug. 24, 1938, *FR 1938*, I, 551; see also Halifax to Lindsay, Aug. 24, 1938, *DBFP*, 3d ser., II, 149.

[13]Kennedy to Hull, Aug. 31, 1938, *FR 1938*, I, 565-566.

[14]On these talks see Note of Conversation between Vansittart and Kleist, Aug. 18, Chamberlain to Halifax, Aug. 19, Note of Conversation between Churchill and Kleist (undated), and Letter given by Churchill to Kleist, Aug. 19, 1938, *DBFP*, 3d ser., II, 683-689. See also Foreign Ministry Memorandum (undated), U.S. Department of State, *Documents on German Foreign Policy, 1918-1945*, series D, 13 vols. (Washington, D.C., 1949-1964), II, 704-710, which includes Churchill's letter and other private statements concerning foreign resistance to a German assault on Czechoslovakia.

Chamberlain desires to adopt he would think right." The next day Kennedy also told Halifax that although Americans would be "shocked" by German aggression, they would not feel that was sufficient reason to plunge Europe into general war.[15] Kennedy himself reported he thought that if Germany attacked Czechoslovakia Chamberlain would try to keep France out and failing that, keep England out as long as he could. Chamberlain, he concluded, looked ill but not jittery, and was the "best bet" against war.[16] To all of these questions and comments, Hull replied only that American sentiments were well known and that nothing could be said about American responses to hypothetical situations.[17]

A few days later Bullitt caused a mild sensation. At a banquet in Bordeaux attended by Bonnet on September 3, the ambassador, speaking in French and extemporaneously, allegedly declared that the United States and France were "indefectively united in war as in peace." Next day, at an unveiling commemorating American aid to France in the First World War, Bullitt declared that in event of war no one could foretell whether the United States would become involved.[18] On September 8, however, Bullitt said that his remarks on September 3 had been misinterpreted, and on September 9 Roosevelt stated at a press conference that it was "100 per cent incorrect" to interpret his policy as associating the United States with France and Great Britain in a front against Hitler.[19] Essentially this assertion was true. Nevertheless, as Lindsay told Halifax on September 12, Roosevelt was "aroused by Germany's brutal diplomacy," and officials in Washington favored England's "making a strong stand against aggression and I anticipate that any compromise with it may bring a certain let-down." This feeling did not preclude a wise accommodation, he cautioned, and Roosevelt had admitted privately that "you may count on us for everything except troops and loans." But Lindsay, who had encouraged his govern-

---

[15]Halifax to Lindsay, Sept. 2, 1938, *DBFP*, 3d ser., II, 212-213.

[16]Kennedy to Hull, Aug. 30, 1938, *FR 1938*, I, 560-561.

[17]Hull to Kennedy, Sept. 1, 1938, *ibid.*, 568.

[18]*New York Times*, Sept. 4 and Sept. 5, 1938.

[19]*Ibid.*, Sept. 9 and Sept. 10, 1938. The corrected version of Bullitt's Sept. 3 remarks appeared Sept. 9: "We are united by our devotion to liberty, democracy, and peace. We are united by an old friendship, by the aid each has brought the other in his hour of need." The French reporter working for the Associated Press said he had misinterpreted Bullitt's remarks. *New York Times*, Sept. 12, 1938. See also John McVickar Haight, Jr., "France, the United States, and the Munich Conference," *Journal of Modern History*, XXXII (Dec. 1960), 345-347.

ment to respond favorably to the American overtures in late 1937 and early 1938, believed that if war came America would enter in "far less" time than it had the first time.[20] Chamberlain remained uninterested in American assistance and the additional warnings that he received through Weizsäcker and Theodor Kordt during the first two weeks of September.[21] On September 4-5 Beneš agreed to virtually all of the demands Henlein had put forth at Karlsbad on April 24; the Sudeten Germans, unprepared for this, thereupon used a minor incident on September 7 to break negotiations.[22] At the same time the London *Times* on September 7 carried a lead article urging that the Czech government cede its German-speaking areas to Germany. Five days later, concluding the Nazi rally at Nuremberg, Hitler, "his words, his tone, dripping with venom," as William Shirer noted, denounced Beneš for playing a "tactical game" and making insufficient "little appeasement presents," and he warned that "the Germans in Czechoslovakia are neither defenseless nor are they deserted, and people should take note of that fact."[23] There followed uprisings by Henlein's followers, Beneš proclamation of martial law (and restoration of order), and Henlein's announcement that the issue was no longer autonomy but return to the Reich.[24]

The French were deeply disturbed, and on September 13 let Chamberlain know they thought a conference "à trois" advisable. Chamberlain instead requested an interview with Hitler himself—much to Daladier's distress, Hitler's surprise, and the amazement of Mussolini, who thought it meant "the liquidation of English prestige"—and on September 15 flew to Berchtesgaden.[25] Bullitt

[20]Lindsay to Halifax, Sept. 12, 1938, *DBFP,* 3d ser., II, 301.

[21]On the controversy concerning the possibility of a *putsch* in September, 1938, cf. Hans Rothfels, *The German Opposition to Hitler: An Appraisal* (Hinsdale, Ill., 1948), 58-63, who blames its collapse largely on Chamberlain's failure to oppose Hitler, and John W. Wheeler-Bennett, *The Nemesis of Power: The German Army in Politics, 1918-1945,* rev. ed. (New York, 1964), 414-424, who sees the plot as vastly exaggerated by its conspirators, who found a scapegoat for their own irresolution and inactivity.

[22]John W. Wheeler-Bennett, *Munich: Prologue to Tragedy* (London, 1948), 90-92.

[23]Entry for Sept. 12, 1938, Shirer, *Berlin Diary,* 126-127; text of speech in Baynes, ed., *Hitler's Speeches,* II, 1487-1499.

[24]Henlein's Statement, Sept. 15, 1938, *DGFP,* D, II, 801-802.

[25]Phipps to Halifax, Sept. 13 and Sept. 14, 1938, *DBFP,* 3d ser., II, 313-314, 329; Hitler's expression of surprise, *"Ich bin vom Himmel gefallen,"* noted in Lewis B. Namier, *Diplomatic Prelude, 1938-1939* (London, 1948), 35; Mussolini's remark in entry for Sept. 14, 1938, in Malcolm Muggeridge, ed., *Ciano's Diary, 1937-1938,* trans. Andreas Mayor (London, 1952), 156.

reported that Bonnet told him the Czechs "had failed to play straight" and the French "would be fully justified in washing their hands of their obligations." On the day of Chamberlain's flight Bullitt concluded that the French generally believed that the Treaty of Versailles was "one of the stupidest documents ever penned by the hand of man," that it would have to be revised to permit "an alteration of the Czech state," and that the French "will support any arrangement that Chamberlain may be able to make with Hitler." [26] Bullitt shared these sentiments. Nevertheless, a while later he reflected to Roosevelt: "The moral is: If you have enough airplanes you don't have to go to Berchtesgaden." [27]

Publicly Hull committed the United States only to observing proceedings with "greatest interest." [28] Roosevelt doubted the wisdom of the conference. He worried, as he wrote Ambassador Phillips (who thought the flight a "fine and courageous thing to do"), that the talks would only postpone the "inevitable conflict," and at a cabinet meeting on September 16 he lamented that Chamberlain was for "peace at any price." [29] Next day he remarked tartly to Ickes that it seemed England and France were going to abandon Czechoslovakia and "wash the blood from their Judas Iscariot hands." Roosevelt said that he thought England and France should refuse Germany's demands and, if war came, announce they would not invade Germany but would blockade its borders and bombard the Germans until they gave in. [30]

A few days after Chamberlain returned from his difficult interview, in which Hitler said he would take the Sudetenland at risk of war but agreed to give Chamberlain a chance to work out a peaceful transfer, the British and French proposed to Czechoslovakia that it cede to Germany all districts in which the German population was 50 percent or more. [31] Kennedy telegraphed an unofficial version of the plan to Roosevelt on the afternoon of September 19. Fifteen

[26]Bullitt to Hull, Sept. 14 and Sept. 15, 1938, FR 1938, I, 595-596, 600-601.

[27]Bullitt to Roosevelt, Sept. 20, 1938, Roosevelt papers, PSF, France: William Bullitt.

[28]Hull Statement in FR 1938, I, 605.

[29]Entry for Sept. 15, 1938, Italian Diary, VIII, and Roosevelt to Phillips, Sept. 15, 1938, William Phillips papers, Houghton Library, Harvard University, Cambridge, Mass.

[30]Entry for Sept. 18, 1938, Ickes, Diary, II, 467-469.

[31]Paul Schmidt, Statist auf diplomatischer Bühne, 1923-1945, 2d ed. (Frankfurt am Main-Bonn, 1964), 394-399. Schmidt Memorandum, Sept. 15, 1938, DGFP, D, II, 786-798; text of Anglo-French plan in Monica Lewis, ed., Documents on International Affairs, 1938, 2 vols. (London, 1942-43), II, 213-214.

minutes later, in a frantic cable, Bullitt elaborated on German military superiority and the destruction of Czechoslovakia and France; the stake, he said, was the entire youth of France and every building in the country. He pleaded that it would be wrong to allow a France misguided by the spirit of a Jacobin or Jeanne d'Arc to "march into the furnace" to keep three million Sudeten Germans under rule of seven million Czechs. Because the United States intended to remain at peace, for any American official to urge the French to resist would be dishonorable.[32]

Roosevelt was not so sure. Without a word to anyone in the State Department, he summoned Lindsay for a secret conference in the White House that night. He felt that the Anglo-French plan demanded "the most terrible remorseless sacrifice" ever demanded of a country, and that it would provoke unfavorable response in America. Nonetheless, Roosevelt remarked, he understood the difficulties confronting the governments of England and France, and if British policy succeeded he would be "the first to cheer." Further, he would not express disapproval of German aggression "lest it might encourage Czechoslovakia to vain resistance." Roosevelt said he feared that Czechoslovakia might provoke war by not giving in; yet, even if Hitler got what he wanted now, he would press demands upon Poland, Denmark, and Rumania until war came. And England, France, and Russia could not win if they fought along classical lines. There seemed to be, then, two alternatives. First, he suggested, the Western powers could call a world conference, which he said he would be willing to attend provided it met somewhere other than in Europe, to reorganize "all unsatisfactory frontiers on rational lines." Second, if the Western powers thought a conference unworkable and elected to fight, they should blockade Germany and close off the North and Mediterranean seas and the Suez Canal. America's contribution to this effort, Roosevelt explained, would be limited. He could not send troops to Europe, nor ignore the Neutrality Act's prohibition on exporting arms and munitions to belligerents. All the President could do under the Constitution and the Neutrality Act was forbid American ships to enter danger zones, except at their own risk.[33] Lindsay reported this conversation to Halifax, who thanked Roosevelt for his interest but questioned the effectiveness of a blockade.[34]

[32]Kennedy to Hull, and Bullitt to Hull, Sept. 19, 1938, *FR 1938*, I, 615-619.
[33]Lindsay to Halifax, Sept. 20, 1938, *DBFP*, 3d ser., VII, 627-629.
[34]Halifax to Lindsay, Sept. 23, 1938, *ibid.*, 630.

Pressed by the English and French, refused their last-minute appeal for a statement from Roosevelt or Hull (on grounds that the United States could not advise a nation to fight), the Czechoslovaks agreed to Anglo-French demands.[35] Chamberlain flew to Godesberg on September 22. Hitler now pressed the demands of Poland and Hungary against Czechoslovakia and insisted that the evacuation of the Sudetenland be started by September 26 and finished by September 28. After sharp exchanges, during which time word came of Czech mobilization, Hitler agreed to extend the deadline to October 1. Chamberlain said he would present the proposal to his government and the government of Czechoslovakia.[36]

Bullitt again pleaded that Roosevelt, in event the British and French rejected Hitler's latest demand and war seemed imminent, summon the heads of state of England, France, Germany, Italy, and Poland—but absolutely not of the Soviet Union—to meet at The Hague with an American representative. But even Bullitt deemed German terms "totally unacceptable" when he learned on the morning of September 25 that in addition to immediate occupation they demanded that the Czechs not remove a single piece of military or factory equipment, not a morsel of food or anything else. Beneš too found the demands unacceptable, and that same morning summoned Carr, told him his people would rather die fighting than accept the terms, and begged him to ask Roosevelt to prevail upon England and France not to desert Czechoslovakia.[37]

Roosevelt's advisers had been conferring all day. Moffat and Assistant Secretary Berle had worked out an "appeal to the American people" in which Roosevelt was to offer his services as mediator rather than summon an international conference. As Moffat recorded, "there was a definite hint of treaty revision in the note, designed like bait to induce Germany to request the President's good offices." Hull agreed to the plan, but Norman Davis took "violent exception" to it; he insisted that it was not the Treaty of Versailles that was the root of all evils, but American failure to ratify. Discussion continued late into the night until Roosevelt

---

[35]Moffat Memorandum, Sept. 20, 1938, *FR 1938*, I, 626-627.

[36]Schmidt, *Statist auf diplomatischer Bühne*, 399-407; Schmidt Memorandum, Sept. 23, 1938, *DGFP*, D, II, 898-908; Note of Conversation between Chamberlain and Hitler, Sept. 22 and Sept. 23, 1938, *DBFP*, 3d ser., II, 463-473, 497-508.

[37]Bullitt to Hull, Sept. 24 and Sept. 25, and Carr to Hull, Sept. 25, 1938, *FR 1938*, I, 641-642, 648-650.

decided to omit the offer of his services on grounds that it was implicit in the exhortation to negotiate.[38] Roosevelt appealed for peace shortly after 1:00 A.M. on September 26, at a time when it appeared that the British and French, no matter how reluctant, would have to fight. He asked the heads of Germany, England, France, and Czechoslovakia not to break negotiations, insisting that no problem was too difficult to be resolved peacefully; at the same time he reaffirmed that the United States had "no political entanglements." Chamberlain, Daladier, and Beneš approved Roosevelt's message.[39] Roosevelt was especially pleased with Chamberlain's warm response, Welles told Kennedy; nonetheless, when the prime minister hinted that his radio address on the current situation, scheduled for the night of September 27, be broadcast directly to the United States, Roosevelt vetoed the idea on grounds that it "might be misconstrued." American stations could pick up the broadcast on their own.[40]

Hitler's reply to Roosevelt reached Washington just after 9:00 P.M. on September 26. The Chancellor agreed with the President's feelings about the unforeseeable consequences of a war, but insisted that Woodrow Wilson had proclaimed self-determination "the most important basis of national life" and that the Sudeten Germans had been deprived of this right. Everyone had agreed that the Sudetenland should join the Third Reich and now the Beneš government was delaying the proceedings. The Germans could wait no longer, Hitler warned, and the decision for war or peace rested with Czechoslovakia alone. That same night, in a near frenzy, Hitler shrieked at the *Sportpalast* in Berlin that "the Czech state began with a single lie, and the father of this lie was named Beneš," and that if the Czechs did not give the Sudeten Germans immediate freedom, "we will go and fetch this freedom for ourselves."[41]

[38]Entry for Sept. 24 and Sept. 25, 1938, Moffat Diary, II, Moffat papers. See also Joseph Alsop and Robert Kintner, *American White Paper: The Story of American Diplomacy and the Second World War* (New York, 1940), 8-9.

[39]Roosevelt's message in *PPFDR*, VII, 531-532; formal replies in Lewis, ed., *Documents 1938*, II, 262-264. Apparently Phipps had to urge Chamberlain to hasten his reply. Phipps to Halifax, Sept. 26, 1938, *DBFP*, 3d ser., II, 546.

[40]Memorandum Welles-Kennedy Conversation, Sept. 26, 1938, *FR 1938*, I, 660-661.

[41]Hitler to Roosevelt, Sept. 27, 1938, *ibid.*, 669-672; Norman H. Baynes, ed., *The Speeches of Adolf Hitler, April 1922-August 1939*, 2 vols. (London, 1942), II, 1508-1527.

On the morning of September 27 the British Foreign Office issued a statement by Chamberlain asking Europe to avoid general war over questions on which agreement already had been "largely obtained," and promising British responsibility for seeing to it that terms agreed to by discussion would be carried out.[42] Shortly after noon (Berlin time) Sir Horace Wilson saw Hitler, who insisted that unless his demands were met he would "smash" Czechoslovakia. Wilson emphasized the advantages that would accrue to England and Germany through a peaceful settlement, and said that if Germany attacked Czechoslovakia, France would be bound to its treaty obligations—although he could not say in what form this commitment would be met—and if French and German troops became "actively engaged," England would be bound to support France.[43]

That, and ensuing general war, were precisely what American diplomats wanted to prevent. Roosevelt called a special meeting of his cabinet and advisers on September 27. Welles and Berle drafted a proposal similar to Bullitt's earlier proposal: a conference at The Hague, on September 29, with the United States sending an observer and committing itself to an economic settlement parallel to a political settlement. Hull opposed the idea, and Roosevelt supported him.[44] They agreed, however, that it would be worthwhile to appeal to Hitler to find some way of preventing war, perhaps by continuing negotiations at a neutral site with the British, French, and Czechs.[45]

No sooner had the meeting ended than the State Department received a cable from Bullitt, at 2:30 P.M., that Bonnet had just "astounded" him by saying that the British and French Foreign Offices were secretly working on a plan to turn over to Germany by

[42]Text of statement in Halifax to Henderson, Sept. 27, 1938, *DBFP,* 3d ser. II, 559-560.

[43]Henderson to Halifax, Sept. 27, and Notes of Hitler-Wilson Conversation, Sept. 27, 1938, *ibid.,* 563-567. See also Schmidt Memorandum of Hitler-Wilson Conversation, Sept. 27, 1938, *DGFP,* D, II, 963-965, and Schmidt, *Statist auf diplomatischer Bühne,* 407-409.

[44]Alsop and Kintner, *American White Paper,* 10.

[45]Entry for Sept. 30, 1938, *The Secret Diary of Harold L. Ickes,* 3 vols. (New York, 1953-55), II, 478. Ickes' contention that no one seriously thought that the appeal would do any good, and that its real purpose was to establish, in event war began, "who was responsible for starting it," tells only part of the story; Roosevelt no doubt wanted to establish a "war guilt," but he desperately wanted to prevent war.

October 1 those regions Czechoslovakia had consented to cede. Bullitt refused to believe that Daladier would agree.[46] Chamberlain, in fact, was about to send two telegrams to Beneš that afternoon, the first warning that Germany would overrun Czechoslovakia if Hitler's demands were not met (and insisting that the British government could not assume responsibility for advising a course of action), and the second urging acceptance of Chamberlain's plan for surrender of the Sudetenland on a schedule close to Hitler's.[47] In the meanwhile, Welles instructed Bullitt and Kennedy to inform Daladier and Chamberlain of Roosevelt's planned appeal and to get their responses; Hull cabled Phillips to tell Mussolini that Roosevelt hoped the Duce would do all he could for peaceful negotiations.[48]

Reports from Europe were frightening. Ambassador Wilson reported on the afternoon of September 27 that Horace Wilson had informed him that Chamberlain was tired and uncertain of what he would say in the House of Commons next day; it appeared that even British and French guarantees that Czechoslovakia would fulfill the terms of the British proposal for ceding the Sudetenland had made no impression on the Germans. Sir Horace thought Roosevelt should urge Chamberlain to keep England out of a war over a matter agreed to in principle. Ambassador Wilson thought that Hitler had burnt his bridges and could not retreat; it was necessary that Czechoslovakia change its attitude.[49] Kennedy could not get an audience with Chamberlain until shortly after 10:30 P.M. (London time) and called Welles back at 5:45 P.M. (Washington time). By then Chamberlain, having appealed through his emissary, Wilson, for direct German-Czech negotiations with the British present as an interested third party, had received Hitler's reply in which he defended his Godesberg demands but left it up to Chamberlain if he

[46]Bullitt to Hull, Sept. 27, 1938, *FR 1938,* I, 680-681.

[47]John W. Wheeler-Bennett, *Munich: Prologue to Tragedy* (London, 1948), 151-152, 154-155.

[48]Memoranda Welles-Bullitt and Welles-Kennedy Conversations, and Hull to Phillips, Sept. 27, 1938, *FR 1938,* I, 675-679. Hull also instructed every American ambassador or minister—except those in Germany, England, France, Italy, Czechoslovakia, Hungary and Poland—to tell the head of state to which he was accredited that the United States, without judging the points at issue between Germany and Czechoslovakia, felt it would be wise for him to urge them to peaceful settlement. Hull to Officers in Charge of American Diplomatic Missions, Sept. 27, 1938, *ibid.,* 677-678.

[49]Wilson to Hull, Sept. 27, 1938, *ibid.,* 683-684.

wished to make a last-hour appeal to the government in Prague.[50] Chamberlain, Kennedy told Welles, found little cheer in Hitler's reply, thought Germany might even march the next day, and saw little prospect for accomplishing anything. If Roosevelt wanted to try there was nothing to lose. Welles replied that Roosevelt would send Hitler a message that night "without fail."[51]

Roosevelt, smoking incessantly, Hull, swearing under his breath, and Welles and Berle, fidgeting from tension, worked in the White House study all evening; by about 9:00 P.M. they finished the draft of an appeal to Hitler, and a half-hour later Roosevelt added the final editorial touches and his signature.[52] The appeal insisted that there was agreement in principle between the German and Czech governments, and that all differences "could and should" be settled peacefully. Roosevelt urged continued negotiation, broadened if need be into a conference at a neutral European site attended by all nations directly interested. The State Department cabled the message at 10:18 P.M. (Washington time) on September 27.[53] Just thirty-two minutes before, as John McVickar Haight, Jr., has pointed out, the State Department received a message from Bullitt that Daladier was "delighted" with the proposed Roosevelt appeal and approved a conference to work out peaceful transfer of Czech territory to Germany, although deep down he did not think there was one chance in a thousand of peace. Yet Haight gives too much credit to Roosevelt and his aides, attaches too much meaning to their appeal, and makes assumptions they dared not make themselves when he says that Roosevelt, while favoring the peaceful transfer of the Sudetenland, supported collective security by standing behind "the Daladier-Bullitt-Welles plan to resist rather than capitulate before the threat of force," and further, that Roosevelt "assumed

[50]Chamberlain to Hitler, Sept. 26, and Hitler to Chamberlain, Sept. 27, 1938, *DGFP*, D, II, 944-945, 966-968. Chamberlain sent a copy of his letter to Roosevelt on September 27, *DBFP*, 3d ser., II, 541n1.

[51]Memorandum Welles-Kennedy Conversation, Sept. 27, 1938, *FR 1938*, I, 679-680.

[52]Alsop and Kintner, *American White Paper*, 11.

[53]Roosevelt to Hitler, Sept. 27, 1938, *FR 1938*, I, 684-685. Celovsky, *Das Münchener Abkommen*, 448-449, attributes Roosevelt's appeal largely to "political" motivation: the desire during an election campaign to appear as one who had taken part in international developments. This emphasis, however, overlooks Roosevelt's dominant motive: the desire to avert war and its attendant catastrophe.

Chamberlain stood with Daladier as an opponent to capitulation" and expected Chamberlain to negotiate at Munich on the basis of "reason and equity." Haight also overstates what occurred at Munich.[54]

To begin, Welles had told Kennedy that Roosevelt would appeal to Hitler even before Bullitt cabled Daladier's approval. Their appeal was written well before word came from Paris, and not in the thirty-two-minute interval between the incoming and outgoing messages. There is no evidence Roosevelt read Bullitt's message before cabling Hitler, nor is there reason to believe that Roosevelt intended to encourage the British and French to be firm, for this might have been interpreted as encouragement to fight and, as the Czechs had learned earlier, he was in no position to proffer such advice. Further, hours before (Washington time) Chamberlain had made his famous broadcast in which he said not only that it was horrible and incredible that the British should be digging trenches and trying on gas masks on account of a quarrel between people "in a far-away country of whom we know nothing," but also that war preparations did not mean war was inevitable or imminent. No matter how much one sympathized with a small country confronted by a big and powerful one "we cannot in all circumstances undertake to involve the whole British Empire in war simply on her account. If we have to fight it must be on larger issues than that."[55] Roosevelt could only have concluded that Chamberlain absolutely did not want to resist Germany, and that though under the circumstances England might have been forced to war if Germany attacked Czechoslovakia and France fought, once a conference was arranged Chamberlain would go to nearly any length to give Hitler those things even Roosevelt recognized everyone had agreed in principle to give him. Roosevelt's chief concern was to encourage further negotiation without committing the United States, and thereby arousing congressional and public wrath, to European political settlements. He also might have suspected that English and French leaders only would have sneered at the head of an uncommitted nation urging them to war.

It is also incorrect to say that there was a "sellout" at Munich, not

[54]Bullitt to Hull, Sept. 27, 1938, *FR 1938,* I, 686-688; Haight, "France, the United States, and Munich," *Journal of Modern History,* 355-356.
[55]Text of address in Lewis, ed., *Documents 1938,* II, 270-271.

only of the Czechs but of Roosevelt's hopes.[56] That conference, as John W. Wheeler-Bennett has stated, was only a ceremony signifying that Hitler, in advance, had won his essential demands.[57] Both Hitler's and Chamberlain's biographers agree that the terms of the Munich settlement varied only slightly from Hitler's Godesberg demands and generally favored Anglo-French demands.[58] That Hitler would violate certain arrangements, not hold a plebiscite, for instance, could not be determined in advance, even if it might have been conjectured. There is no reason to believe, however, that the settlement, or events of the next few weeks, disappointed Roosevelt. On October 11 he wrote the prime minister of Canada, MacKenzie King, that he rejoiced that war had been averted. Explicitly and plainly he told Phillips six days later: "I want you to know that I am not one bit upset over the final result."[59] Certainly Roosevelt had misgivings; he likened Poland's demand for Teschen to a cruel kick at a small boy who was being held down by a bully.[60] But by and large Roosevelt had convinced himself that Munich opened the way to a new and better world.[61]

There is nothing in diplomatic records to indicate that the President's aides disapproved the Munich settlement—the evidence, in fact, indicates the opposite. Hull later would say that he urged Roosevelt, against Welles's pressure, to "go slow" and not, through appeals, associate himself with Chamberlain's appeasement.[62] But if Hull had misgivings at the time, he did not express them in council,

[56]Haight, "France, the United States, and Munich," *Journal of Modern History,* 358, suggests that the cautious nature of American diplomatic statements had an impact upon the French that was actually opposite the real wishes of American leaders. To some extent this is true, but again, Roosevelt knew how little material support he could offer, and, for example, on September 16 Welles apparently told Daladier and Bonnet that they would not get "a single soldier, nor a sou of credit." Georges Bonnet, *Défense de la Paix: De Washington au Quai d'Orsay,* 2 vols. (Geneva, 1946-48), I, 212.

[57]*Munich,* 173.

[58]Alan Bullock, *Hitler: A Study in Tyranny,* rev. ed. (New York, 1962), 469; Iain Macleod, *Neville Chamberlain* (New York, 1961), 253.

[59]Roosevelt to King, Oct. 11, and Roosevelt to Phillips, Oct. 17, 1938, *FDRL,* II, 816-819.

[60]Roosevelt to Hull, Sept. 29, 1938, Roosevelt papers, PSF, State Department Files: Cordell Hull.

[61]William L. Langer and S. Everett Gleason, *The Challenge to Isolation, 1937-1940* (New York, 1952), 35.

[62]*The Memoirs of Cordell Hull,* 2 vols. (New York, 1948), I, 591-595.

nor seek to slacken the President's pace. [63] In his press statement on September 30, Hull said only that the results at Munich afforded "a universal sense of relief," and that the United States would not judge the dispute itself. [64] Welles was more certain. In a national broadcast on October 3 he said there was now more opportunity to establish "a new world order based upon justice and upon law" than at any time during the last twenty years. [65] Moffat, head of the European desk in the State Department, wrote Ambassadors Wilson and Kennedy that he did not sympathize with those Americans who criticized arrangements at Munich; a country that had no intention of fighting, he said, had no business criticizing decisions of other countries that were "nearer the abyss." [66]

Viewed in this light, the meaning of Roosevelt's "Good man" cable, sent through Kennedy on the afternoon of September 28 after Chamberlain had accepted Hitler's invitation to Munich, is clear. [67] Only a few hours before Chamberlain took off, the British apparently asked that Roosevelt publicly endorse the move. Hull, Moffat, and Messersmith adamantly opposed giving a "blank check"; the British, they felt, were trying to get them to share responsibility in case ultimate arrangements proved unpopular. [68] Nonetheless, Roosevelt and his aides knew Hitler's Godesberg demands, had agreed to transfer of the Sudetenland to Germany, knew that Czechoslovakia would not be at the conference to defend itself, knew that Hitler would not and could not back far off his demands, and knew that Chamberlain and Daladier could not and would not push Hitler because England and France were desperate not to fight. Nor did the Americans want them to fight. Mistakenly or not, diplomats in Washington sought, if not peace at any price, peace with honor; but above all, peace. Chamberlain claimed to stand for an honorable peace, and when he agreed to go to Munich Roosevelt told him sincerely that he was a "good man."

Bearing in mind that the European powers could discount American military intervention, what was Roosevelt's contribution to the events of September 26-28? His first message of September

[63]Julius W. Pratt, *Cordell Hull,* 2 vols. (New York, 1964), I, 296-298.

[64]*FR 1938,* I, 703.

[65]*New York Times,* Oct. 4, 1938.

[66]Moffat to Wilson, Oct. 5, and Moffat to Kennedy, Oct. 7, 1938, Jay Pierrepont Moffat Papers, Houghton Library, Harvard University.

[67]Hull to Kennedy, Sept. 28, 1938, *FR 1938,* I, 688.

[68]Entry for Oct. 14, 1938, Moffat Diary, II, Moffat papers.

26 to the heads of the German, English, French, and Czech states contributed in a general way to continuing negotiations, but was by no means decisive. On September 27 Dieckhoff sent a cable insisting that Hitler would get "practically all he is demanding" if he agreed to negotiations, and reiterating his persistent theme that in the event of war the United States would choose the appropriate time to enter on the side of England.[69] Several hours later there followed Roosevelt's second appeal to Hitler, which arrived at the Foreign Ministry at 9:45 A.M. (Berlin time) on September 28 and went unanswered.[70] Afterward, however, Captain Fritz Wiedemann, Hitler's *aide-de-camp,* did tell Ambassador Wilson that the telegram had been translated by 10:00 A.M. and that Wiedemann "supposed it had already been brought to the Chancellor" sometime between then and 11:00 A.M., when his interview with Ambassador François-Poncet began. Hitler had probably read it, then, about a half-hour before François-Poncet arrived and about an hour before the Italian ambassador, Bernardo Attolico, interrupted with Mussolini's request that mobilization be delayed twenty-four hours; Hitler had Roosevelt's message well over an hour before Ambassador Henderson arrived with Chamberlain's request for a conference.[71]

Mussolini usually has been credited with making the decisive intervention, and this assumption probably is correct.[72] The major influences on Mussolini's decision, in addition to the important facts that he neither wanted war at that time nor was prepared for it, were the two British requests to him made by the British ambassador in Rome, Lorth Perth, through Ciano. The first request reached Mussolini around 10:30 A.M.; the second, a personal message from Chamberlain, around noon.[73] Frequently overlooked is Roosevelt's message to Mussolini, transmitted via the State Department and Ambassador Phillips on the afternoon of September 27, asking him

[69]Dieckhoff to Foreign Ministry, Sept. 27, 1938, *DGFP,* D, II, 981-982.

[70]Printed *ibid., 983-985.*

[71]Wilson to Welles, Oct. 21, 1938, *FR 1938,* I, 727-729. On Mussolini's intervention, see Erich Kordt, *Wahn und Wirklichkeit* (Stuttgart, 1948), 125, and André Francois-Poncet, *The Fateful Years: Memoirs of a French Ambassador in Berlin, 1931-1938,* trans. Jacques Le Clercq (New York, 1949), 266-267.

[72]*Memoirs of Ernst von Weizsäcker,* trans. John Andrews (Chicago, 1951), 153, attributes the "credit" for bringing about the Munich Conference to "many people," including Roosevelt. Weizsäcker also recalls that as late as August 31, 1938, he told Attolico "Mussolini was the only man in Europe who could influence Hitler." *Memoirs,* 147.

[73]Entry for Sept. 28, 1938, Ciano, *Diary,* 165-166.

to intervene in behalf of a negotiated settlement.[74] Because of differences in time between Washington and Rome, the message did not reach the American embassy until after midnight, and Phillips did not present it to Mussolini until nearly 4:00 P.M., September 28.[75] But as Phillips reported afterward, he had learned "positively" that Mussolini and Ciano were "thoroughly aware" of the message's contents before 10:00 A.M., or about an hour before the English, through Perth, prevailed upon the Duce. The cable from Washington, Phillips said by way of explaining Mussolini's knowledge, had been sent in a "well known" code.[76] Roosevelt replied that he knew well when he ordered the message sent that it would not reach Rome until after midnight and that Phillips would not be able to get an audience with Mussolini at least until the morning of September 28. The President expressed no surprise or upset that the Italians knew of his message by 9:45 A.M., and he seemed delighted that "we actually got in about one hour ahead of Perth"; the American press was wrong in thinking that he had "missed the boat" with an appeal that reached Mussolini only after others had persuaded him to intervene.[77] One can only conclude that it was no accident that the message was sent in a well-known code.

How much the appeal influenced Mussolini is difficult to estimate; clearly he did not act until he heard from the English. Roosevelt, however, gave him one more good reason to intervene at the eleventh hour. The incident further emphasizes how strongly Roosevelt wanted negotiations, the outcome of which could not be in much doubt.

* * *

The thought that somehow, somewhere along the line, the war that Churchill branded "unnecessary" might have been prevented

[74]Hull to Phillips, Sept. 27, 1938, *FR 1938,* I, 677.

[75]After Phillips had left, Ciano noted that Mussolini remarked: "As you can see, I am only moderately happy, because, though perhaps at a price, we could have liquidated France and Great Britain forever. We now have overwhelming proof of this." Entry for Sept. 28, 1938, Ciano, *Diary,* 166.

[76]Phillips to Roosevelt, Oct. 6, 1938, Department of State files, number 760. F62/1462 1/2, National Archives, Washington, D.C. At 9:45 A.M. on September 28 the embassy counselor called the Italian Foreign Office and asked that an interview be arranged for Phillips with Mussolini. The Italians were not told the contents of Roosevelt's confidential message, but they were given "an unmistakable intimation of its purport." Phillips to Hull, Oct. 1, 1938, *FR 1938,* I, 703-704.

[77]Roosevelt to Phillips, Oct. 17, 1938, *FDRL,* II, 818-819.

will probably haunt men forever. Many people have argued that there were at least three or four critical situations when England and France could have halted Germany, called Hitler's "bluff," and perhaps caused the Nazi regime to collapse. Such speculation must take account of the disillusioning aftermath of the First World War and the gripping fear of repeating mistakes that had led to it, the effect of the Great Depression, the popular desire to resolve difficulties peacefully and the faith that this could be done, the widespread legitimate revulsion in the face of warfare's horrors, and belief that at least some of Germany's grievances were real and demands just. These factors affected Americans as profoundly as they did Europeans. Under the circumstances the especial lure and challenge of appeasement—defined by Chamberlain's biographer as neither a foolish nor ignoble hope but a moral imperative not to accept war until every effort had been made to redress legitimate grievances peacefully—is readily understood.[78] But American diplomats, as surely as their British and French colleagues, committed mistakes that went beyond justifiable appeasement, and kept them from achieving the ends they sought.

Perhaps it was natural in 1933 to regard Hitler, as Davis did, as a relative moderate among radicals making legitimate, if overstated, claims, or to assume, as did even Messersmith for about a year, that Hitler's regime could not last if it did not follow traditional economic and diplomatic guidelines. But America's policy makers and analysts, especially the President, were wrong to throw away almost carelessly their opportunity to place their nation in position to cooperate in a system of collective security, and were wrong to be more sympathetic toward German demands for equality of armaments than the French need for security. The implications of Germany's abandonment of the Disarmament Conference and the League of Nations (the latter of course was an embarrassing issue for the United States) were not entirely clear in autumn 1933. But American diplomats might have urged a more cautious if not firmer policy on the British and French instead of immediately retreating behind a public declaration of lack of involvement in European political affairs and almost wistfully hoping that Germany's action would have a "sobering" effect and make the French less rather than more recalcitrant.

American diplomats disapproved of Germany's unilateral

[78]Macleod, *Neville Chamberlain,* 209.

decision to rearm, but they also questioned the wisdom or effectiveness in 1935 of the restriction of the Treaty of Versailles. They wished neither to protest Germany's action nor to encourage the Stresa[79] conferees—whom they suspected of meeting only to "blow off steam," as Bingham had put it—to take serious action. It was wrong, however, to approve the Anglo-German Naval Agreement a few months later, thus condoning both German rearmament and British revisionist policy, the latter so politically ill conceived at that juncture. Even more mistaken was the failure to take a more aggressive position during Italy's assault on Ethiopia. The President and the State Department made various diplomatic efforts and invoked their moral embargo, but they counted too heavily on British and French pressure, and would not risk a political fight over an oil embargo which, if successful, might have forced others to follow suit and probably would have ended the drive of Mussolini's forces. As noted before, Erich Kordt's claim that the outcome of the Italian-Ethiopian conflict determined whether Europe would have war or peace is overstatement, but Italy's unchecked aggression contributed significantly to setting the stage first for the reoccupation of the Rhineland, then for the march into Austria and the confrontation, as Hassell noted even in 1935, between the "static" and "dynamic" powers.

During the Spanish civil war, and the attendant German and Italian assault, the United States exhibited incredible political blindness. The British and French did not play their proper roles, but the United States went beyond even the legal requirements of its neutrality legislation. Had aid been forthcoming from the United States and from England and France, considering that Hitler's position on aid to Franco was not firm at least until November 1936, the Spanish Republicans could well have triumphed. Instead, Germany gained every advantage from the Spanish civil war: fascism triumphed over democracy, France was ringed with a third hostile neighbor, and the groundwork was more securely laid for the Rome-Berlin-Tokyo alliance. The United States succeeded only in making itself increasingly vulnerable to war in Europe and Asia.

The American government in 1937 and early 1938 tried to make up for time and opportunity lost by achieving a joint policy with

---

[79]In April 1935, representatives of England, France, and Italy met at Stresa, Italy, and "condemned"—but did nothing else—Germany's announcement in March 1935 of its rearmament in violation of the Treaty of Versailles. [Editor's note.]

England that might appease or curb Germany. The Americans and English had failed to agree in major areas of economics and disarmament. The State Department and Foreign Office in 1933 had failed to agree on a joint policy for the sale of airplanes to Germany. The British in 1934 secured a bilateral debt settlement with Germany without considering how it would affect Germany's other creditors. By the spring of 1937 Chamberlain was in power, and for several years before that time his attitude toward an American contribution to the search for peace had been derisive. His response to Roosevelt's first overture in 1937 was standoffish. But the State Department's pious response to his request for changes in American trade and neutrality policies, and assistance in the Far East, was no better. Significantly, when Japan went to war against China in July 1937, both the United States and Great Britain felt their vital interests were threatened, but neither knew how to cope with the problem. Roosevelt wanted to "quarantine" the aggressor, but was afraid of sanctions and feared having American policy appear to be a "tail to the British kite." Hull scotched Welles's Armistice Day scheme. Chamberlain opposed sanctions against Japan, the French would do nothing unless assured of military support in Indochina, and the Brussels Conference, which might have served as a useful example for European developments, collapsed.

Chamberlain next threw a deadly damper on Roosevelt's conference proposal in January 1938, although its formal burial did not occur until after Eden's resignation—which the proposal ironically hastened—and the *Anschluss*. What Roosevelt might have accomplished had he taken advantage of his slim opportunity to summon an international conference is questionable. The Welles-Lindsay exchange in February and March 1938 demonstrated that the United States was uncertain about recognizing Italy's conquest of Ethiopia. Recognition was central to Chamberlain's appeasement policy. Even Welles admitted that once the nations had gathered around the conference table and agreed to a code of international ethics—a noble undertaking—he did not know what would come next. If it was to be concessions to Germany, and the evidence indicates he intended that, there is little reason to think those concessions would have contained German aggression any more than the ones England and France were about to make.

In the matter of Czechoslovakia and the Munich Conference, American diplomats displayed no more insight or foresight than anyone else. They did not see that the stake was more than commitment to a nation's life; it was the entire system of French, if not European, security and the opening of eastern Europe to German economic and political domination, to say nothing of the forcing of the Soviet Union to alter its foreign policy. A. J. P. Taylor is correct: Americans, whatever misgivings they might have had at the time, only later condemned the British and French for doing what they would have done in their place.[80]

Some Americans quickly perceived the threat of Nazi Germany to the United States and the world: Dodd especially, and Bowers and Morgenthau. In a year's time Messersmith became perhaps his country's most astute diplomatic analyst, and by the middle of the decade Davis had become a strong proponent of collective security. Others did not see so well or quickly. Hull, of course, loathed every form of German brutality and international aggression, but failed to recognize that his economic liberalism and moral persuasion were insufficient to combat Germany's new order. His responses to the crises and chaos of his era were excessively cautious. Roosevelt was able, shrewd, and farsighted, but expended most of his energy on domestic problems and belatedly and without daring or dash turned to foreign policy. Early and often he talked about blockade, boycott, and economic sanctions to bring pressure on Germany, but there is little reason to believe he took these schemes seriously. If he did, he demonstrated his naïveté about the Third Reich and international problems. In addition, as he remarked to Phillips in mid-September of 1938, he felt that the United States could do nothing except wait for Europe to blow itself up and then have America "pick up the pieces of European civilization and help them to save what remains of the wreck—not a cheerful prospect."[81] That idea, tragically, was a popular one. Further, to a shocking degree those responsible for planning and executing their nation's foreign policy did not heed Messersmith's charge that they were responsible for informing and guiding the public in its own interest.

It is impossible to know precisely in what way bolder policy might have caused Hitler to revise his distorted assessment of the United States or to alter his foreign policy; as it was, he disregarded the more realistic, if sometimes exaggerated, assessment of German diplomats, and American behavior during 1933-1938 tended to

[80]*Origins of the Second World War,* 191.

[81]Roosevelt to Phillips, Sept. 15, 1938, Roosevelt papers, PSF, Italy: William Phillips.

reinforce his ill-founded conclusions. Other studies have shown that even as the United States pursued a more belligerent policy during 1939-1941 Hitler remained largely unable or unwilling to grasp the implication of the American balance of power. Nevertheless, it is clear that whatever Hitler's larger designs, during 1933-1938 he improvised according to the opportunities he saw, and he was frequently fearful of foreign response and prepared to alter immediate policy. Bolder American policy might not only have encouraged others to greater daring and resistance, but could have changed, in a way highly advantageous to the democracies, the critical political circumstances in which German, and European, policy developed.

Underlying these failures is the inescapable conclusion that from Roosevelt, through Hull and Welles, and down through the ranks of the State Department, in the Congress, and in all walks of life, with too few exceptions, there persisted a belief that Europe's problems were Europe's, that an ocean three thousand miles wide separated the New World from the Old. As a rule Americans cared about Europe's troubles only within their limited framework; they would render what assistance they could by disarmament talks or reciprocal trade programs. When the great crises came, Americans, as Chamberlain had said of his countrymen, regarded them as being in a faraway country between people they did not know. Indeed, when war began in Europe Americans naïvely declared their independence.

III Between Peace and War, 1939-1941

Once war began in Europe, the Roosevelt administration and probably most of the American people feared that a German victory over England and France (which did surrender in June 1940), combined with Japan's conquest of China, would leave Europe and Asia in the hands of two aggressive "Axis" powers, and the United States isolated and vulnerable. But neither the Roosevelt government nor the American people ever found a satisfactory way to resolve the dilemma created by their desire to remain neutral in the world conflict yet support one side over the other. This problem is dealt with skillfully and honestly in Part III in selections from William E. Leuchtenburg's *Franklin D. Roosevelt and the New Deal, 1932-1940* (1963) and William L. Langer and S. Everett Gleason's *The Undeclared War, 1940-1941* (1953). Leuchtenburg, in two of his chapters—"The Fascist Challenge" and "An End to Isolation"—deals with the repeal of the arms embargo neutrality legislation in September 1939, the "stormcellar" neutrality position of the United States up to the German blitzkrieg of 1940, and then the gradually hardening American line toward Japan and the linking of the German and Japanese peril in the fall of 1940. Following his re-election in November 1940, Roosevelt for the first time began to fashion a global foreign policy and "quasi belligerency shaded into war." The excerpts from Langer and Gleason pick up the story of "The Shooting War" and the American resolve to defeat Germany by aiding England, and carry it through the increasing involvement of the United States in belligerent activities through convoying British supplies, German assaults on American ships, Roosevelt's less than candid report on the *Greer* incident to justify "shoot on sight" orders to the Navy, and finally the arming of American merchant ships and declaration of the end of combat zones. By autumn 1941 the United States and Germany were engaged in undeclared war in the Atlantic. Roosevelt accepted this state of affairs, indeed intended it, and yet there remained his belief, shared by many others, that the war in Europe could be resolved without formal American entry—as though the determination could bring about the reality. One should point out that although Langer and Gleason both had a commitment to the Roosevelt administration, and they wrote before our 1957 "cutoff" line, their book is still the most thorough one on the subject and they do not fail to point out the Roosevelt administration's inconsistencies and deceptions.

WILLIAM E. LEUCHTENBURG
Franklin D. Roosevelt and the New Deal, 1932-1940

William E. Leuchtenburg (born 1922) is Professor of History at Columbia University. He is author of *Flood Control and Politics* (1953), *The Perils of Prosperity, 1914–1932* (1958), and many articles.

IN THE SUMMER of 1939, people tuned in the newly popular portable radios to hear the reports of H. V. Kaltenborn and Raymond Gram Swing on the impending war in Europe. When, on August 24, the Nazis signed a pact with the Soviet Union which separated Russia from the West, war could no longer be very far off, yet people still could not believe that the nightmare of World War I would be repeated. One American diplomat noted in his diary: "These last two days have given me the feeling of sitting in a house where somebody is dying upstairs. There is relatively little to do and yet the suspense continues unabated."[1] On the hot Saturday of September 2, crowds hemmed in parked taxicabs to catch the latest radio bulletins; almost every broadcast was interrupted by a fresh dispatch on Danzig and the Corridor. Through the day, fears that war would come alternated with suspicions that Britain and France would abandon Poland and there would be no war. Sunday morning at 6:10 A.M. Eastern Standard Time, the waiting ended. Neville Chamberlain announced to the British people over the radio: "I have to tell you now that this country is at war with Germany."[2]

No one doubted where American sympathies lay; a Gallup poll revealed that 84 per cent of respondents wanted an Allied victory, 2 per cent a Nazi triumph, while 14 per cent had no opinion.[3] So strong was the identification with the Allied cause, so faithfully did the alignments of 1939 appear to repeat those of 1917, that many

[1]Jay Pierrepont Moffat MS. Diary, August 26-27, 1939. Moffat noted: "The issues involved are so terrible, the outlook so cloudy, the probability of ultimate Bolshevism so great, and the chances of a better peace next time are so remote that if one stopped to think one would give way to gloom." *Ibid.,* September 1, 1939.

[2]"A.D. 1939," *Fortune,* XXI (January, 1940), 93.

[3]*Public Opinion Quarterly,* IV (1940), 102.

From pp. 293-298, 299, 301-310, 323-325, *Franklin D. Roosevelt and the New Deal, 1932-1940* by William E. Leuchtenburg. Copyright ©1963 by William E. Leuchtenburg. By permission of Harper & Row, Publishers, Inc.

were overcome by the fatalistic feeling that, whether they willed it or not, the United States would inevitably be drawn into the war on the Allied side. One observer noted, "But everyone—everyone— little people like taxi drivers and drugstore clerks and farmers down in the Shenandoah and the like are saying we'll sure get into it."[4] Indeed, the country seemed to fear nothing so much as its own sentiments. Raoul de Roussy de Sales wrote: "The average American apparently visualized himself as the Greeks did: his will was set one way, but he felt that the gods would be stronger than his will. . . . Isolationists and their opponents acted as if the American people might be tempted to go to war the way a man who was once addicted to drink is suddenly seized with terror at the sight of a bottle of whiskey."[5]

Three weeks after the invasion of Poland, the President asked Congress, summoned into special session, to repeal the arms embargo and apply the cash-and-carry principle to munitions as well as raw materials. The President's request touched off an explosion of isolationist propaganda, much of it sparked by Coughlinites, which was remarkable for the violence of its imagery and the bitterness of its Anglophobia. "Hitler is an Angel compared to John Bull," a Massachusetts woman wrote Senator Taft. Hundreds of thousands of letters implored senators: "Keep America Out of the Blood Business."[6] Roosevelt, impressed by the intensity of isolationist passions, bent his argument to emphasize not aid to the Allies but keeping America out of war. He dismissed the contention that repeal of the embargo would lead to armed intervention as "one of the

[4]Maxine Davis to Florence Jaffray Harriman, September 7, 1939, Harriman MSS., Box 4.

[5]Raoul de Roussy de Sales, "America Looks at the War," *Atlantic Monthly,* CLXV (1940), 153. Alistair Cooke has pointed out that "Americans were more afraid of their sympathies than of a military threat to the continental United States if the Nazis won. They had to keep up a separate annoyance at the British and French as at potential seducers who have the run of the house." Cooke, *A Generation on Trial* (New York, 1950), p. 29.

[6]Mrs. Ann Gath to Robert Taft, September 24, 1939, Taft MSS.; Mrs. Andrew Dillman to Taft, September 25, 1939, Taft MSS. Cf. Maxine Davis to Florence Jaffray Harriman, September 27, 1939, Harriman MSS., Box 4. "The sole purpose of amending the Neutrality Act," Henry Ford insisted, "is to enable munitions makers to profit financially through what is nothing less than mass murder." *The New York Times,* September 21, 1939. Many of the letters in the Taft manuscripts at Yale University are striking for their curious unrelatedness; they speak, for example, of saving "the flower of American manhood."

worst fakes in current history." The President stated: "The simple truth is that no person in any responsible place . . . has ever suggested . . . the remotest possibility of sending the boys of American mothers to fight on the battlefields of Europe."[7]

So persistent was the conviction that the real menace confronting the country lay not abroad but in Roosevelt's desire for dictatorial power that the President felt compelled to heed the advice of administration senators that he stay in the background during the debate and let them lead the fight. He kept his New Deal advisers off the Hill and deliberately cultivated conservative Democratic senators who would support his international position. Senator Bailey confided: "I have rather important assurances that he is not going to run for a third term." He asked Lord Tweedsmuir, the Governor General of Canada, to pospone a visit to the United States until the debate ended. "I am almost literally walking on eggs," he explained.[8] By pursuing such cautious tactics, the President carried the day. After six weeks of acrimonious controversy, Congress, over substantial Republican opposition, repealed the arms embargo.

Roosevelt got what he wanted; the Allies could buy the munitions they needed. But the isolationists won significant concessions too. The Allies would have to pay cash and haul the arms away themselves; United States citizens could not sail on belligerent vessels; American ships could not sail to belligerent ports and might be forbidden to enter combat zones. When on November 4 the President defined the entire Baltic and the Atlantic from southern Norway to the northern coast of Spain as a combat zone, Hitler was relieved of the threat of conflict with the most important neutral carrier, could brush aside the rights of the smaller neutrals, and was free to launch unrestricted submarine warfare with little risk. "By taking our ships off the seas," noted one writer, "the bill aided the German blockade of Britain as effectively as if all our ships had been torpedoed." In the midst of war, the Neutrality Act of 1939 marked

[7]Samuel I. Rosenman, comp., *The Public Papers and Addresses of Franklin D. Roosevelt,* 13 vols. (New York, 1938-50), VIII, 557.

[8]James MacGregor Burns, *Roosevelt: The Lion and the Fox* (New York, 1956), 396; William L. Langer and S. Everett Gleason, *The Challenge to Isolation, 1937-1940* (New York, 1952), pp. 227-231; Theodore Carlson to Stephen Chadwick, November 2, 1939, Chadwick MSS.; Bailey to Dr. Julian Ruffin, September 18, 1939, Bailey MSS., Personal File; F.D.R. to Tweedsmuir, October 5, 1939, in Elliott Roosevelt, ed., *F.D.R.: His Personal Letters, 1928-1945.* 2 vols. (New York, 1950), II, 46.

one final effort at neutrality by statute to apply the lessons of World War I.[9]

The United States hoped—by neutrality legislation and by inter-American agreement—to insulate the Western Hemisphere from the European war. At the First Meeting of Foreign Ministers of the American Republics, the United States scored a notable triumph. On October 3, 1939, delegates adopted unanimously the Declaration of Panama, which created a zone around the Americas, south of the Canadian border, from 300 to 1,000 miles wide, in which belligerents were warned not to undertake naval action. Since neither side would recognize this "chastity belt," and since the American republics were not prepared to command recognition by force, the Declaration of Panama had little practical effect, although Hitler did give his commanders secret orders not to initiate action within this zone.[10] The Declaration marked an important step in collective action by the American nations and in the "multilateralization" of the Monroe Doctrine; it signified too the hold of the ancient illusion that the United States could, simply by fiat, isolate itself from Europe's quarrels.[11]

Even the Soviet invasion of Finland on November 30, 1939, failed to break the spell of isolationism, despite the nearly unanimous sympathy of the country for the Finns. Finland had won affection by being the one nation which had paid its war debts to the United States, thereby tapping the vast well of sentimentality of the American people. "By last week," observed *Time* in March, 1940, "a U.S. Citizen who had neither danced, knitted, orated, played bridge, bingo, banqueted or just shelled out for Finland was simply nowhere socially." President Roosevelt, who referred privately to

[9]Denna Frank Fleming, "Arms Embargo Debate," *Events,* VI (1939), 342; Langer and Gleason, *Challenge to Isolation,* pp. 231-235; Robert A. Divine, *The Illusion of Neutrality* (Chicago, 1962), pp. 286-335; Philip Jessup, "The Neutrality Act of 1939," *American Journal of International Law,* XXIV (1940), 95-99; L. E. Gleeck, "96 Congressmen Make up their Minds," *Public Opinion Quarterly,* IV (1940), 3-24.

[10]H. L. Trefousse, *Germany and American Neutrality, 1939-1941* (New York, 1951), p. 41; U.S. Navy Department, *Fuehrer Conferences on Matters Dealing with the German Navy, 1940* (5 vols., Washington, 1947), II, 46.

[11]Langer and Gleason, *Challenge to Isolation,* pp. 210-212; Donald Drummond, *The Passing of American Neutrality, 1937-1941* (Ann Arbor, Mich., 1955), 119-121. The foreign ministers met under authority of the Declaration of Lima of 1938, which gave substance to the principle of consultation adopted at Buenos Aires in 1936 by providing that, in the event of war or other threats to security, any American foreign minister could call an emergency meeting.

"this dreadful rape of Finland," denounced the Russian incursion as a "wanton disregard for law." He placed Finland's annual debt installment in a separate account, extended the Finns $10 million in credits to buy farm surpluses and supplies in the United States, and applied a "moral embargo" against the U.S.S.R.[12] But what the Finns really needed was not agricultural credits but, as the Finnish minister explained, cold cash to buy arms in Sweden. Roosevelt refused to antagonize isolationists by asking for an unrestricted loan, and Congress quickly proved that the President's caution was well founded. When Senator Prentiss Brown of Michigan filed a bill to lend the Finns $60 million to buy arms, Congress so mutilated the measure that in the end the "Finnish aid bill" did not mention Finland at all, and limited the Finns to another $20 million credit for nonmilitary supplies. The Senate approved the bill on February 13, as the Red Army was breaking through the Mannerheim Line; the House passed it on February 28, as the Russians started mopping-up operations. In the end the Finns, by capturing Russian arms on the battlefield, received more military aid from the Soviet Union than from their friends. In March, 1940, a Finnish leader commented that the sympathy of the United States and its other well-wishers proved so great that "it nearly suffocated us."[13]

America's commitment to "stormcellar" neutrality rested on a series of assumptions which seemed wholly reasonable—that the war would quickly settle down to a protracted state of siege, with the Germans unable to crack the Maginot Line, and the Allies unable to pierce German defenses; that the British would maintain control of the seas; and that Hitler would be defeated in a war of attrition. In the first months of the war, this appeared to be precisely what was happening; some Americans even protested the lack of excitement in the "bore" war. The war itself, and the threat of Hitler, seemed far distant. When the British cruiser *Orion* chased the German

[12] *Time,* XXXV (March 11, 1940), 16; Max Jakobson, *The Diplomacy of the Winter War* (Cambridge, 1961), pp. 191-192; F.D.R. to Lincoln MacVeagh, December 1, 1939, FDRL PPF 1192; *The New York Times,* December 2, 1939; Langer and Gleason, *Challenge to Isolation,* pp. 329-331.

[13] *The New York Times,* March 17, 1940; Langer and Gleason, *Challenge to Isolation,* pp. 334-340; Mrs. Florence Jaffray Harriman to F.D.R., February 27, 1940, Harriman MSS.; W. R. Castle to David I. Walsh, March 1, 1940, Walsh MSS. For a different view, see Robert Sobel, *The Origins of Interventionism* (New York, 1960).

merchantman *Arauca* along the Florida coast in late December, 1939, a newspaper ran the headline: "SEA INCIDENT AT MIAMI'S FRONT YARD DRAWS GAY HOLIDAY CROWD TO DOCK."[14] The unreal quality of the war left Roosevelt in a quandary. How, he asked William Allen White, could he persuade the nation of the danger it faced without "scaring the American people into thinking that they are going to be dragged into this war?"[15] As time passed, not only the country, but Roosevelt too, came to lose the fatalistic feeling of September that the country would inevitably be drawn into the conflict. The President came to think of the United States as the Great Neutral, giving its aid to one side but determined to stay out of the war. In the early months of 1940, an eerie stillness fell over the White House. "Things here are amazingly quiet," Roosevelt wrote in March, 1940.[16] That same month, as American diplomats traveled by train through Germany, they could see both French and German trenches within a short distance of one another. "Not a gun was fired, not a disturbing sound broke the stillness," one envoy noted in his diary. "Men, women, and children were in the fields, or tying up the vines in the vineyards." In Paris, fowl was plentiful, and one drank champagne as an apéritif; in London, Englishmen enjoyed a warm spring afternoon in the park.[17] The character of the European war served to reinforce the illusion of isolation. Only a revolutionary change in the nature of the European struggle could explode that illusion.

* * *

At dawn on April 9, 1940, Nazi troops crossed the Danish border and emptied out of barges and troopships all along the Norwegian coast. They overran Denmark in a matter of hours, Norway in a few weeks. On May 10, the Germans struck swiftly at the Low Countries and, through them, into France. In five days Holland surrendered, in eighteen days Belgium; in less than three weeks, the Nazis had driven the British armies out of France. As the Panzer divisions, supported by siren-blowing dive bombers, careened toward Paris, Premier Reynaud pleaded vainly with the United States for "clouds

[14] *Time,* XXXV (January 1, 1940), 8.
[15] F.D.R. to White, December 14, 1939, White MSS., Box 324.
[16] F.D.R. to John Boettiger, March 7, 1940, in *Personal Letters,* II, 1006.
[17] Nancy Harvison Hooker (ed.), *The Moffat Papers* (Cambridge, 1956), pp. 295-298. Cf. Sumner Welles, *The Time for Decision* (New York, 1944), pp. 73-147.

of planes." A week later, on June 22, 1940, in the very same railway car in the Compiègne forest where Germany had agreed to the 1918 armistice, France capitulated to Hitler. In the United States, the national mood changed overnight. In Times Square, great crowds, grim-faced, awesomely silent, blocked traffic as they spilled into the middle of Broadway to stare up at the bulletins on the Times Building. Suddenly the country felt naked and vulnerable. Only the British stood between Hitler and the United States. If Germany struck across the Channel with the same ferocity and cunning that had annihilated opposition in western Europe in a few weeks, Britain might well be flying the swastika by the end of the year, and Admiral Raeder might be commanding the British fleet. . . .

In the spring of 1940, Roosevelt moved toward a crisis government of national unity. On June 19, he startled the nation by naming two prominent Republicans to the key defense posts in his cabinet: Henry Stimson as Secretary of War and Frank Knox as Secretary of the Navy. In making these appointments, Roosevelt not only stole a march on the Republicans on the eve of their national convention but also shored up the foreign-policy militants within his administration. Knox and Stimson had both taken positions well in advance of any yet assumed by Roosevelt; Stimson, in fact, had just come out in favor of using the American fleet to convoy munitions to Britain.[18]

Although Roosevelt did not go as far as Stimson, he was just as determined to speed all possible aid to Britain, a resolve he proposed to expound to the nation in his address to the graduating class of the University of Virginia. Just before departing for Charlottesville, the President received word that Italy was about to declare war on France. Roosevelt was infuriated, not least because he had labored so assiduously to detach the Duce from Hitler. Only a few days earlier, he had sent a personal message to Mussolini with an offer to mediate between Italy and the Allies and to hold himself personally responsible for the execution of any agreements. Count Ciano noted that he had told Ambassador Phillips: "It takes more than that to

[18]Elting Morison, *Turmoil and Tradition* (Boston, 1960), pp. 477-486; Louis Brownlow, *A Passion for Anonymity* (Chicago, 1958), pp. 433-454; Henry Stimson MS. Diary, June 25, 1940; Langer and Gleason, *Challenge to Isolation,* pp. 509-511. The G.O.P. national chairman promptly read Knox out of the party, although no one could recall when he had been vested with the power of excommunication.

dissuade Mussolini. In fact, it is not that he wants to obtain this or that; what he wants is war, and, even if he were to obtain by peaceful means double what he claims, he would refuse." On May 29, Bullitt cabled Roosevelt: "Al Capone will enter war about the fourth of June, unless you can throw the fear of the U.S.A. into him."[19] Three days before, Mussolini told his generals that he had already promised Hitler he would intervene. "I need only a few thousand dead to enable me to take my seat, as a belligerent, at the peace table," the Duce explained.[20]

On the train to Charlottesville, the President's anger at the fascists mounted. As he afterward said, he became "so hot" he was "grumbling about it." In his formal oration, he pledged that America would not only step up its own defense preparations but would "extend to the opponents of force the material resources of this nation." The United States, he premonished, could not hope to remain an island of democracy in a totalitarian sea, "a people lodged in prison, handcuffed, hungry, and fed through the bars from day to day by the contemptuous, unpitying masters of other continents." At the conclusion of his speech, Roosevelt ad-libbed one stinging sentence: "On this tenth day of June, 1940, the hand that held the dagger has struck it into the back of its neighbor."[21]

In making the Charlottesville commitment to aid Britain, the President risked a good deal. Polls revealed that only 30 per cent of the nation still believed an Allied victory possible. Senator Pittman, chairman of the Senate Foreign Relations Committee, announced it was futile for Britain to continue to fight on in England, and even a pro-British senator like Josiah Bailey wrote that under no circumstances could Britain hope to dislodge Hitler from his conquests on the Continent.[22] The Joint Planners of the War and Navy Departments pointed out the slim prospects for Britain's survival, and

[19]Hugh Gibson (ed.), *The Ciano Diaries* (New York, 1946), p. 255; Langer and Gleason, *Challenge to Isolation,* p. 462. Cf. Bullitt to R. Walton Moore, April 18, 1940, Moore MSS., Box 3.

[20]Pietro Badoglio, *L'Italie dans la Guerre Mondiale* (Paris, 1946), pp. 38-39.

[21]Henry Stimson MS. Diary, December 29, 1940; *Public Papers,* IX, 261-264; William Bullitt to Cordell Hull, May 31, June 10, 1940. FDRL, Tully Safe File; William Phillips MS. Diary, June 11, 1940, XV, 4010.

[22]*The New York Times,* June 26, 1940; Bailey to Dr. Julian Ruffin, July 24, 1940, Bailey MSS., Personal File. The former ambassador to Italy, Breckinridge Long, commented on the Charlottesville address: "If we are not very careful we are going to find ourselves the champions of a defeated cause. . . . France has utterly collapsed. It may not be but a few weeks before England collapses and Hitler stands rampant

General Marshall warned that if the United States stripped its defenses to help Britain, and the British capitulated, leaving this country to face unarmed an Axis invasion, Roosevelt's policy could never be justified to the American people. The United States had only 160 P-40 planes for the 260 pilots waiting for them; it had no antiaircraft ammunition, and would not for six months.[23]

All that summer the Nazis rained bombs on British cities as a prelude to the invasion scheduled for September. Alone, beleaguered, the British desperately needed to maintain control of the seas to keep military supplies flowing into the country. By the end of July, they had lost nearly half of the hundred destroyers available for home waters. Prime Minister Winston Churchill beseeched Roosevelt to let him have fifty or sixty "overage" World War I destroyers to use against the Nazi submarines.[24]

Roosevelt hesitated. He had already turned down similar entreaties from Norway and France—and for compelling reasons.[25] Not only might the ships be needed for American defense, but the lease of ships of war to a belligerent would almost certainly violate international law. Even if he overcame these objections, he faced nearly insurmountable difficulties. The Walsh Act of June 28, 1940, stipulated that equipment could be released for sale only if the Navy certified it was useless for defense; and naval officials had just testified to the value of the destroyers in order to prevent Congress from junking them. The President was convinced it would require an act of Congress to permit even their indirect sale; yet if he went to Congress, Senator David I. Walsh and the isolationists might very well block the proposal. Such a rebuff, taken as an index to the

---

across the continent of Europe." Breckinridge Long MS. Diary, June 13, 1940. Long noted that Ambassador Phillips believed Germany would win, and hence there should be no more provocative statements; that Ambassador Kennedy was "quite a realist and he sees England gone"; and that Ambassador Cudahy was "sure Germany will win. . . . " Kennedy, Long set down, thought the United States should approach Germany and Japan for "an economic collaboration," while Ambassador Cudahy "sees no disadvantage to us if Germany wins. . . . " Breckinridge Long MS. Diary, August 16, November 6, 1940.

[23]Langer and Gleason, *Challenge to Isolation,* pp. 487-488, 566-569, 654.

[24]Winston Churchill, *Their Finest Hour* (Boston, 1949), p. 402; Langer and Gleason, *Challenge to Isolation,* pp. 744-749. Cf. William Allen White to Fiorello La Guardia, July 29, 1940, La Guardia MSS.

[25]F.D.R. to Mrs. Florence Jaffray Harriman, January 9, 1940, Harriman MSS., Box 4; William Bullitt to Cordell Hull, May 18, 1940, FDRL, Tully Safe File; F.D.R. to Sumner Welles, June 1, 1940, FDRL PSF 24.

views of the American Congress, would deal a mean blow to Allied morale.[26]

Roosevelt found a way out of one part of his dilemma by taking an old isolationist scheme and giving it a new twist. He suggested a deal with Great Britain in which the United States would exchange the destroyers for bases in the British possessions in the Western Hemisphere.[27] Unhappily, he could not obtain a firm warranty of Republican support for a destroyer-base bill, and without such assurance he risked a costly defeat in Congress. As Nazi bombers blackened the skies over Britain, Roosevelt made a bold decision: to bypass Congress entirely and negotiate a compact with Churchill on his own. On the strength of an opinion from Attorney General Robert Jackson, military leaders were persuaded they could certify the destroyers were not essential to national security, since the bases would be still more valuable. "This is the time," Admiral Stark penciled at the end of his memorandum approving the transfer, "when a 'feller' needs a friend."[28]

Yet this did not end Roosevelt's troubles. Winston Churchill now insisted that the United States make a free gift of the destroyers, and Britain make a present of the bases. He feared that if the transaction was presented as a *quid pro quo,* Britons would think he had made a bad bargain in bartering historic possessions for overage vessels. Moreover, he was unwilling to have the agreement pivot on a public pledge that the British fleet would not be surrendered in the event of a Nazi conquest, since even to discuss such an eventuality would be demoralizing. Roosevelt believed he could avoid congressional wrath only by presenting the exchange as a sharp bargain, and asked Hull to explain to "former Naval person" that he had no authority to give away any ships. The United States proposed a compromise, which Churchill reluctantly accepted. The bases would be divided into two lots; the British would lease Bermuda and Newfoundland as outright gifts; leases on the remaining bases in the Caribbean

---

[26]Benjamin Cohen to F.D.R., July 19, 1940, F.D.R. to Frank Knox, July 22, 1940, FDRL PSF 19; Langer and Gleason, *Challenge to Isolation,* pp. 744-746.

[27]Memorandum, August 2, 1940, FDRL PSF 19; Henry Stimson MS. Diary, August 2, 1940; *The Secret Diary of Harold Ickes* (3 vols., New York, 1953-54), III, 292-293.

[28]Harold Stark to F.D.R., August 21, 1940, FDRL PSF 19. Jackson's opinion was roughly handled by international lawyers. See especially Herbert Briggs, "Neglected Aspects of the Destroyer Deal," *American Journal of International Law,* XXXIV (1940), 569-587.

would be traded for the fifty destroyers. At a later time, Churchill would reaffirm his vow to Parliament of June 4 that the British fleet would not be surrendered or scuttled under any circumstances. On September 3, the President electrified the country by announcing the details of the deal. "This is the most important action in the reinforcement of our national defense that has been taken since the Louisiana Purchase," Roosevelt declared.[29]

The parallel to Jefferson and Louisiana was less than perfect. While the response to the disclosure of the transfer was generally enthusiastic—even the Chicago *Tribune* approved it—many were disturbed by the method Roosevelt had chosen. Critics charged that he had flouted the authority of Congress, whose rights in the matter he had previously conceded; that he had acted without taking the people into his confidence; and that he had transgressed international law.[30] At a time when Britain faced annihilation, Roosevelt and his supporters had little patience with animadversions based on Edwardian conventions of international law. To his admirers, the transaction was a magnificent stroke of daring statesmanship. They rejoiced in the abandonment of traditional neutrality and the fusion of British and American interests. Henceforth, as Churchill told the Commons, the United States and Great Britain would be "somewhat mixed up together."[31]

Fresh from his triumphs in Europe, Hitler warned Latin American governments that by autumn Britain would be vanquished, and Latin America would have to depend on the Reich for markets. To appease Berlin, Brazil, Argentina, Chile, and other countries refused

[29]F.D.R. to Hull, August 28, 1940, in Elliott Roosevelt (ed.), *F.D.R., His Personal Letters, 1928-1945* (2 vols., New York, 1950), II, 1061; *Public Papers,* IX, 391. See F.D.R. to David I. Walsh, August 22, 1940, Walsh MSS.; Langer and Gleason, *Challenge to Isolation,* pp. 764-770; Eugene Gerhart, *America's Advocate: Robert H. Jackson* (Indianapolis, 1958), pp. 216-217: Sumner Welles to F.D.R., August 8, 1940, FDRL PSF 19. The deal also stipulated that the United States would give twenty torpedo boats, five heavy bombers, thirty million pounds of ammunition and other supplies. By a fantastic inadvertent error these were left out of the agreement.

[30]"Mr. Roosevelt today committed an act of war," the St. Louis *Post-Dispatch* declared in a full-page advertisement in newspapers across the country. "He also became America's first dictator." St. Louis *Post-Dispatch, September 3, 1940.*

[31]"I do not view the process with any misgivings. I could not stop it if I wished; no one can stop it. Like the Mississippi, it just keeps rolling along. Let it roll. Let it roll on—full flood, inexorable, irresistible, benignant, to broader lands and better days." James Burns, *Roosevelt: The Lion and the Fox* (New York, 1956), p. 441. Cf. 365 H. C. DEB 5S 39.

to send their foreign ministers to the Havana Conference in July. Roosevelt was compelled to recognize that repentance did not constitute a Latin American policy. By the end of 1940, the United States had worked out defense agreements with every South American nation save Argentina, and Congress had expanded the lending authority of the Export-Import Bank to finance exports to countries south of the border. In August, 1940, an Office for Co-ordination of Commercial and Cultural Relations between the American Republics was established under the direction of Nelson Rockefeller, although it was not until after Pearl Harbor that we began to send professors, tennis players, and ballet companies to Latin America to prove that we were a cultured people. The Havana Conference, too, scored another success for the Good Neighbor policy. The delegates accepted the historic "no transfer" principle of the Monroe Doctrine; agreed to Hull's appeal to take steps to establish a "collective trusteeship" over European possessions in the Caribbean; and, during the emergency, gave the United States a blank check to take what action it deemed necessary.[32]

The American Army of 1940 could hardly cope with an invasion, let alone protect Latin America. In August, 1940, when the Army conducted its greatest peacetime maneuvers in history in St. Lawrence County, New York, the troops were virtually weaponless. Pieces of stovepipe served as antitank guns, beer cans as ammunition, rainpipes as mortars, and broomsticks as machine guns. The attempt to simulate conditions of blitzkrieg warfare failed miserably. The Army had only one fully armored unit, and it was tied down at training centers in the South; no combat planes were available; and, for Panzer divisions, men maneuvered trucks bearing placards with the word "TANK."[33]

The United States Army numbered little more than a half-million men, including the National Guard. Chief of Staff General George Catlett Marshall wanted a force of at least two million, yet enlistments had been falling off sharply. In May, 1940, a group of eastern gentry, who had voluntarily undertaken military training at a camp in Plattsburg, New York, in 1915, turned the occasion of their twenty-fifth reunion into the start of a campaign for peacetime

[32]Langer and Gleason, *Challenge to Isolation,* pp. 629-637, 689-700, and *The Undeclared War* (New York, 1953), pp. 151-158, 162-169; John A. Logan, Jr., *No Transfer* (New Haven, 1961), pp. 330-345; Percy Bidwell, *Economic Defense of Latin America* (Boston, 1941); Arthur Whitaker, *The Western Hemisphere Idea* (Ithaca, 1954), pp. 147-149. The Export-Import Bank had been created in 1934.

[33]*The New York Times,* August 1-27, 1940.

conscription. Neither Roosevelt, in an election year, nor Marshall, who did not want to jeopardize War Department appropriations or break up seasoned units in order to train draftees, would support such an unpopular proposal. The Plattsburg group, headed by Grenville Clark, a prominent New York attorney, and Colonel Julius Ochs Adler, publisher of *The New York Times,* framed their own bill and had it introduced late in June by Senator Edward Burke, an anti-New Deal Democrat from Nebraska, and Representative James Wadsworth, a New York Republican.[34]

Opposition to the selective service bill crossed a wide spectrum from conservatives like Robert Taft to progressives like George Norris. Senator Wheeler admonished: "If this Bill passes—it will slit the throat of the last Democracy still living—it will accord to Hitler his greatest and cheapest victory. On the headstone of American Democracy he will inscribe—'Here Lies The Foremost Victim Of The War Of Nerves.'"[35] A peacetime draft, opponents charged, could only signify a step toward involving the United States in the European war, since this country was not imperiled.[36] A conscript force, military experts like Hanson Baldwin argued, would be useless for modern warfare, which required not mass armies but skilled, mobile striking forces. Senator James Murray of Montana protested: "A conscript army made up of youths trained for a year or two, compared to Hitler's army, is like a high school football team going up against the professional teams they have in Chicago and New York."[37]

[34]Langdon Marvin, Columbia University Oral History Collection, Columbia University Library; James Wadsworth, COHC, pp. 434 ff.; Henry Hooker to Missy LeHand, May 23, 1940, FDRL PPF 482; Langer and Gleason, *Challenge to Isolation,* p. 680; Mark S. Watson, *Chief of Staff: Prewar Plans and Preparations* (Washington, 1950), pp. 189-192.

[35]Burton K. Wheeler, "Marching Down the Road to War," *Vital Speeches,* VI (1940), 692.

[36]"Whom do we fear?" Hamilton Fish asked, "Do we fear Hitler, who seems afraid to attack England over 20 miles of sea, when he would have 3,000 miles to cross over here?" *Congressional Record,* 76th Cong., 3d Sess., p. 11361.

[37]Hanson Baldwin, "Wanted: A Plan for Defense," *Harper's,* CLXXXI (1940), 225-238; James Murray to Hugh Daly, August 31, 1940, Murray MSS. Senator Gillette of Iowa declared: "This idea of letting the boys sit around for a year playing stud poker and blackjack is poppycock." *Time,* XXXVI (August 12, 1940), 13. John L. Lewis denounced the proposal as "a fantastic suggestion from a mind in full intellectual retreat." *The New York Times,* June 20, 1940. See National Council for the Prevention of War files, Drawer 84.

Over the summer, as the Nazis poised to invade Britain, support for the bill mounted. Although mail to congressmen ran 90 per cent against the measure, polls indicated a rapid shift of opinion in favor of selective service.[38] Secretary Stimson, another Plattsburg alumnus, converted President Roosevelt and General Marshall to the conscription cause.[39] In mid-September, Congress passed the Burke-Wadsworth bill. On October 16, men between the ages of twenty-one and thirty-five registered for America's first peacetime draft. Ten days later, Secretary Stimson, blindfolded, reached into a fishbowl to pluck out the first of the numbers which would determine the order men would be called into the armed services.

The Japanese viewed the Allied reversals in Europe with unconcealed delight. With France and Holland overrun, and Britain threatened with extinction, Japan might now free itself of dependence on America for vital resources by reaching into the rice paddies of French Indochina, the oil fields of the Netherlands East Indies, and the rubber plantations of Malaya. On June 25, 1940, the War Minister, General Shunroku Hata, one of the more moderate of the Japanese military men, declared: "We should not miss the present opportunity or we shall be blamed by posterity." In July, Tokyo compelled the British to close the Burma Road for three months, cutting off the trickle of munitions and gasoline to China. That same month, the military precipitated the fall of the Yonai cabinet and persuaded Emperor Hirohito, against his better judgment, to name the Army's choice, Prince Fumimaro Konoye, as Premier. Konoye picked one of the Army hotspurs, General Hideki Tojo, as his new War Minister, and another of the Army's favorites, Yosuke Matsuoka, as his Foreign Minister. The Japanese policy of moderation had been unable to survive the Nazi triumphs in Europe, which, as Grew later noted, had "gone to their heads like strong wine."[40]

Japan's new militance sharpened a division within the administration over Far Eastern policy. One faction, led by Morgenthau and Stimson, pressed for the imposition of economic sanctions on Japan, while Hull and Sumner Welles in the State Department and Am-

[38]Rowena Wyatt, "Voting Via the Senate Mailbag," *Public Opinion Quarterly,* V (1941), 373-374.
[39]Stimson MS. Diary, July 9, 1940, *et seq.*
[40]Langer and Gleason, *Challenge to Isolation,* pp. 599, 603, 719-720; F. C. Jones, *Japan's New Order in East Asia* (London, 1954), pp. 165-170; *Japan Chronicle,* July 4-19, 1940; Joseph Grew, *Turbulent Era,* ed. Walter Johnson (2 vols., Boston, 1952), II, 1125.

bassador Grew in Tokyo warned that an embargo would not only destroy what little strength the moderates in Japan still held but would drive the Nipponese to attack Singapore and the Indies. Through the first eight months of 1940, Hull held the upper hand. When in July the President signed a proclamation, drafted by Morgenthau, banning the export of oil and scrap metals, Welles persuaded Roosevelt to modify the edict sharply to restrict it to aviation gasoline and only high-grade iron and steel scrap.[41]

Yet as the Japanese in the late summer of 1940 moved toward an alliance with the fascist powers, and tightened the vise on French Indochina, even their warmest American friends lost faith in their peaceful intentions. On September 12, Ambassador Grew sent his "Green Light" message. Long an advocate of patient negotiations with Tokyo, and an eloquent opponent of sanctions, Grew had come to feel that Japan could be deterred only by "a show of force, together with a determination to employ it if need be." Less than two weeks later, Nipponese soldiers invaded Indochina. Roosevelt responded on September 26 by slapping a total embargo on the shipment of iron and steel scrap to Japan. The following day, at a great ceremony in Berlin, Japan signed a treaty of alliance with the Rome-Berlin Axis. The Tripartite Pact, one section of which appeared to be aimed directly at the United States, explicitly linked events in Europe and the Far East. There was now only one war, Roosevelt concluded, and the democracies had to unite against a common peril, worldwide in its scope.[42]

* * *

Roosevelt, returned to an unprecedented third term, now sought to fashion a global foreign policy to contain the fascists. In Tokyo, Joseph Grew, who felt that his eight years of work for peace had "been swept away as if by a typhoon with little or nothing remaining to show for it," cautioned that Japan would not be deterred by bluff. "Only if they become certain that we mean to fight if called upon to do so," he wrote the President, "will our preliminary measures stand

---

[41]Langer and Gleasoṇ, *Challenge to Isolation,* I, 721-722; Herbert Feis, *The Road to Pearl Harbor* (Princeton, 1950), pp. 89-93.

[42]Grew, *Turbulent Era,* II, 1229; Robert Aura Smith, "The Triple-Axis Pact and American Reactions," *Annals of the American Academy of Political and Social Science,* CCXV (1941), 127-132; "Axis Alliance, 1940," Hugh Byas MSS. For the thesis that the United States misinterpreted the Pact, see Paul Schroeder, *The Axis Alliance and Japanese-American Relations 1941* (Ithaca, 1958).

some chance of proving effective and of removing the necessity of war—the old story of Sir Edward Grey in 1914."[43] Within the Administration, advocates of a hard policy pressed for that final economic sanction, an embargo on oil. "We did not keep Japan out of Indo-China by continuing to ship scrap-iron, nor will we keep Japan out of the Dutch East Indies by selling it our oil," Harold Ickes remonstrated.[44]

But the main burden of advice Roosevelt received still cautioned restraint toward Japan. "Any strength that we might send to the Far East would, by just so much, reduce the force of our blows against Germany and Italy," Admiral Stark pointed out.[45] Admiral James Otto Richardson, in command of the fleet at Hawaii, even wished to return naval forces to the Pacific Coast. Roosevelt believed that the Japanese should be met with firmness—he ordered Richardson to hold the fleet at Pearl Harbor to deter Japan—but he agreed that a showdown with Tokyo should be eschewed. Despite the entreaties of men like Ickes, he continued to permit oil to flow to the island empire.[46]

Since resistance to Hitler had priority, the President directed the energies of the government to converting the United States into a "great arsenal of democracy." He not only announced that half the country's future war production would be allotted to Britain but, in response to an urgent plea from Winston Churchill, unveiled the startling proposal to lend arms directly to Britain on the understanding that they would be returned or replaced when the war ended.[47] The nation still hoped that such subvention would be enough; that without any commitment of American military or naval forces, the Allies would be able to overcome the Axis and thus spare the United

---

[43]Grew, *Turbulent Era,* II, 1256-1257.

[44]Ickes to F.D.R., October 17, 1940, FDRL PSF 17. "Now we've stopped scrap iron, what about oil?" Eleanor Roosevelt asked. Eleanor Roosevelt to F.D.R., Nov. 12, 1940, FDRL PSF 35.

[45]Stark to F.D.R., November 12, 1940, FDRL Tully Safe File. "If Germany should win in Europe, Japan will run amuck in the Far East," observed Francis Sayre, High Commissioner in Manila, "whereas if England wins, I doubt if Japan will thereafter present much of a problem in this part of the world. . . . Under no circumstances," Sayre advised, should the United States "play into Hitler's hands by being sucked into a war with Japan." Sayre to F.D.R., November 13, 1940, FDRL PSF 17.

[46]U.S. Congress, *Pearl Harbor Attack,* Hearings before the Joint Committee on the Investigation of the Pearl Harbor Attack, 79th Cong., 1st Sess., pursuant to S. Con. Res. 27, Part 1, November 15-21, 1945 (Washington, 1946), pp. 264-266; F.D.R. to Eleanor Roosevelt, November 13, 1940, FDRL PSF 35.

[47]*Public Papers,* IX, 563, 605-613, 643; Churchill, *Their Finest Hour,* pp. 557-569.

States the need to fight. When the William Allen White Committee in November, 1940, suggested it might be necessary for the U.S. Navy to convoy merchant ships to Britain, White, after first approving the statement, backed down in a public letter in which he called the convoy scheme "a silly thing, for convoys, unless you shoot, are confetti and it's not time to shoot now or ever. . . . If I was making a motto for the Committee to Defend America by Aiding the Allies," White added, "it would be 'The Yanks Are Not Coming.'" Early in January, after Fiorello La Guardia accused him of "doing a typical Laval," White resigned as committee chairman.[48]

White's irresolution represented the feeling of the average American at the end of 1940. He wanted to help Britain, even at the risk of war, yet he wished too to remain at peace. But it was by no means clear that economic aid alone would suffice. At a meeting in October, 1940, Secretary Knox burst out: "I can't escape saying that the English are not going to win this war without our help, I mean our miltary help." In December, Secretary Stimson reflected that it would be impossible to expand production to the levels needed "until we got into the war ourselves." By January, even White was writing: "The dictators are greedy for our wealth and have scorn for our liberty. Sooner or later we shall have to meet them with arms, how and when I don't know."[49] Increasingly, Washington discussed not "whether" but "when" we would enter the war. In the Pacific, the decision to impose sanctions on oil would not long be postponed. Even if such measures halted the Japanese advance toward the South Seas, war might come over American insistence on the liberation of China.[50] In the Atlantic, it seemed absurd to ship arms to Britain and then permit U-boats to send them to the bottom of the ocean. Inevitably, lend-lease would lead to convoying, and if the Nazi wolfpack menaced the convoy, would not U.S. naval vessels have to shoot? As the new Atlantic Fleet, organized on February 1, 1941, extended its patrol from the blue Caribbean to the icy waters of Greenland, quasi-belligerency shaded into war.

[48]Walter Johnson, *William Allen White's America* (New York, 1947), pp. 544, 547; F.D.R. to White, June 16, 1941, White MSS., Box 324.

[49]Charles Tansill, *Back Door to War* (Chicago, 1952), p. 602; Theodore Carlson to Stephen Chadwick, December 21, 1940, Chadwick MSS.; Langer and Gleason, *Undeclared War,* p. 187; Stimson MS. Diary, December 13, 29, 1940; White to Rev. Allen Keedy, January 3, 1941, Walter Johnson (ed.), *Selected Letters of William Allen White* (New York, 1947), p. 422.

[50]Schroeder, *Axis Alliance,* pp. 203-204.

WILLIAM L. LANGER and S. EVERETT GLEASON
The Undeclared War, 1940-1941

William L. Langer (born 1896) was Professor of History at Harvard University. He worked in the Office of Coordinator of Information, the Office of Strategic Services, and the State Department during 1941-1946, and was Assistant United States Secretary of State in 1946 and Assistant Director of National Estimates for the Central Intelligence Agency, 1950-1951. He has written many works, including *European Alliances and Alignments* (1931), *The Diplomacy of Imperialism* (1935), *Our Vichy Gamble* (1947), and, with S. Everett Gleason, *The Challenge to Isolation, 1937-1940* (1952). S. Everett Gleason (born 1905) was Associate Professor of History at Amherst College and worked for the Office of Strategic Services during 1943-1945. He was Historian for the Council on Foreign Relations, 1946-1950, and Deputy Executive Secretary of the National Security Council, 1950-1959. Since 1962 he has been Historian in the Historical Office of the Department of State. He has written *Ecclesiastical Barony of the Middle Ages* and coauthored two books with William L. Langer.

BY THE AUTUMN of 1941 the American public had gone far toward identifying itself with the opposition to Nazism and the Axis. It was united in its desire and determination to see Nazism destroyed and was all but unanimous in holding that Britain must be sustained, if only in the interest of American and hemisphere defense. Under Lend-Lease seven billion dollars had been appropriated to provide the opponents of Hitler with the tools of victory. In October, 1941, another six billion dollars was voted for the same purpose, almost without opposition. But the American people, while willing to supply material aid and even prepared to accept measures for ensuring the safe arrival of munitions in Britain, still clung to the hope that material sacrifice would spare them the horror of full-fledged hostilities. Public opinion polls showed that some 75 to 80 percent of the population still strenuously opposed direct participation in the war.[1]

[1]See particularly the editorial in *The New York Times,* October 1, 1941.

From William L. Langer and S. Everett Gleason, *The Undeclared War, 1940-1941* (New York: Harper and Bros., for the Council on Foreign Relations, 1953).

If the man in the street persisted in his self-delusion, it was certainly not for want of enlightenment or admonition. Individuals and newspapers in ever increasing numbers pleaded with the public to face the facts. William C. Bullitt, among others, argued for an immediate declaration of war on Germany, a step which, he pointed out, was inevitable sooner or later: "We are going to war, whether you like it or not. . . . We are doing a job that is really not good enough. Why? We are caught in a conflict of emotions so deep we cannot resolve it. We want to defeat Hitler, but we do not want to go to war. These viewpoints are incompatible. . . . It's a sad thing to say, but the only way we can defeat Hitler is by the United States putting all its resources into this fight and going to war now."[2] Similarly, newspapers like the *New York Post* reasoned that a declaration of war would have a devastating psychological effect on the Germans:

It would be an icy hand to snatch hope from every soldier in Hitler's line. It would install despair as a permanent guest in every German home. It would uphold the bleeding hands of Russia certainly until the snow flies—more effectively than swarms of planes and fresh divisions of troops. It would enable Britain to pour out her hoarded reserves. And in the resentful lands under conquest,what a backfire it would kindle.[3]

But the American public, generally speaking, refused to be persuaded. True, isolationism had long been on the wane and some of its leaders were being discredited by their anti-Semitic utterances and by the revelations of abuse of the franking privileges of Congressmen for the benefit of Nazi propaganda.[4] Nevertheless, many Americans, intent above all on avoiding involvement in war, were prone to heed the positive assertions of Colonel Lindbergh and his ilk and to suspect the President of maneuvering the country into

---

[2] *The New York Times,* October 24, 1941.
[3] Editorial, October 10, 1941.
[4] On September 26, 1941, a Federal Grand Jury exposed the mechanism of Nazi agitation. See also the *Chicago Daily News,* October 13 and 14, 1941, on the publication of *Scribner's Commentator* and other ostensibly isolationist but clearly pro-Nazi tracts at Geneva, Wisconsin. On October 6, 1941, the *New Republic* called for a Congressional investigation of America First, charging that organization with having become the general staff of all Fascist, semi-Fascist and proto-Fascist elements in America, as well as the focal point of anti-Semitism. President Roosevelt shared suspicions of the organization (*F.D.R.: His Personal Letters,* II, 1241-42).

war without the approval of Congress. Senator Robert A. Taft quickly seized upon the Atlantic Charter to argue that the pledge to destroy the Nazi tyranny could be fulfilled only "by sending our soldiers to Berlin." On balance, it appears that the country at large, while firmly committed to almost any move "short of war," hardened in opposition to intervention as the implications of current policies became ever more obvious. Lord Beaverbrook, after visiting Washington in August, was unable to send any but the most discouraging reports to London: there was not the slightest chance of the United States entering the war unless forced to do so by direct attack, which would probably not occur until after Soviet Russia and Britain were already defeated.[5]

The British Government and people, sensing the trend of American sentiment, were much disheartened, especially when it appeared that the dramatic Atlantic Conference had produced nothing but a declaration of general principles. Mr. Mackenzie King, returning from a visit to England, reported the Government absolutely confident that Hitler could not defeat Britain, but quite unable to see how Britain could defeat Germany without the active participation of the United States.[6] Mr. Churchill and his associates had tried to dispel misapprehensions on this score during the Atlantic meeting, but to no avail. Doubtless the Prime Minister, like Lord Halifax, thought and hoped that more positive leadership by Mr. Roosevelt would carry the American public along the desired course. Mr. Churchill's speech in the House on September 30, 1941, suggests that he had become impatient with the tides of public opinion, for he remarked: "Nothing is more dangerous in wartime than to live in the temperamental atmosphere of a Gallup poll, always feeling one's pulse and taking one's temperature. . . . There is only one duty, only one safe course, and that is to try to be right and not to fear to do or say what you believe to be right."[7] Privately he wrote Mr. Harry Hopkins that a "wave of depression" had come

---

[5]Robert E. Sherwood: *Roosevelt and Hopkins* (New York, 1948), 368. Secretary Ickes, after a long tour around the country, wrote the President, September 17, in despair over the popular lack of a wish to fight or will to victory (*Roosevelt Papers: Secretary's File*, Box 73).

[6]*Moffat Diary (MS).* September 18, 1941, reporting a talk with the Canadian Prime Minister.

[7]Winston S. Churchill: *The Unrelenting Struggle* (Boston, 1942), 272. For Lord Halifax's opinion we rely on the *Moffat Diary* (MS.), August 20, 1941, reporting the Ambassador's observations at lunch.

over British Government circles and warned that "if 1942 opens with Russia knocked out and Britain left again alone, all kinds of dangers may arise."[8]

Mr. Hopkins took this opportunity to remind the President that if the British lost hope of American intervention, a critical moment might come and the appeasers might stage a comeback. Mr. Roosevelt may well have discounted this argument, but it is altogether probable that he too was profoundly concerned by the dilemma confronting him. Mr. Churchill has recorded his conviction that after the Atlantic Conference the President desired above all things to bring the United States into the fight for freedom, but was unable to see how this could be encompassed.[9] Others, mostly hostile critics, have made the same assertion, usually with the addition that Mr. Roosevelt was at a loss as to how to deceive his countrymen and circumvent Congress. It seems hardly necessary, however, to ascribe such ignoble motives to the President. It may safely be assumed that from countless conferences with his own military advisers, as well as from his correspondence and discussion with Mr. Churchill, he had been driven to abandon his earlier hopes that America's role could be confined to that of the Arsenal of Democracy. His military advisers, in their contemporary strategic estimates, were at one in stating that Britain might well be defeated unless the United States intervened militarily and that Germany could almost certainly not be defeated without the commitment of American forces on a large scale. It should be noted at once, however, that these same experts were unequivocally of the opinion that early entry of the United States into the war would serve no useful purpose, since the new Army as yet consisted of only two or three divisions ready for action and was therefore far too weak to undertake significant operations.[10]

It is impossible to speak with certainty of Mr. Roosevelt's views and intentions, but the evidence, fragmentary though it is, suggests that he was reluctant to accept the thesis that Hitler could be defeated only by a large-scale Anglo-American invasion of the Continent. Secretary Stimson noted in his diary that Mr. Roosevelt

[8]Sherwood: *Roosevelt and Hopkins*, 373.

[9]Winston S. Churchill: *The Grand Alliance* (Boston, 1950), 539.

[10]The military view was expressed most comprehensively in the American comments on the British General Strategy Review, which were sent to London on September 25, 1941. For a detailed discussion see Mark S. Watson, *Chief of Staff: Prewar Plans and Preparations* (Washington, 1950), 345 ff., 406 ff.

"was afraid of any assumption of the position that we must invade Germany and crush Germany."[11] This impression would seem to be bolstered by the fact that in late September the President reviewed with Secretary Stimson and General Marshall the planned strength and organization of the Army in the hope of finding ways and means to allot more equipment to Britain and Soviet Russia through reduction of United States combat forces and overseas garrisons. Such reduction appeared inadvisable, but the very fact that it was considered reflects the trend of Mr. Roosevelt's thought at this time.[12] It is probably not far from the mark to say that by September, 1941, he realized that the defeat of Hitlerism, so ardently desired by the American people, could not be achieved without active military participation on the part of the United States, but that he still hoped the American contribution could be restricted to naval and air support and material assistance. Had he not still deluded himself with the idea that heavy loss of American lives might be avoided, he would hardly at so critical a juncture have reconsidered the 1940 plans for building a large, modern Army. It is certainly worth noting that the President at no time prior to Pearl Harbor suggested further increase of the Army which, according to the existing program, was designed for national and hemisphere defense rather than for overseas operations against Nazi Germany.

* * *

At the time of the enactment of the Lend-Lease legislation Hitler had announced that he would frustrate the program of American aid to Britain by sinking every ship carrying supplies to British ports. The havoc which was in fact raised by Nazi submarines during the spring of 1941 was eloquent proof of the Fuehrer's determination. It left the American Government and people little doubt that if their support of Britain were to be fully effective, something would have to be done sooner or later to ensure the safe arrival abroad of the war materials produced at such expense. The question of using American naval vessels to escort convoys across the Atlantic was an obvious corollary of the Lend-Lease program. As the preceding narrative has indicated, the issue was publicly debated again and again and was of deepest concern to the President. Realizing the full

---

[11] *Stimson Diary (MS.)*, September 25, 1941.
[12] For details see Watson: *Chief of Staff: Prewar Plans and Preparations*, 362 ff., which, however, requires some correction in the light of the Conn MS. study on *Defense of the Americas.*

implications of American naval escort, Mr. Roosevelt had repeatedly recoiled from a clean-cut decision. However, a number of battleships had been withdrawn from the Pacific so as to strengthen the patrol system in the Atlantic and after the occupation of Iceland early in July American naval escort of United States and Icelandic shipping as far as Iceland had been initiated. Secretary Knox, Admiral Stark and others had at that time hoped fervently that the President would put an end to the uncertainty by extending the new escort system to all friendly shipping, but they had once again been disappointed. Not until the Atlantic Conference was the decision made to permit American warships to escort other than American shipping as far as Iceland. Although the official orders were not issued until September 13 (effective September 16), the new system had in fact been introduced by August 26, 1941.[13]

It may be observed that this important departure took place at a time when the British had fairly well mastered the submarine menace in the North Atlantic. Mr. Churchill was stating publicly that sinkings had dropped to one third the figure reached in the spring and that, in view of the increased construction of new shipping, the net loss was only one fifth.[14] It should be remembered, however, that the Nazi wolf packs had carried their attacks far into the western Atlantic and that, when effectively opposed there, they had begun to shift their operations to the vicinity of the Cape Verdes and Canaries. In order to hold in check their depredations in the North Atlantic the British Navy was obliged to employ all available destroyers and corvettes, many of which were badly needed elsewhere and would indeed be essential for countering the submarine menace off the African coasts. By the summer of 1941 yet another aspect of the situation had emerged: if supplies were to be sent to the Soviet Union, the British and other shipping required would have to be escorted northward along the Norwegian coast to Archangel or Murmansk. This additional mission would be beyond British naval capabilities unless some measure of relief were provided in the Atlantic.[15]

[13]See above, Chapters XVIII and XX. For the implementation of the new system we have used the MS. study by Captain Tracy Kittredge on *United States-British Naval Coöperation*. See also Samuel E. Morison: *The Battle of the Atlantic* (Boston, 1947), 79 ff.

[14]Churchill's speeches in the House, September 9 and 30, November 12 and December 11, 1941 *(The Unrelenting Struggle,* 246 ff., 264 ff., 300 ff., 345). See also Churchill: *The Grand Alliance,* 516-18, and the statistical table on p. 522.

[15]We rely here chiefly on the Kittredge MS. study cited above.

President Roosevelt was, of course, kept fully informed by Mr. Churchill of all important features of the situation. Being unable or unwilling to satisfy British expectatons of full-scale participation in the war, he was evidently eager to do what he could to relieve the strain on British naval forces and in general to bolster British morale. Hoping still to avoid the commitment of large American expeditionary forces, he could at least press for greater war production and ensure that American supplies reached their destinations safely. Furthermore, he may by this time have convinced himself that Hitler would not accept the challenge presented by American escort of British shipping, at least before Soviet Russia were defeated. In short, Mr. Roosevelt may have concluded that substantial additional support could be given to Britain without entailing serious consequences.

Having made his decision, the President had no alternative but to inform the country and try to justify the grave measure he had now adopted. His Labor Day address (September 1) was clearly a preparatory move, for it referred to Hitler openly as the enemy and warned Americans in these words:

> We are engaged on a grim and perilous task. Forces of insane violence have been let loose by Hitler upon this earth. We must do our full part in conquering them. For these forces may be unleashed on this nation as we go about our business of protecting the proper interests of our country. . . . I know that I speak the conscience and determination of the American people when I say that we shall do everything in our power to crush Hitler and his Nazi forces.

But Mr. Roosevelt was to be spared the unpleasant task of springing on his countrymen the announcement of the new system of escort. On September 4 there occurred a German submarine attack on the *USS Greer* which provided him a perfect opportunity to underline the above-quoted passage of his Labor Day speech.

The facts of the *Greer* episode were briefly as follows: the American destroyer was en route to Iceland with passengers and mail when it was notified by a British patrol plane that a Nazi submarine lay submerged some ten miles ahead. The *Greer* thereupon located and trailed the submarine for several hours, periodically broadcasting its position. Eventually the harassed submarine commander fired two torpedoes, both of which missed their mark. In reply the *Greer* dropped depth bombs, with unknown effect. The incident had occurred about 175 miles southwest of

Iceland, within the zone proclaimed by the Germans as a war zone, but also well within the area in which American warships had been ordered to attack and destroy surface raiders. The *Greer's* commander could not reasonably be blamed for reacting, once the submarine had fired its torpedoes. On the other hand, it is difficult to appreciate the indignation with which news of the episode was received in American official and private circles. Considering that the *Greer* had sought out the submarine, had trailed it doggedly for hours, and had given British planes information to facilitate their attack, it would have been astounding if the prospective victim had not finally turned on her pursuers.[16]

The President seized on the incident with alacrity, even before all the facts were known. In a statement to the press on September 5 he emphasized that the attack on the *Greer* was deliberate, and revealed that orders had been issued to "eliminate" the guilty submarine. On the same day he conferred with Secretary Hull and Mr. Hopkins about an important speech which he proposed to make on the subject. Mr. Hull was duly outraged by the attack and made appropriately stern comments. Thereupon the President requested him to write out his remarks for use in the speech, only to find on receiving the text, that Mr. Hull had quickly lost his ardor and made no recommendation for specific action.

At this point delay was occasioned by the President's unavoidable absence at Hyde Park to attend the funeral of his mother. Meanwhile, however, Mr. Hopkins, Judge Rosenman and Assistant Secretary of State Berle tried their hands at a draft, keeping in touch with Mr. Roosevelt by telephone. The text was finally completed after the President's return to Washington (September 10) and included important passages from Mr. Roosevelt's own pen. After dinner on the evening of September 10 the address was read to Secretaries Hull, Stimson and Knox, all of whom concurred heartily in thinking it "the most decisive one which he [the President] had made." On the following morning Mr. Roosevelt read it again, this time to a group of Congressional leaders, who evidently took no exception to it. To be sure, at the last moment Secretary Hull was again beset by qualms and urged the omission of all reference to shooting. But the President's mind was made up; on the evening of

---

[16]The facts, as presented to a Congressional committee by Admiral Stark on September 20, 1941, are given in *Documents on American Foreign Relations*, IV, 93 ff., and in Morison: *The Battle of the Atlantic*, 79 ff.

September 11 he delivered his address over a worldwide radio hookup.[17]
The speech took its departure from the *Greer* incident. Despite what the Nazi propaganda machine might assert, said the President, the facts were "that the German submarine fired first upon this American destroyer without warning, and with deliberate design to sink her." This, he concluded, was "piracy, legally and morally." Recalling the earlier sinking of the *Robin Moor* and of other American or Panamanian vessels, he argued that these episodes were all part of a Nazi plan to abolish freedom of the seas and acquire control of the oceans as a prelude to domination of the United States and the Western Hemisphere. It was time, declared the President, for all Americans in all the Americas to stop deluding themselves with the romantic notion that the Americas could go on living happily and peacefully in a Nazi-dominated world: "No tender whisperings of appeasers that Hitler is not interested in the Western Hemisphere, no soporific lullabies that a wide ocean protects us from him—can long have any effect on the hard-headed, farsighted and realistic American people." The time had come to call a halt. Diplomatic notes and protests were patently useless. But the United States would refuse to be intimidated:

> No act of violence or intimidation will keep us from maintaining intact two bulwarks of defense: first, our line of supply of matériel to the enemies of Hitler, and second, the freedom of our shipping on the high seas.
> No matter what it takes, no matter what it costs, we will keep open the line of legitimate commerce in these defensive waters.
> We have sought no shooting war with Hitler. We do not seek it now. But neither do we want peace so much that we are willing to pay for it by permitting him to attack our naval and merchant ships while they are on legitimate business.

The next was one of the passages drafted by Mr. Roosevelt himself:

> Do not let us split hairs. Let us not ask ourselves whether the Americas should begin to defend themselves after the fifth attack, or the tenth attack, or the twentieth attack.
> The time for active defense is now.

[17]Sherwood: *Roosevelt and Hopkins,* 370 ff. *The Memoirs of Cordell Hull,* 2 vols., (New York, 1948), II, 1046 ff.; *Stimson Diary* (MS.), September 9,10,11,1941; *Berle Diary* (MS.), September 9, 10, 11, 1941, containing various drafts of the speech.

Then, continuing:

> If submarines or raiders attack in distant waters, they can attack
> equally well within sight of our own shores. Their very presence in
> any waters which America deems vital to its defense constitutes an
> attack.
>
> In the waters which we deem necessary for our defense, American
> naval vessels and American planes will no longer wait until Axis
> submarines lurking under water, or Axis raiders on the surface of the
> sea, strike their deadly blow—first.
>
> Upon our naval and air patrol now operating in large number over a
> vast expanse of the Atlantic Ocean—falls the duty of maintaining the
> American policy of freedom of the seas—now. That means, very
> simply and clearly, that our patrolling vessels and planes will protect
> all merchant ships—not only American ships but ships of any
> flag—engaged in commerce in our defensive waters.

At this point the President made reference to the attitude and action
of some of his predecessors in like situations and then denounced
the idea that his decision involved an act of war: "It is not an act of
war on our part when we decide to protect the seas which are vital to
American defense. The aggression is not ours. Ours is solely
defense." The speech concluded with a crucial warning, again in the
President's own language: "But let this warning be clear. From now
on, if German or Italian vessels of war enter the waters the
protection of which is necessary for American defense, they do so at
their own peril."

The official orders to the Commander in Chief of the Atlantic
Fleet (September 13) were only the logical implementation of the
President's statement. Thenceforth the Fleet was to protect not only
American convoys to Iceland, but also "shipping of any nationality
which may join such convoys between United States ports and
bases and Iceland." Furthermore, American warships were
authorized to escort convoys which included no American ships,
and American ships, in turn, were permitted to sail under Canadian
escort. The Atlantic Fleet was instructed to assure "protection
against hostile attack of United States and foreign flag shipping
(other than German and Italian shipping) by escorting, convoying
and patrolling as circumstances may require, or by destroying
German and Italian naval, land, and air forces encountered."[18]

---

[18]Kittredge MS. study on *United States-British Naval Coöperation;* Morison: *The
Battle of the Atlantic,* 79 ff.

Thus was the long-standing issue of American naval escort resolved by the declaration of the shooting war. The immediate effect was to relieve some forty British destroyers and corvettes for use elsewhere.[19] This in itself was an important contribution to Britain's war effort. But in a larger sense the President's speech and the subsequent orders to Admiral King constituted the proclamation of a naval war between the United States and the two European members of the Axis. Neither the President nor his advisers were under any misapprehension about the implications of the "shoot-on-sight" orders. Indeed, in concluding his address Mr. Roosevelt had made a point of saying: "I have no illusion about the gravity of this step. I have not taken it hurriedly or lightly. It is the result of months and months of constant thought and anxiety and prayer." Similarly Secretary Knox, in his speech to the American Legion Convention at Milwaukee (September 15), took pains to underline the fact that Hitler had now been left with "the grim choice" of leaving the bridge of ships intact or adding the American Navy to his foes. The attack on the *Greer* had dispelled all doubt as to the Fuehrer's decision and the American response was therefore inevitable:

> Beginning tomorrow, the American Navy will provide protection as adequate as we can make it for ships of every flag carrying lend-aid supplies between between the American Continent and the waters adjacent to Iceland. The Navy is ordered to capture or destroy by every means at its disposal Axis-controlled submarines or surface raiders encountered in these waters. That is our answer to Mr. Hitler.

In a letter to Admiral Kimmel a few days later (September 22) the Chief of Naval Operations made the same point in even fewer words: "So far as the Atlantic is concerned, we are all but, if not actually in it. The President's speech of September 11, 1941, put the matter squarely before the country, and outlined what he expected of the Navy. We were ready for this; in fact our orders had been issued."[20] Finally, this was also Mr. Churchill's understanding, as expressed in a letter to Field Marshal Smuts (September 14): "Hitler

[19]Mr. Churchill's letter to Field Marshal Smuts, September 14, 1941 (Churchill: *The Grand Alliance,* 517).

[20]*Pearl Harbor Attack. Hearings Before the Joint Committee on the Investigation of the Pearl Harbor Attack,* 79th Congress 2nd Session, 39 parts, (Washington, 1946), V, 2217. For Admiral Stark's Testimony to the same effect, see *ibid.,* pp. 2292 ff., 2310 ff.

will have to choose between losing the Battle of the Atlantic or coming into frequent collision with United States ships and warships."[21]

It was inevitable that isolationist leaders, who had long anticipated the likelihood of American naval escort and had done their utmost to forestall the final decision, should have lodged vigorous protests against the President's words and deeds. Former President Herbert Hoover, in a radio broadcast of September 16, objected violently to Mr. Roosevelt's "edging our warships into danger zones" without the approval of Congress, and Senator Tobey of New Hampshire declared at an America First rally in New York City (September 17) that the American people was "being deceived in a gigantic conspiracy to drive them into war." The *Chicago Tribune* openly charged the President and "the belligerent old men in his Cabinet" with hoping to create an incident that would bring about war without the need of Congressional action.[22] These and kindred indictments have been repeated by a number of postwar writers who would have their readers believe that Mr. Roosevelt deceived the American people, bypassed Congress, violated his election pledge of 1940, and purposely maneuvered an unwilling and unsuspecting country into war.

The historian can hardly evade the responsibility of pronouncing on this crucial and controversial matter. Basically his opinion will depend on whether or not he agrees with Mr. Roosevelt's conclusion that Hitlerism constituted a menace to the United States and to the principles on which the nation was founded, and that therefore it was in the national interest to support the opponents of Nazism and contribute to Hitler's defeat. The policy of aid to the victims of aggression having been accepted by Congress at the time of the Lend-Lease debates, the conclusion was almost inescapable that sooner or later steps would have to be taken to ensure the safe delivery of the aid which was then thought of as America's contribution to the common cause. Approaching the issue from this angle, posterity is likely to be surprised not so much that the decision to escort was taken, but that it was taken so late.

Viewing the problem in a narrower context, the reader should remember that Mr. Roosevelt, before delivering his radio broadcast,

---

[21]Churchill: *The Grand Alliance,* 517.

[22]*Chicago Tribune,* September 24, 1941; similarly the *New York Journal-American,* September 25, 1941.

had read it to Democratic leaders of Congress and had secured at least their tacit assent. Furthermore, public opinion polls throughout the summer of 1941 had indicated at least a slight majority as favoring the introduction of naval escort.[23] Following the *Greer* incident and the President's speech a Gallup poll revealed that 62 percent of those queried approved the stand taken by the President, while a survey conducted by *The New York Times* indicated wide and growing support of the Administration policy throughout the country. It is hardly fair, therefore, to charge Mr. Roosevelt with having acted without reference to the Congress and the country. No doubt the American people were still opposed to involvement in the war and particularly averse to having their boys sent overseas. But the evidence would suggest that they were agreeable to the steps taken by the President to defeat Hitler, even though acceptance of those steps meant that the line between "short of war" and actual war now became so blurred as to lose all significance.

On the other hand it can hardly be gainsaid that Mr. Roosevelt's devious procedure exposed him to criticism. Whether he honestly believed that, in attributing the "attack" on the *Greer* to the Germans, he was released from his election pledges, it is, in the present state of the evidence, impossible to say. However, the strained interpretation put upon the *Greer* incident gives color to the charge. Certain newspapers unfriendly to the Administration were at the time quick to seize upon the discrepancies between Mr. Roosevelt's statements on September 11 and Admiral Stark's account to a Congressional committee on September 20. Secretary Knox attempted to explain by stating that the President based his remarks of September 11 on the best information available to the Navy Department at that time, and that this information had proved incomplete.[24] This does not, however, exonerate the President of the charge of having exploited the incident without awaiting a detailed report.

Some reservation must also be made with respect to the assertion by the President and Secretary Knox, an assertion repeated in

[23]Gallup polls: May 30, 52 percent in favor; June 14, 55 percent; September 2, 52 percent.

[24]Memo of the President to Admiral Stark, September 18, 1941, commenting on the Admiral's proposed answers to questions submitted by the Congressional committee (*Roosevelt Papers:* Secretary's File, Box 77), and Secretary Knox's report to the President on his correspondence with the *New York Daily News* apropos of an editorial of October 29, 1941 (*ibid.,* Box 73).

Secretary Hull's memoirs, that the "attack" on the *Greer* revealed a systematic Nazi plan to sink American vessels. While it is true that Hitler had publicly threatened to do so, the President by September, 1941, must certainly have been convinced that Hitler, deeply involved in his campaign in the east, was intent on avoiding provocation of the United States. The astounding thing was not that there had been a few sinkings of American ships, but that there had not been many more. Actually it has now been established, from the German records, that Hitler steadfastly rejected all pleas of Admiral Raeder for all-out operations against the Anglo-American supply lines. Even after the President's declaration of September 11 Raeder failed to move his chief. In a concise memorandum the Nazi Chief of Naval Operations had stressed the point that thenceforth there would be no difference between British and American ships, and that "the order to fire signifies that the U.S.A. has gone over from silent partnership and only indirect assistance to open participation in the war." Raeder therefore urged that all restrictions on the operations of German submarines be lifted and that the Pan American Safety Zone be ignored except for a strip twenty miles wide along the American coasts. But Hitler remained adamant. He was firmly convinced that Soviet Russia would soon be defeated and that, pending that happy event, trouble with the United States should at all costs be avoided. He therefore requested that care be taken "to avoid any incidents in the war on merchant shipping before the middle of October."²⁵ These statements on Hitler's part cannot, of course, be taken as demonstrating that the United States and the Western Hemisphere were in no danger from Nazism. The Fuehrer's naval decisions were based squarely on the assumption that Soviet Russia would soon be defeated. Had the Nazis succeeded in liquidating opposition in the east, it is all but certain that they would soon have turned in full force on Britain and probably also on West Africa and South America.

In the introductory paragraphs of the present section an effort was made to determine President Roosevelt's motives in finally making the decision to employ American naval forces to escort not only American but belligerent British shipping over a major part of the Atlantic trade routes. By way of summary it may be noted that in so

---

²⁵U.S. Navy Department, *Fuehrer Conferences on Matters Dealing with the German Navy, 1939-1945.* 7 vols. (Washington, 1947), II, 33 ff; Anthony Martienssen: *Hitler and His Admirals* (New York, 1949), 118.

doing he was in full accord with the highest military opinion. The significant Joint Board Estimate of September 11, the very date of Mr. Roosevelt's speech, put the major considerations in these succinct terms:

> The sea communications can continue to support the United Kingdom only if the damage now being inflicted upon them is reduced through increases in the strength of the protective sea and air forces based in the British Isles, Iceland, and positions in the central and eastern Atlantic. Unless the losses of British merchant ships are greatly reduced, or unless there is an internal collapse in Germany, it is the opinion of the Joint Board that the resistance of the United Kingdom can not continue indefinitely, no matter what industrial effort is put forth by the United States. Therefore, the immediate and strong reënforcement of British forces in the Atlantic by United States naval and air contingents, supplemented by a large additional shipping tonnage, will be required if the United Kingdom is to remain in the war. These contingents must be manned by Americans, since the reserves of British manpower for employment in Europe are practically exhausted.[26]

It is quite possible, however, that to these compelling reasons should be added a further one deriving from the rapid deterioration of the situation in the Far East. By the terms of the Tripartite Pact Japan was obliged to come to Germany's assistance in the event of the latter's being attacked by the United States. True, this provision left open the question of what constituted an attack. Therefore one of the main issues in dispute between Tokyo and Washington was whether or not what the United States Government regarded as defensive action against German submarines in the Atlantic would be interpreted by Japan as constituting an attack upon Germany. No doubt Japanese authorities were themselves unable to answer the question if put in general terms, but obviously the President and his advisers had to reckon with the possibility that Japan might resort to war while Hitler continued to stand aloof. Since American military authorities had long since decided that Germany was the primary enemy and that American offensive action should be centered in the Atlantic while maintaining a strategic defensive in the Pacific, it was essential to avoid involvement with Japan and the commitment of America's main strength in the Far East.

[26]Sherwood: *Roosevelt and Hopkins,* 416.

Considering this problem, Admiral Stark's Plan Dog of November, 1940, had already developed the idea that if war eventuated from a Japanese attack, the United States should initiate steps to bring Germany also into the war. This concept had been reaffirmed by the Joint Board in December, 1940, and had been tacitly accepted by the President as well as by the Secretaries of War and the Navy. There is little if anything in the presently available records to show whether this aspect of the problem was considered in reaching the decision on American naval escort in September, 1941, but in view of the acuteness of the Far Eastern situation and particularly of the discussions at the Atlantic Conference, it seems improbable that it was far from the minds of the President and his military advisers. It may well be that the introduction of American naval escort was intended in part to keep relations with Germany at least one step ahead of relations with Japan. The President made his decision in his capacity as Commander in Chief and there can be little doubt that the crucial departure of September, 1941, was based primarily on strategic considerations.[27]

The revision of the Neutrality Act in November, 1941, came as a distinct anticlimax to the "shoot-on-sight" orders and the introduction of naval escort of convoys. Like the question of escort, the issue of revising the existing neutrality legislation had been under consideration for many months. President Roosevelt and Secretary Hull had long been convinced that those sections of the law which excluded American shipping from proclaimed combat areas and forbade the arming of American merchantmen were major and now altogether illogical obstacles to the implementation of the Lend-Lease program. But they could not bring themselves to submit the matter to Congress, lest it provide the isolationists a new springboard for attack.[28]

Within the general framework of American policy the neutrality legislation had certainly become anachronistic, for the country was no longer neutral except in the most rigorously legalistic sense. With the Lend-Lease Act the last tatters of neutrality had been discarded, as everyone recognized. On the very eve of the *Greer* incident *The New York Times* could write editorially (September 3): "The United States is no longer a neutral in this war. It is no longer on the

[27]On this aspect of the matter see the testimony of Admiral Richmond K. Turner, in *Pearl Harbor Attack*, VI, 2842. We have made use also of notes provided by Captain Tracy Kittredge, U.S.N.R.

[28]Hull: *Memoirs*, II, 943, 1046 ff.

sidelines. It has made its choice. It is a belligerent today, in the sense, and to the degree that it has become a part of the service of supply that leads from its own factories to the battlelines."

Yet the Neutrality Act of 1939 remained on the statute books and from the President's viewpoint its revision had become progressively more urgent. The *Greer* incident seemed to provide an ideal opportunity to dispose of this issue as well as to put over the decision on naval escort. On September 5 the press was already reporting that the President would soon request Congress to amend the existing law and after the noteworthy radio address of September 11 it soon became known that Mr. Roosevelt had already discussed the matter with Congressional leaders.[29] The news was received with jubilation by the interventionists. *The New York Times* hastened to point out once again the contradiction between the law and the Lend-Lease policy approved by Congress: "These self-denying ordinances," it concluded, "are worth as much as a thousand submarines to Hitler. From his point of view they accomplish the same purpose." The *New York Post* likewise demanded that "this hoary and decrepit antique" be scrapped, while the *New York Herald Tribune* insisted that "the Neutrality Act . . . has ended its usefulness; it has ended its reason for being, and has become a stench in the nostrils of anyone for whom two and two still add up to four. It should be repealed *in toto* and at once."[30]

By the last week in September the issue, so far as the President was concerned, was simply whether to ask for total repeal, for the repeal of Sections II, III and VI, or only for the abolition of Section VI. Total repeal was unnecessary and in some ways actually undesirable, for the Act contained several provisions (restrictions on the solicitation and collection of funds, control of munitions export, regulation of financial transactions, etc.) which the Administration itself desired to retain. Total repeal would, of course, make a deep impression, both at home and abroad, but it might also provoke unnecessary opposition. The essential thing was the elimination of Sections II, III and VI, among which the repeal of Section VI could be almost certainly counted on. This section prohibited the arming of American merchant ships. Now that naval escort had been introduced it was patently absurd not to arm for self-defense the very ships which the American Navy was assigned to protect.

[29] *The New York Times,* September 5 and 6, 1941.
[30] *The New York Times,* September 17; the *New York Post,* September 17; the *New York Herald Tribune,* September 24, 1941.

Mr. Roosevelt was for some time undecided as to how comprehensive to make his request. After numerous conferences with Secretary Hull and Congressional leaders he concluded that it would be best to take no chances, with the opposition in Congress, for which he continued to have profound respect. Senate leaders were optimistic about the chances for repeal of all three of the sections in question, but sentiment in the House appeared less favorable. Evidently the President and his Congressional advisers finally arranged that if the repeal of Section VI were carried in the House by a strong majority, a request for repeal of all three sections should be laid before the Senate, in the hope that after favorable action in that body the House too could be brought to accept it.[31]

Meanwhile the issue had become the subject of public debate. The American Legion Convention passed a resolution favoring total repeal and Secretary Knox, speaking at the launching of the battleship *Massachusetts* (September 23), pleaded for immediate action: "The time is now for all of us to face facts which no longer can be ignored. The time has come to do away with the Neutrality Law. We can waste no time in repealing that law. It must be repealed. We must remove the restrictions upon our Chief Executive. Our Army must be used wherever and whenever it is needful." Many leading newspapers chimed in, calling for total repeal and an end to "the whole outworn farce of American neutrality." In an editorial the influential *New York Times* argued (October 3):

> Our relationship with the European war has passed the stage when it can be affected by "incidents." We are not formally at war with Hitler. We may never be formally at war with him. But we are already at war with him in the sense that we are mobilizing our entire economy in order to beat him. The remnants of "neutrality" now on our statute books do not make us less his enemy by one period or comma. They merely hamper our defense and our lend-lease activities—which unavoidably has now become a single activity.

There was evidently considerable sentiment throughout the country for total repeal or at the very least for drastic amendment of a law which, for whatever reasons, had become completely incongruous. According to a Gallup poll of October 5 some 70 percent of those consulted thought it more important to defeat Hitler than to

---

[31]Hull: *Memoirs*, II, 1046 ff.; *Berle Diary* (*MS.*), September 23, 30 and October 2-6, 1941; *The New York Times*, October 1, 2, 3, 8, 9, 1941.

keep the country out of war. Though public opinion seems to have been more ready than the Congress to support the President's policy, it was thought by some that even on Capitol Hill there was a strong tendency to line up behind the President, the more so in view of the stand taken by the American Legion.[32] Democratic leaders were certainly optimistic.

Senator Connally came out publicly in favor of the abolition of combat zones and the arming of American merchant ships, while Senator McKellar introduced a resolution calling for complete repeal on the theory that the whole Neutrality Act had been a mistake and contravened the principle of freedom of the seas.[33]

But the isolationists were not to be silenced. Following a well-reasoned radio address by former President Hoover (September 16), the opposition in the Senate began to mobilize. Senator Robert A. Taft took the stand that repeal of the Neutrality Act would be tantamount to a declaration of war or would at least authorize the President to carry on an undeclared war. Senator Robert La Follette railed at the Administration for not knowing "whether to bury it completely or leave a skeleton hanging up." The veteran isolationist leader, Senator Hiram Johnson, supported his colleagues in his usual vehement fashion. Before long the whole anti-interventionist group was in full cry. As a result the outlook, even in the Senate, became less favorable. According to an informal poll of Senate opinion early in October only twenty-nine members were well disposed toward total repeal or the elimination of Sections II, III and VI, and only thirty-five were prepared to vote even for the arming of merchantmen. Twenty were opposed to any change and the remainder expressed themselves as undecided. When one remembers that relatively few Senators were needed to kill the bill by filibuster, one can hardly escape the conclusion that Mr. Roosevelt was well advised in trying to make progress slowly.[34]

On October 9 the President laid his proposals before the Congress. His message recalled the erroneous assumptions on which the Neutrality Act had been based and noted that once the war in Europe had broken out the American people had ceased being neutral in thought or indifferent to the fate of Hitler's victims. On the contrary, the country had become increasingly aware of the threat to its

---

[32]Arthur Krock in *The New York Times,* September 21, 1941.
[33]*The New York Times,* September 25 and 26, 1941.
[34]*The New York Times,* September 26 and 28, October 5, 1941.

traditions and institutions, to its territory and to the entire hemisphere. It had become the nation's policy to defend itself wherever defense appeared necessary:

> Therefore it has become necessary that this Government should not be handicapped in carrying out the clearly announced policy of the Congress and of the people. We must face the truth that the Neutrality Act requires a complete reconsideration in the light of the known facts.
>
> The revisions which I suggest do not call for a declaration of war any more than the Lend-Lease Act called for a declaration of war. This is a matter of essential defense of American rights.
>
> In the Neutrality Act are various crippling provisions. The repeal or modification of these provisions will not leave the United States any less neutral than we are today, but will make it possible for us to defend the Americas far more successfully, and to give aid far more effectively against tremendous forces now marching towards conquest of the world.

The message then remarked on the futility of combat zones but, without pursuing that issue, asked specifically only for repeal of Section VI so as to permit the arming of American merchant ships:

> The arming of our ships is a matter of immediate necessity and extreme urgency. It is not more important than some other crippling provisions in the present act, but anxiety for the safety of our crews and of the almost priceless goods that are within the holds of our ships leads me to recommend that you, with all speed, strike the prohibition against arming our ships from the statute books.
>
> There are other phases of the Neutrality Act to the correction of which I hope the Congress will give earnest and early attention. One of these provisions is of major importance. I believe it is essential to the proper defense of our country that we cease giving the definite assistance which we are now giving to the aggressors. For, in effect, we are inviting their control of the seas by keeping our ships out of the ports of our own friends.
>
> It is time for this country to stop playing into Hitler's hands and to unshackle our own.
>
> I earnestly trust that the Congress will carry out the true intent of the Lend-Lease Act by making possible for the United States to help deliver the articles to those who are in a position effectively to use

them. In other words, I ask for Congressional action to implement Congressional policy. Let us be consistent.

Hitler has offered a challenge which we as Americans cannot and will not tolerate. We will not let Hitler prescribe the waters of the world on which our ships may travel. The American flag is not going to be driven from the seas either by his submarines, his airplanes, or his threats.

We cannot permit the affirmative defense of our rights to be annulled and diluted by sections of the Neutrality Act which have no realism in the light of unscrupulous ambition of madmen. We Americans have determined our course. . . . [35]

The President's message left no doubt that the abolition of combat zones and the employment of American ships for the transport of supplies to friendly ports were just as much at issue as the arming of American merchantmen. As noted, the request for repeal only of Section VI was intended to spearhead the larger program, for even avowed opponents of the President's policies, like Senator Taft and Representative Fish, were ready to accept the arming of American ships as an obviously defensive measure.

The Administration proposals were given preferred and urgent treatment by Congress. The House Foreign Affairs Committee heard testimony from Secretary Hull on October 13 and thereafter from Secretaries Stimson and Knox. Before appearing on the Hill, Mr. Hull took the precaution of obtaining from Admiral Stark a memorandum analyzing the advantages and disadvantages of the combat zones, of naval escort all the way across the Atlantic, and of a declaration of war by the United States. This memorandum, dated October 8, is of some interest as reflecting current thinking in naval circles. The Chief of Naval Operations referred to the obvious advantages of being able to send American ships to Great Britain and noted the moral effect to be expected from the operation of American warships in British waters. On the other hand he pointed out that a declaration of war could not be followed immediately by major operations and that it might bring Japan into the conflict, which would be a highly undesirable development. Nonetheless, he reiterated his firm conviction that Hitler could not be defeated until the United States was "wholeheartedly in the war" and therefore favored intervention as soon as possible, even at the cost of

[35]*Documents on American Foreign Relations,* IV, 23 ff.

hostilities with Japan: "I might finally add that I have assumed for the past two years that our country would not let Britain fall; that ultimately in order to prevent this we would enter the war and as noted above I have long felt and have stated that the sooner we get in, the better." After all, he concluded, there was little chance that Hitler would attack until he had calculated coldly that it would be to his advantage to do so. He already had all the pretexts he needed.[36]

Little if any of this reasoning was reflected in Mr. Hull's testimony, which was a carefully worded statement of the weakness of the existing law and of the factors making its modification imperative. The Secretary emphasized that "the Neutrality Acts did not remotely contemplate limiting the steps to be taken by this country in self-defense, especially were there to develop situations of serious and immediate danger to the United States and to this hemisphere." His argument culminated in the assertion that "the theory of the neutrality legislation was that by acting within the limitations which it prescribed we could keep away from danger. But danger has come to us—has been thrust upon us—and our problem is not that of avoiding it, but of defending ourselves against a hostile movement seriously threatening us and the entire Western hemisphere."[37]

Though Secretaries Hull, Stimson and Knox all expressed themselves in favor of repeal of Section II as well as Section VI, the House was called upon to vote only on the latter. Just before the termination of the limited debate, on the night of October 16-17, the United States destroyer *Kearny* was struck by a German torpedo and suffered many casualties. The *Kearny,* together with other American destroyers and one British destroyer, had been despatched to the aid of a westbound convoy which was under heavy attack by a pack of German submarines about four hundred miles south of Iceland. The escorting warships were dropping depth bombs indiscriminately, while the submarines were taking an impressive toll of the merchant ships. A full-scale naval action was in progress and there was nothing surprising in the fact that the *Kearny* was struck. But this made little difference to the American public, for whom the important fact was that an American warship had been "attacked." Congress was clearly impressed. On October 17 the House voted repeal of Section VI of the Neutrality Act of 1939 by a

---

[36]Text in *Pearl Harbor Attack,* XVI, 2216 ff. See also Hull: *Memoirs,* II, 1049.
[37]*Documents on American Foreign Relations,* IV, 102 ff.

majority (259-138) larger than had been expected. Only 21 Democrats opposed the measure, while the Republicans voted 39 in favor and 113 in opposition.[38]

The stand of the Republicans in the House outraged Mr. Willkie and that wing of the party which supported the Administration in matters of foreign policy. Willkie promptly appealed for an end of "the shame and deception of the hypocritical Neutrality Laws" and on October 20 three Republican Senators (Bridges, Austin and Gurney) introduced an amendment calling for outright repeal of the Act. On the following day Mr. Willkie and a hundred leading Republicans from some forty states called on their colleagues in Congress to abolish the neutrality legislation as "hypocritical and degrading." Their message declared:

> The requirement of America today is for a forthright, direct, international policy, designed to encompass the destruction of totalitarianism by whatever means necessary. This policy should be presented to us by our elected leader frankly and not by doses as though we were children. . . . Millions upon millions of Republicans are resolved that the ugly smudge of obstructive isolationism shall be removed from the face of their party so that it may not be hampered in forwarding these high and important purposes.[39]

The relatively favorable outcome of the vote in the House on repeal of Section VI and the revolt of the nonisolationist wing of the Republican Party encouraged Senators Glass and Pepper to come out openly for total repeal of the Neutrality Law, described by Mr. Glass as "a craven piece of poltroonery." But the Democratic leaders of the Senate, no doubt following advice from the White House, contented themselves with a resolution to repeal only Sections II, III and VI, the only sections really objectionable from the Administration's standpoint. On October 25 the Senate Foreign Relations Committee voted thirteen to ten in favor of the resolution. Two days later, just as the resolution came to the floor, Mr. Roosevelt delivered a Navy Day address in which he made the most of the *Kearny* incident, as he had previously exploited the "attack" on the *Greer*.

---

[38] *The New York Times,* October 18, 1941. For the facts of the *Kearny* incident see Admiral Stark's letter to Admiral Kimmel in *Pearl Harbor Attack,* XVI, 2214 ff., and Morison: *The Battle of the Atlantic,* 92-93. We have used also a tel. from MacVeagh (Reykjavik), October 19, 1941, addressed to the President.

[39] *The New York Times,* October 19, 21, 22, 1941.

We have wished to avoid shooting. But the shooting has started. And history has recorded who fired the first shot. In the long run, however, all that will matter is who fired the last shot. America has been attacked. The *USS Kearny* is not just a Navy ship. She belongs to every man, woman and child in this nation. . . . The forward march of Hitler and Hitlerism can be stopped—and it will be stopped.

Very simply and very bluntly—we are pledged to pull our own oar in the destruction of Hitlerism. . . .

I say that we do not propose to take this lying down.

Our determination not to take it lying down has been expressed in the orders to the American Navy to shoot on sight. These orders stand.[40]

These fighting words no doubt helped further to arouse the country, but they made the isolationist elements all the more angry and irreconcilable. In the course of a ten days' debate in the Senate the opposition rang all possible variations on the basic theme that the decision of Congress would necessarily settle the question "whether America deliberately and consciously shall go all the way into a 'shooting war'—probably upon two oceans."[41] Much was made of the argument that American security would not be directly threatened even if Soviet Russia and Britain went under and that, even if the menace were real, it would be better to cut through all subterfuges and declare war at once. One member of the opposition after another charged the President with willful deceit and with making arrangements for an American Expeditionary Force because he knew that Hitler could not be defeated without the active military aid of the United States. Senator Wheeler embroidered this theme for almost nine hours and Senator Brooks, urging his colleagues not to overlook the implications of the resolution, declared: "You cannot shoot your way a little bit into war any more than you can go a little bit over Niagara Falls."[42]

It is unlikely that the pleas of the isolationists influenced the supporters of the Administration policy any more than the appeals

[40] *Documents on American Foreign Relations,* IV, 27 ff.

[41] *The New York Times,* October 28 and 29, 1941, reporting the remarks of Senators Vandenberg and Taft.

[42] *The New York Times,* October 30, November 6 and 7, 1941. The debates on the resolution are summarized in Charles A. Beard: *President Roosevelt and the Coming of the War* (New Haven, 1948), Chapter VI.

of Willkie and his followers impressed the old guard Republicans. When the tally was taken on November 7 it turned out that the resolution had passed the Senate by a vote of only fifty to thirty-seven. Six Republicans voted in its favor, while twenty-one registered opposition. The Senate majority was smaller than on any major foreign policy issue since the beginning of the war in Europe. What deductions to draw from this fact it is hard to say. Mr. Roosevelt, writing to King George on October 15, expressed the opinion that public sentiment was distinctly "better" than it had been six months before and that it was more strongly with the Administration than was the Congress.[43] A Gallup poll published early in November pointed in the same direction, for it showed that 81 percent favored the arming of American merchant ships and 61 percent the use of American ships in transporting supplies to Britain. In the opinion of many newspaper editors Congress was lagging behind the public, which was thought to be more determined than ever to see the crisis through. The inescapable fact, however, was that in both houses of Congress there was still formidable opposition to the Administration's policy. An out-and-out proposal to declare war would certainly have been defeated even on the very threshold of the Pearl Harbor attack.

A lurid light was thrown on the situation when the House reopened debate on the Senate resolution, which was much more comprehensive than the measure originally passed by the House. Irritated no doubt by the previous efforts of the White House to put over the larger program and evidently incensed by the President's lenient attitude toward labor disputes in key war industries, many members of the House let themselves go in bitter criticism. While isolationists argued that the resolution meant war at a time when the country was still woefully unprepared, others accused the British of wanting to push the United States into action while they themselves were unwilling to risk opening a second front to relieve the Soviet forces. To quote Representative Charles L. South of Texas: "Let's tell England: 'We know you're in distress and we're sorry for you. But get in there and fight like hell for yourself for a while and then we'll see if anything else should be done.'"

Representative Eaton (Republican) did his utmost to combat this simple-minded view, but the House became more and more intractable. Even Democrats showed an inclination to defect until their

[43] *F.D.R.: His Personal Letters,* II, 1223 ff.

leaders induced the President to send Congress a message reminding it that "the world is obviously watching the course of this legislation," and to follow this up with another message promising early action to quell labor troubles. When the issue was finally brought to vote (November 13), the majority again proved alarmingly small. The vote was 212 in favor and 194 opposed. Of the Republican members only 22 approved the bill, as against 137 who opposed it. Even more noteworthy was the fact that more Democrats voted in opposition than at the time of the Lend-Lease bill. An analysis of the vote revealed that while the southern states were strong in support of the resolution, the Midwest was generally hostile and the Far West rather evenly divided. Even the large industrial states of the East split their votes in a most unusual fashion: Massachusetts, 7-6; New York, 25-20; New Jersey, 5-9; Pennsylvania, 10-20. Clearly the President was justified in refusing to share the easy optimism of many of his advisers, both inside and outside Congress. Nevertheless, it would probably be a mistake to ascribe the strength of the opposition solely to the realization that retreat from the neutrality legislation might lead to war, or to strong sentiment against involvement on any terms. If there is reason to suppose that the vote in the House did not accurately reflect the sentiment of the country, there are also grounds for thinking that many members opposed the resolution because of their disgust with the Administration's labor policy and their fear that the country might be dragged into war long before it was economically or militarily prepared.

Despite the closeness of the vote, the essential features of the ill-starred Neutrality Law had now gone into the discard. "No decision of greater importance has been made in this country since the beginning of the war," declared *The New York Times* (November 14), while its London counterpart pronounced revision of the Neutrality Act "the greatest contribution to the defeat of Hitlerism since the passing of the Lend-Lease Act." Surely no one could look back with real satisfaction on the effort to legislate neutrality. According to one eminent student of international law:

It can fairly be said that there was no instance of the application of this theory of neutrality in which it contributed to maintaining the peace of the United States, the peace of the world, respect for international law, or the interests of a free and stable world order. Its effect, as anticipated by most informed observers, was to give

American opinion a sense of frustration inducing belligerency, to encourage aggression by the despots in Europe and Asia, and to thwart the democracies from achieving a unity of purpose in the defense of their interests and principles.[44]

In terms of international law the repeal of the key sections of the Neutrality Law meant return to the principle of freedom of the seas. The United States now resumed its traditional right to send its ships wherever it pleased and to arm and protect them in every way possible. There was nothing novel or revolutionary about the revision and it would therefore be misleading to attach too much importance to it. The really significant decision was the one to employ American naval forces in the escort not only of American but of belligerent shipping. The revision of earlier legislation merely indicated a turn in the road already chosen. Such significance as it had derived chiefly from the fact that, unlike the introduction of naval escort, it required Congressional approval. Though the vote was extremely close, the fact remains that that approval was given. To that extent one can say that the country, through its elected representatives, accepted the President's policy, despite the general realization that the arming of merchantmen, the escort of convoys, and the despatch of American ships to the ports of belligerent powers would inevitably result in armed clashes with German submarines.

It may well be argued, then, that by November 13, 1941, the President, the Congress and the country had made the decision to accept war. No doubt, if Mr. Roosevelt had taken up the challenge thrown down by his opponents and had asked Congress for a formal declaration of war, he would have been voted down. As it was, the revision of the Neutrality Act gave him substantially what he and his advisers had come to regard as essential in view of the world situation, namely, acceptance by the nation of genuine involvement in the world conflict. Although one can rarely be apodictic about such matters, the evidence suggests that the American people, perhaps more surely than their representatives, "knew the score." Generally speaking they had come to realize that they could not permit a Nazi victory and must therefore sustain Britain at all costs. They did not want war and shunned that ugly word as much as ever.

[44]Quincy Wright: "Repeal of the Neutrality Act" (*American Journal of International Law*, XXXVI, 1942, 8-23).

But they were willing to accept the reality in thin disguise and probably found the President's gradualism and artifice more palatable than the frank and forthright leadership for which Mr. Roosevelt's friends so often clamored.

By way of epilogue it may be well to repeat that in shaping the national policy the President, like many leaders of American opinion, probably calculated that Hitler would not react with a declaration of war or the initiation of hostilities against the United States. By this time it had become sufficiently clear that he would move against the United States whenever it suited his purposes, but not before. In the autumn of 1941 the evidence indicated that the Fuehrer would stay his hand until he had finally subjugated Soviet Russia. The Nazi press denounced the *Kearny* affair as "a clumsy swindle on the part of Mr. Roosevelt" and accused the President of rigging incidents in order to put through the revision of the Neutrality Law. But there was no suggestion that Hitler intended, for the moment, to take reprisals. In his long address of October 3, 1941, the Fuehrer spoke at length about the campaign in the east but made only a few oblique references to the United States. On October 18, the day after the Senate vote on revision, he delivered a great annual address at Munich but again confined himself to defensive and on the whole noncommittal remarks: "President Roosevelt has ordered his ships to shoot as soon as they sight German ships. And I have ordered German ships, upon sighting American vessels, not to shoot but to defend themselves as soon as attacked. . . . If, therefore, an American ship shoots . . . it will do so at its own peril. The German ship will defend itself, and our torpedoes will find their mark."

It may be taken as certain that the President and for that matter most Americans were not deceived by Hitler's proclamation of virtuous self-restraint. It is more likely that they pondered another passage in Hitler's October 3 address, a remark made not with reference to the United States but easily applicable to the relationship between the two countries: "When I see the enemy levelling his rifle at me, I am not going to wait till he presses the trigger. I would rather be the first to press the trigger."

IV The Nuances of Negotiations, 1941

In the spring of 1941 the United States and Japan made a major effort to resolve their differences, and avoid a military confrontation, over the issues which long antedated and were now exacerbated by the Sino-Japanese war. The Americans and the Japanese entered into bilateral negotiations, which were held in the informal atmosphere of Secretary of State Cordell Hull's Washington hotel apartment and stretched out over nine months. The problems that plagued the negotiators were more than just substantive issues; there were also dimly perceived but no less critical problems of language, communication, and understanding, as is made clear in Part IV in Robert J. C. Butow's article, "The Hull-Nomura Conversations: A Fundamental Misconception" (1960) and in an excerpt from Paul W. Schroeder's *The Axis Alliance and Japanese-American Relations, 1941* (1958). Butow, who has thoroughly explored Japanese sources, explains the internal problems of language and communication that the Japanese suffered, and how the failure of Japan's negotiator in Washington, Ambassador Kichisaburo Nomura, to report adequately to his government the famous "four principles" that Hull marked out in April 1941 led the Japanese in the fall of 1941 to think that the United States was escalating its demands for a proposed settlement of the Sino-Japanese war when in fact the Americans were reiterating the position that they had taken at the outset of the talks. Schroeder, in the first half of his chapter on "The American Policy and Public Opinion," counterbalances Butow's revelation by showing that the American negotiating position over the Sino-Japanese conflict gradually evolved from a "defensive" one, i.e., seeking to halt hostilities and the further southward movement of the Japanese, to an "offensive" one, i.e., seeking by principle to force Japan to withdraw its troops from China as a basis for negotiations. This change, neither underhanded nor even carefully planned, Schroeder explains, ultimately "made the crucial difference between peace and war." The juxtaposition of Butow's and Schroeder's analyses provides an interesting example of how both sides, convinced that they were negotiating over the same principles and issues, were frequently talking past one another on separate planes, with tragic consequences for all.

ROBERT J. C. BUTOW

The Hull-Nomura Conversations
A Fundamental Misconception

Robert J. C. Butow (born 1924) is Professor of History in the Far Eastern and Russian Institute at the University of Washington. He has written *Japan's Decision to Surrender* (1954), *Tojo and the Coming of the War* (1961), and various articles.

IN THE DIPLOMATIC TALKS between Japan and the United States which were begun in the spring of 1941, the government of Prince Fumimaro Konoye chose to be represented by a retired admiral rather than by a career diplomat. Ambassador Kichisaburō Nomura had met Franklin D. Roosevelt years before, when the former had seen service in Washington and the latter had been Assistant Secretary of the Navy. The admiral, who had other prominent American friends, had also held the foreign portfolio in the short-lived cabinet of General Nobuyuki Abe (August 30, 1939-January 15, 1940), which had been entrusted with the task of trying to improve relations with the United States. Because of these connections, it was thought that Nomura might be able to win understanding for Japan's case. Such experience as he had acquired during his brief tenure at the Foreign Office would stand him in good stead.

Knowing that the navy did not want to risk its fleet unnecessarily, some Japanese leaders seem also to have believed that having an admiral in Washington might prevent matters from getting out of hand. Nomura's personal reluctance to accept the proffered ambassadorial post was largely overcome by the persuasive efforts of naval colleagues, who encouraged him with assurances that the imperial navy did not intend to fight the United States.[1]

---

[1]Background material on Admiral Kichisaburō Nomura and his appointment as ambassador is contained in Takushirō Hattori, *Dai-Tōa Sensō Zenshi* [A Complete History of the Greater East Asia War] (4 vols., Tokyo, 1953), I, 109; Kenryō Satō, "Dai-Tōa Sensō wo Maneita Shōwa no Dōran" [The Shōwa Upheavals Which Brought on the Greater East Asia War] in *Kingu*, XXXII (Oct. 1956), 114; Cordell Hull, *The Memoirs of Cordell Hull* (2 vols., New York, 1948), I, 723, II, 987-88, 996;

From *The American Historical Review*, LXV (July 1960). Reprinted by permission of Robert J. C. Butow.

Although these various reasons may have appeared sound at the time, the posting to Washington of an ambassador who was far more at home in dealing with naval matters than in handling problems of foreign relations simply added one more complication to an already tangled situation. Nomura's sincerity of purpose and good intentions proved incapable of coping successfully with the many intricate aspects of a diplomatic mission that would have tried the powers of an accomplished senior member of Japan's foreign service. This point is perhaps best illustrated by an extraordinary development that occurred at the very outset of his undertaking.

The Hull-Nomura conversations, which began on a fairly regular basis in March 1941, were an outgrowth of the private endeavors of two Maryknoll missionaries, Bishop James E. Walsh and Father James M. Drought, who had been in touch with Foreign Minister Yōsuke Matsuoka, Major General Akira Muto of the War Ministry, and a number of other influential Japanese. The last-named, generally unidentified individually, had emphasized their interest in seeing a peace agreement reached with the United States. Although Matsuoka personally had not been very definite about the terms of such an agreement, "other officials and spokesmen" had suggested an effective Japanese withdrawal from the Tripartite Pact—in fact, if not in name—and a restoration of Chinese territorial and political integrity through the removal of all Japanese military forces from China.[2]

Papers Relating to the Foreign Relations of the United States: Japan, 1931-1941 [hereafter cited as FR: Japan 1931-1941] (2 vols., Washington, D. C., 1943), II, 128-29, 387-89; Joseph C. Grew, Ten Years in Japan (New York, 1944), 350-51, 367; Frederick Moore, With Japan's Leaders, an Intimate Record of Fourteen Years as Counsellor to the Japanese Government, Ending December 7, 1941 (New York, 1942), 157-61, 185, 210-14; Herbert Feis, The Road to Pearl Harbor (Princeton, N.J., 1950), 172.

[2]See International Military Tribunal for the Far East, "Transcript of Proceedings" [hereafter cited as IMTFE, "Transcript"] (48,412 pages, Tokyo, 1946-48), 32978-85 (Walsh affidavit), 10747-48, 10854-57 (Joseph W. Ballantine affidavit and cross-examination); Hull, Memoirs, II, 984; FR: Japan, 1931-1941, II, 328-31; Foreign Relations of the United States: Diplomatic Papers, 1941, IV, The Far East [hereafter cited as FR: Diplomatic Papers, 1941] (7 vols., Washington, D. C., 1956-), IV, 113-14; Teiji Yabe, Konoye Fumimaro (2 vols., Tokyo, 1952), II, 237-47; Reijirō Wakatsuki, Kofūan Kaiko-roku [Memoirs] Tokyo, 1950), 406-11; Tokuzō Aoki, Taiheiyō Sensō Zenshi [A Complete History of the Pacific War] (3 vols., Tokyo, 1953), III, 101-102. Bishop Walsh (at present, incommunicado in Shanghai) and Father Drought (since deceased) also met, among others, former Premier Baron Reijirō Wakatsuki, the financier Seihin Ikeda, and Taro Terasaki, the chief of the American bureau of the Foreign Office.

Following their return to the United States from Japan early in 1941, Bishop Walsh and Father Drought had conferred with Postmaster General Frank C. Walker, who was "one of the most prominent Catholics in the Administration," and with several members of the Japanese embassy. The two priests had subsequently placed the matter before the President during an interview at the White House which had been arranged by Walker and at which he and the Secretary of State were present.

Despite the fact that optimistic reports had been received before without result, Roosevelt and Hull had decided that Walsh and Drought, together with Walker, "should continue their contacts with the Japanese Embassy on a purely private basis and [should] seek to reduce to writing *what the Japanese had in mind.*" More than two months later, on April 9, a so-called "Draft Understanding" was delivered to Secretary Hull through the Postmaster General, who had been acting as go-between.[3] Although this document was regarded by the State Department as a product of informal and unofficial discussions between the Maryknoll fathers and Japanese representatives in Washington, it was basically the work of an imperial army colonel, on temporary duty at the Japanese embassy.[4]

The presence of this officer on the scene stemmed from Admiral Nomura's belief that the China problem was the main issue between Japan and the United States. Before departing for the American capital, Nomura had traveled on the Asian continent, visiting key Japanese generals and their staffs in Korea, Manchuria, and China in order to discuss his new assignment with them, to pick up ideas, and to obtain the "understanding" of the armies in the field (a revealing indication of the role of field commanders in the formulation of Japan's foreign policy in the period in question.)[5]

[3]Hull, *Memoirs,* II, 984-86, 991 (the source of the quotation; italics mine); *FR: Japan, 1931-1941,* II, 328-31, 387-98; *FR: Diplomatic Papers, 1941,* IV, 14-18, 21-27, 51-55, 57-58, 61-81, 95-107, 111-17, 119-28, 130-39; IMTFE, "Transcript," 32978-85 (Walsh affidavit), 10747-48, 10854-57 (Ballantine affidavit and cross-examination).

[4]This point will be developed in the text that follows, but the basic references are *Kyokutō Kokusai Gunji Saiban Sokki-roku* [The Stenographic Record of the International Military Tribunal for the Far East] (416 *gō,* Tokyo, 1946-48), Section 312, p. 14 (Iwakuro affidavit and cross-examination) [hereafter cited as *Sokki-roku,* 312: 14]; Iwakuro's responses to questions from the author; IMTFE, "Transcript," 32984-85 (Walsh affidavit); *FR: Diplomatic Papers, 1941,* IV, 17-18, 52, 70, 114-15, 119-22, 127, 174.

[5]Nomura visited Generals Jirō Minami, Yoshijirō Umezu, and Toshizō Nishio (governor-general of Korea, commander of the Kwantung army, and commander in

Upon his return to Tokyo Nomura had also spoken with Chief of the Army General Staff Gen Sugiyama and Vice-Minister of War Korechika Anami. He had expressed the hope that he would receive the cooperation of the authorities at the "center" (the army's top leadership). He had also specifically requested that an officer with a thorough knowledge of the China Incident, and of problems pertaining thereto, be sent to Washington to assist him.[6] Since the army at that time had reason to share Nomura's desire for success, the admiral's request had received prompt and favorable consideration. On the recommendation of Major General Mutō (the chief of the military affairs bureau), War Minister Hideki Tōjō had ordered Colonel Hideo Iwakuro (the then chief of the army affairs section of that bureau) to proceed to the American capital to help the ambassador in his difficult mission.[7]

Iwakuro was well qualified for the assignment by virtue of having kept abreast of the activities and views of Walsh and Drought while they were still in Tokyo. His informant had been Mr. Tadao Ikawa, described by an American Foreign Service officer as "apparently a sincere and ardent Christian . . . believed to be married to an American woman." Ikawa had acted as interpreter for the Maryknoll fathers and was known to them as "a friend and unofficial representative" of Konoye. As the event turned out, Ikawa also traveled to the United States to render his assistance in bringing the two countries to an understanding.[8]

---

chief of the Japanese forces in China, respectively). See Kichisaburō Nomura, "Kafu Kaisō [Reminiscences of Washington] in *Dai Nippon Teikoku Shimatsu-ki* (Saron rinji zōkangō, Tsūkan 38, Tokyo, Dec. 15, 1949), I, 21.

[6]*Ibid.; Sokki-roku,* 312: 14 (Iwakuro affidavit); Hattori, *Dai-Tōa Sensō Zenshi,* I, 109-10; Aoki, *Taiheiyō Sensō Zenshi,* III, 100.

[7]On the attitude of the services (especially the role of Major General Akira Muto and his naval counterpart Rear Admiral Takasumi Oka), see *Sokki-roku,* 315: 10 (Kenji Tomita affidavit), 312: 14-15 (Iwakuro affidavit), 312: 16 (Iwakuro re-direct), and IMTFE, "Transcript," 3278-91 (Walsh affidavit).

According to Hull, "Iwakuro had all the virtues and shortcomings of a Japanese Army officer. He was a very fine type, honest, calmly poised, very sure of himself without being annoyingly self-confident. He could, of course, see only his Army's viewpoint, not ours or the real interest of Japan." *Memoirs,* II, 1003.

[8]Iwakuro's responses to questions from the author; *FR: Diplomatic Papers, 1941,* IV, 51-53 (a letter-report to the Secretary of State by the assistant commercial attaché in Japan), 113-17 (Ballantine memorandum); IMTFE, "Transcript," 32980 (Walsh affidavit). The name of Tadao Ikawa (since deceased) occasionally appears as "Tadao (Paul) Wikawa" in English-language sources.

In Toshikazu Kase, *Mizuri-Gō e no Dōtei* [Journey to the *Missouri*] (Tokyo, 1951),

Although the record is not explicit, the evidence suggests that there had been a considerable amount of loose talking in Tokyo on the part of all concerned. The desire to create an atmosphere favorable to negotiations had existed on both sides. Since the discussions had been informal and unofficial, the participants (mostly amateurs with respect to diplomatic affairs) had tended to go quite far at times in speaking of the concessions that might be made in certain eventualities. There is no doubt that Walsh and Drought had come away with a rather misleading view of the extent to which the Japanese government was prepared to compromise. They steadfastly remained hopeful despite the skepticism later expressed in Washington. At times their enthusiasm betrayed them into reporting, at third hand, trivial items which would have been of no significance even if they could have been verified. On one such occasion, the Secretary of State was told in all seriousness, "Prince Konoye has hung on the wall of his private bedroom a photograph of President Roosevelt."[9]

The evidence also suggests that statements made by Walsh and Drought while still in Tokyo had encouraged some members of the Japanese group to form more optimistic conclusions about the attitude of the United States than were justified by the facts. Drought appears to have mentioned more than once that he was acting with the approval of "top personnel" in the American government. As a consequence, Ikawa imprudently treated statements made by Drought as representing President Roosevelt's personal views. Iwakuro seems not to have gone quite that far, but he believed that the President was at least aware of what was taking place. At any rate, Iwakuro followed Ikawa's reports with interest. Various suggestions made by Walsh and Drought in conversations with others proved helpful to the colonel in formulating his own ideas for a "draft understanding." By the time he left Tokyo to assume his new duties in Washington, the framework of a proposal had already taken shape in his mind.

After his arrival in the United States Iwakuro learned from Ikawa

---

79, Ikawa is described, without being identified by name, as a man "of rather unsavory reputation." Hull's impression was that Ikawa "was of the 'slick politician' type whom the Japanese themselves did not seem to respect for integrity." *Memoirs,* II, 1003.

[9]*Ibid.,* 984-85, 991; *FR: Japan, 1931-1941,* II, 330-31; *FR: Diplomatic Papers, 1941,* IV, 17-18, 71-74 (the source of the quotation), 117; William L. Langer and S. Everett Gleason, *The Undeclared War, 1940-1941* (New York, 1953), 468.

that Walsh and Drought were in close touch with Postmaster General Walker and that Walker, in turn, was on "intimate terms" with the President (for instance, Walker could see Roosevelt at any time and the Postmaster General was always talking about his "boss"). Both Iwakuro and Ikawa thus concluded that they could interpret remarks made by Walker as reflecting the President's opinions.[10] The danger of so doing apparently did not cross their minds.

The first draft of the document conveyed to Hull on April 9 was prepared in Washington between April 2 and April 5. Iwakuro's Japanese text was translated orally by Ikawa for the benefit of Drought, who then wrote down an English equivalent. Discussions with regard to content took place primarily between Iwakuro and Drought (with Ikawa acting as interpreter), but according to the colonel's own postwar estimate the document that finally resulted was "90%-95% identical" with the outline he had had in mind when he left Japan.[11]

As Hull and his Far Eastern experts studied the "Draft Understanding" their "disappointment was keen." It was "much less accommodating" than they "had been led to believe it would be, and most of its provisions were all that the ardent Japanese imperialists could want."[12] The Secretary nevertheless decided to pursue the matter. He "concluded that, however objectionable some of the points might be, there were others that could be accepted as they stood and still others that could be agreed to if modified."[13]

Feeling that "no opportunity should be overlooked that might lead to broad-scale conversations with Japan," Hull invited Nomura to

[10]Iwakuro's responses to questions from the author; Shigenori Tōgō, *Jidai no Ichimen* [An Aspect of the Times] (Tokyo, 1952), 160; Mamoru Shigemitsu, *Shōwa no Dōran* [The Upheavals of the Shōwa Period] (2 vols., Tokyo, 1952), II, 58-59.

[11]See the references cited in n. 4. Fumimaro Konoye, *Ushinawareshi Seiji* [Lost Politics] (Tokyo, 1946), 53, is incorrect in stating that the proposal of April 9 was a "second tentative draft" prepared by the Japanese side in answer to a "first tentative draft" presented by the American side on April 8.

[12]Hull, *Memoirs*, II, 991. The text of the proposal of April 9, which became known in Japan as the "Draft Understanding" of April 18 (the date of its arrival in Tokyo), is printed in *FR: Japan, 1931-1941*, II, 398-402. For the Japanese version ("Nichi-Bei Ryokai-an"), see Gaimusho (Hensan), *Nihon Gaiko Nenpyo narabi ni Shuyo Bunsho* [Chronological Tables and Major Documents Pertaining to Japan's Foreign Relations] (2 vols., Tokyo, 1955), II, 492-95. A detailed comparison of the English and Japanese texts is beyond the scope of this paper, but there are several omissions in the Japanese version that might bear further investigation.

[13]Hull, *Memoirs*, II, 993-94.

call on him, on April 14, at his apartment in the Wardman Park Hotel. At this meeting Hull emphasized a very important fact: the entirely informal and noncommittal nature of the proceedings. He told Nomura that he had received "unofficial proposals" and that he had been informed "that the Ambassador himself had participated in and associated himself with" that effort. He wanted to be clear in his own mind, Hull said, as to the extent of Nomura's "knowledge of the document containing the proposals and whether it was his [Nomura's] desire to present it officially as a first step in negotiations."

The admiral "promptly replied he knew all about the document, he had collaborated to some degree with the various Japanese and American individuals who drew it up, and he would be disposed to present it as a basis for negotiations." The proposal had not yet been sent to Tokyo, Nomura said, "but he thought his Government would be favorably disposed toward it." Hull then remarked that there were "certain points" the United States would wish to raise "prior to negotiations, such as the integrity and sovereignty of China and the principle of equality of opportunity in China," and that Nomura "could then communicate these to his Government and ascertain whether it agreed that there was a basis for negotiations."[14]

Two days later, at another meeting at the Secretary's apartment, Hull handed Nomura the now-famous four principles on which the United States insisted any agreement with Japan must be based: "(1) respect for the territorial integrity and the sovereignty of each and all nations; (2) support of the principle of non-interference in the internal affairs of other countries; (3) support of the principle of equality, including equality of commercial opportunity; (4) non-disturbance of the *status quo* in the Pacific except as the *status quo* may be altered by peaceful means."[15]

Hull emphasized that the United States wanted "a definite assurance in advance" that the Japanese government had "the willingness and ability to go forward with a plan for settlement" along the lines being proposed. The United States also wanted a positive indication from Japan that it was prepared "to abandon its

[14]The quoted remarks are all from *ibid.*, 994. See also Hull's memorandum of his conversation with Nomura on Apr. 14 in *FR: Japan, 1931-1941,* II, 331-32, 402-406; *FR: Diplomatic Papers, 1941,* IV, 135-39, 146-47; IMTFE, "Transcript," 10857, 10859-60 (Ballantine affidavit).

[15]For these and other details relating to the Hull-Nomura conversation of Apr. 16, 1941, see Hull, *Memoirs,* II, 994-96; *FR: Japan, 1931-1941,* II, 406-10; *FR: Diplomatic Papers, 1941,* IV, 152-54.

present doctrine of military conquest," forsake the use of force as an instrument of policy, and adopt the principles that the American government had been proclaiming "as the foundation on which all relations between nations should properly rest."[16] Once Japan had adopted those principles, Hull said, if the ambassador "submitted to his Government the informal document prepared by the individual Americans and Japanese, and if his Government approved it and instructed him to propose it to us, it would afford a basis for starting conversations. We would thereupon offer counter proposals and independent proposals. We would then discuss these with Nomura, along with the Japanese proposals, and talk them out to a conclusion one way or the other in the friendly spirit that unquestionably should and would characterize the conversations."[17]

A rather extended exchange ensued on various issues raised by the four principles. Nomura suggested that the question of equality might be discussed in connection with the negotiations, but Hull immediately replied that this "would be impossible." The United States "could not think of entering into negotiations" if the Japanese government "should even hesitate in agreeing" to the principle of equality. Nomura referred to the "special relations" enjoyed by the United States with South America—relations of a type that Japan, he said, would not be allowed to maintain in the Far East. Hull endeavored, at some length, to convince the ambassador that there was "a great misapprehension and misunderstanding" in that regard.

Nomura then turned to the principle of nondisturbance of the *status quo* except by peaceful means. He stated that acceptance would interfere with the situation in Manchuria. The Secretary "replied that the question of non-recognition of Manchuria would be discussed in connection with the negotiations and dealt with at that stage, and that this *status quo* point would not, therefore, affect 'Manchukuo,' but was intended to apply to the future from the time of the adoption of a general settlement."[18]

Despite Nomura's remarks, Hull "was not sure" whether his statements regarding the four principles were fully understood by the ambassador. The Secretary had earlier found that Nomura "spoke a certain—sometimes an uncertain—amount of English." On

[16]Hull, *Memoirs*, II, 994.

[17]*Ibid.*, 995.

[18]The quotations are from Hull's memorandum of the conversation in *FR: Japan, 1931-1941*, II, 408-409. See also Hull, *Memoirs*, II, 995-96.

the day in question (April 16) Nomura's command of the language struck Hull as being "so marginal" that he "took care to speak slowly and often to repeat and reemphasize some of [his] sentences."[19]

Nomura wanted the Secretary to indicate whether he would approve, for the most part, the specific proposals contained in the document of April 9. Hull answered that the United States could approve several; others would have to be changed or dropped. The United States would also want to offer some proposals of its own. "But if your Government is in real earnest about changing its course," Hull declared, "I can see no good reason why ways could not be found to reach a fairly satisfactory settlement of all the essential questions presented."[20]

In this conversation with Nomura on April 16 Hull again went out of his way to stress that the United States and Japan had "in no sense reached the stage of negotiations" and that he and the ambassador were, at the moment, "only exploring in a purely preliminary and unofficial way what action might pave the way for negotiations later." "You tell me," Hull said, "that you have not submitted the document in question to your Government, but that you desire to do so. Naturally, you are at the fullest liberty to do this, but, of course, this does not imply any commitment whatever on the part of this Government with respect to the provisions of the document in case it should be approved by your Government."[21]

For all the good this did, Hull might have saved himself the time and the effort. Not one matter of substance out of all that he had said, with care and purpose, was transmitted to the Japanese government. In fact, hardly even a single word uttered by the Secretary trickled through to Tokyo. Nomura simply took the draft proposal, of which he was already fully cognizant, and cabled it to Japan's Foreign Ministry with a request for instructions and with a

[19]*Ibid.,* 987, 996; *FR: Japan, 1931-1941,* II, 409; Ballantine correspondence. Joseph W. Ballantine, a State Department expert on Japan, entered the conversations in May, on the occasion of the presentation of Japan's first formal proposals. From that point on, all vital matters, including those previously discussed, were repeated to the ambassador in Japanese. Ballantine had earlier met and talked with Iwakuro, who did not speak or understand English. Ballantine therefore believes that Nomura "clearly understood" the American position.

[20]Hull, *Memoirs,* II, 996.

[21]See Hull's memorandum of his conversation with Nomura on Apr. 16 in *FR: Japan, 1931-1941,* II, 406-10, esp. 407, from which the above statements are quoted.

strong recommendation in behalf of a favorable response. In a single, longish, and rather ambiguous sentence of a type not infrequently encountered in the Japanese language, Nomura explained that "behind-the-scenes maneuvers" with respect to the proposal he was forwarding had been in progress for some time; the "approval" of the American government had been "sounded" out; he personally had "privately participated" after he had been able to affirm that Hull had "on the whole no objections" to the draft; as a result of "various negotiations" undertaken at his direction, this proposal had been "agreed upon."[22]

The ambassador also informed Tokyo that Hull had said the United States was willing to go ahead with the negotiations on the basis of the draft and had asked him to request instructions from his government. Here, too, Nomura's brief account gave not the slightest hint of the innumerable statements with which Hull had patiently built up his position like a mason carefully laying one stone upon another. The ambassador's few clipped words did not even report the sense of what he had been told by the American Secretary of State.

Hull had merely suggested to Nomura that he ask his home government to look at the "Draft Understanding" of April 9 so that Tokyo could decide whether it wished to instruct Nomura *to present that document to the United States* as a basis for starting conversations, in the course of which many specific items would be subject to revision or elimination. But in the Nomura cable this salient point is nowhere to be found.[23] The entire dispatch contains only one short sentence that even approaches anything that was

---

[22]"Hon-Rōkai-an ni tsuite wa kanete yori naimen kōsaku wo okonai Beikoku seifu-gawa no san-i wo 'saundo' shi oritaru tokoro 'Haru' chōkan ni oite mo daitai kore ni igi naki mune tashikame etaru ni yori honshi ni oite mo naimitsu ni kan'yo shi shuju sesshō seshimetaru kekka hon-an wo yakushitaru mono nari" (Nomura Cable No. 233, Apr. 17, 1941, as copied from the original in the Foreign Office archives). In Tōgō, *Jidai no Ichimen,* 159, the concluding phrase, "hon-an wo yakushitaru mono nari," appears as "hon-an wo etaru mono nari." The text of the "Draft Understanding" was transmitted separately, in Japanese, as Cable No. 234. Since Matsuoka was then in Europe, Konoye was acting concurrently as Foreign Minister.

[23]Nomura's cable answers a question in this regard raised by Feis, *Road to Pearl Harbor,* 192. A statement in Langer and Gleason, *Undeclared War,* 470, to the effect that Hull "made a rather serious mistake in requesting Nomura to send the informal program to Tokyo with the inquiry whether the Imperial Government would accept it as a basis for negotiation . . . " requires revision.

said, and then only in far less specific terms than Hull had used. The reference is to a remark made during the meeting at the Wardman Park on April 16. According to Hull's memorandum of the conversation, "The Ambassador seemed not to understand why I could not now agree to some of these proposals· in his document [the "Draft Understanding"]. I sought repeatedly to make clear to him, in the first place, that we have not reached the stage of negotiations, he himself agreeing that he thus far has no authority from his Government to negotiate; and in the second place, that if I should thus out of turn agree to a number of important proposals in the document and these proposals should be sent to Japan and the military or extremist groups should ignore them, I and my Government would be very much embarrassed."[24]

In Nomura's report this latter thought was restated in a way that contextually implied a certain American eagerness to push ahead on the basis of the proposal he was forwarding. The Secretary of State had advised him, Nomura cabled, that the United States government would be placed in a difficult position if Tokyo should convey its disavowal *after* the conversations had been in progress in Washington. The phrasing employed by Nomura throughout his cable tended to suggest that the "Draft Understanding" was essentially an American product prepared as a response to the various inside moves initiated by Nomura and his staff, that Hull himself had had a hand in the matter, or, at the very least, that the United States was taking the initiative in making a proposal to Japan.[25]

Ambassador Nomura also refrained from giving his government any indication of the basic American position emphatically defined by Hull in the form of the four principles and discussed at length by the two men on April 16. Despite Hull's concern as to whether the ambassador had "fully understood each statement . . . in regard to the four points laid before him," Nomura had informed the Secretary at the end of the conversation that he did comprehend the situation.

[24]*FR: Japan, 1931-1941*, II, 410.

[25]Nomura Cable No. 233, Apr. 17, 1941 (Foreign Office archives). Nomura's comments and recommendations in the latter half of the cable confirm the implication to the effect that the ambassador was forwarding a proposal suggested by the Americans. Upon reading the original dispatch after becoming Foreign Minister in October 1941, Tōgō interpreted Nomura's April report as indicating that Hull had personally participated in the preparation of the "Draft Understanding." *Jidai no Ichimen*, 160.

He had also made it clear, or so Hull thought, "that he would [now] proceed in his own way to consult his Government regarding the four points. . . . "[26]

As a matter of fact, however, it was not until May 8, three weeks later, that Nomura quoted the four principles in a cable to the Foreign Office. He then advised Tokyo that the United States had stubbornly advocated those points during discussions relating to the "Draft Understanding." But he also added a disarming remark implying that he had been able to curb the American effort in that regard by proposing that the two sides avoid becoming deeply involved in arguments over principles so that they might concentrate instead on the solution of practical problems.[27] The impression given to Tokyo was that Nomura had successfully shelved the issue.

Four months were to pass before the Japanese government finally learned how important Hull's principles actually were in the American approach to a settlement. It was only on September 4, 1941, that Tokyo realized, from a so-called oral statement which had been handed by the President to Nomura for communication to his government, that the four principles constituted a definite problem—indeed, a major stumbling block—in the negotiations.[28]

Is it any wonder, then, that the "Draft Understanding" cabled to Tokyo by Nomura in mid-April was received there with open arms "like welcome rain in the desert," as a veritable "boon from Heaven," or that the eyes of the former premier, Baron Reijirō Wakatsuki, are said to have filled with tears of joy upon his being informed of the proposal just received from Washington?[29]

The "Draft Understanding" was immediately discussed at a liaison conference between the cabinet and the supreme command.

[26]FR: Japan, 1931-1941, II, 409-10.

[27]Nomura Cable No. 277, May 8, 1941 (Foreign Office archives). Statements in Hull, Memoirs, II, 996, and Langer and Gleason, Undeclared War, 470, to the effect that Nomura sent Hull's four principles to Tokyo in April, together with the "Draft Understanding," represent what would normally have been a logical assumption in the circumstances.

[28]Nomura's Cable No. 777, Sept. 3, 1941 (Foreign Office archives); FR: Japan, 1931-1941, II, 589-91, esp. 590. The "oral statement" given to Nomura by the President on September 3 arrived in Tokyo on the afternoon of September 4.

[29]In the order quoted: Japanese Research Division, "Interrogations of Japanese Officials on World War II" (2 vols., Tokyo, ca. 1949-51), I: 49157, Seizō Arisue, 40-41; Stō, "Dai-Tōa Sensō wo Maneita Shōwa no Dōran," 112; Saburō Kurusu, Nichi-Bei Gaikō Hiwa: Waga Gaikō-shi [The Secret Story of Japanese-American Relations: A History of Our Diplomacy] (Tokyo, 1952), 164.

A decision was postponed pending the return of Matsuoka from Europe, but the general feeling inclined toward "acceptance in principle." Several days later the document was subjected to careful study at a joint conference between the leaders of the Army General Staff and the War Ministry. In addition to Nomura's report to the Foreign Office, the army had at its disposal a cable from Iwakuro recommending that favorable consideration be given to an adjustment of Japanese-American relations on the basis being proposed. It was the understanding of all present that the private American citizens who had been involved in "drafting" the document had maintained close and continuous contact with Roosevelt, Hull, and Walker and that the President and Secretary of State had no objections regarding the purport of the proposal! The army leaders therefore concluded that his draft was "in reality . . . a plan submitted by the American Government."[30]

As Tōjō later expressed it, since the President and Hull "had knowledge" of the proposal and the Secretary of State had asked Nomura to obtain instructions from Tokyo as to "whether or not it would be all right to go ahead with the negotiations on the basis of this proposal we looked upon it as an official document. That is to say, we regarded the Japanese-American negotiations as having begun from the moment we were asked to indicate our attitude with respect to this proposal."[31] It is therefore apparent that the inadequacies of Nomura's reporting were further compounded by the manner in which the decision makers in Tokyo drew unwarrantable conclusions from even the few substantial facts that were available to them.

Thus, from the very beginning of the Hull-Nomura conversations, the opportunity for peace inherent therein was impaired by a fundamental misconception on the part of Japan's leaders. The generally poor communication existing among them by virtue of the indirection and vagueness traditional in Japanese thought and

---

[30]On the reaction of the leaders in Tokyo, see Konoye, *Ushinawareshi Seiji*, 52-54, 62-70; *Sokki-roku*, 293: 7-8 (Kido affidavit); Kurusu, *Nichi-Bei Gaikō-Hiwa*, 164-65; Tōgō, *Jidai no Ichimen*, 154, 159-61; Shigemitsu, *Shōwa no Dōran*, II, 62-75 (Shigemitsu's account is based on what he learned after the war); Japanese Research Division, "Interrogations. . . . ," I: 49157, Seizō Arisue, 40-41; Satō, "Dai-tōa Senso wo Maneita Shōwa no Dōan," III-13, 116-18; Satō correspondence; *Sokki-roku*, 343: 4-5 (Tōjō affidavit); Hattori, *Dai-Tōa Sensō Zenshi, I, 121-23*; Yabe, *Konoye Fumimaro*, II, 255-65.

[31]*Sokki-roku*, 343: 4 (Tōjō affidavit).

speech was now rivalled by an equally serious problem of communication between Japan and the United States. The officials in the American capital never realized the nature of the Japanese error, nor, for that matter, did the leaders in Tokyo. The army conference in question produced a decision in favor of going ahead on the basis of "the American plan." The navy was consulted and found to be in general agreement. Konoye, who believed implicitly that he was dealing with an American proposal, was also of the same view. Following his return from Europe, Matsuoka proved to be a major stumbling block and, consequently, a continuing source of difficulty for his colleagues. In view of what is now known about Iwakuro's role in formulating that proposal, the Foreign Minister's assessment of the "Draft Understanding" as representing 30 per cent good will and 70 per cent evil intent provides perhaps the ultimate irony. In the end, Matsuoka's objections were overcome, thanks, in part, to the efforts of Major General Mutō and Rear Admiral Oka, the Chiefs of the powerful military and naval affairs bureaus of the War and Navy Ministries.[32] As a result, on May 12, 1941, Japan finally and rather tardily submitted her "answer" to the "American proposal" of mid-April.

Not until after the Pacific war had ended, more than four years later, did a few of those who had been in high places in Tokyo in 1941 come to realize that what had been intended as Japan's "answer" had been received in Washington on May 12 as Japan's initial offer. The decision makers within the Japanese government had always regarded their communication of that date as an official revision of the earlier "American" proposal. Only from postwar American testimony did they belatedly learn that their "answer" had been interpreted in Washington as Japan's first "official propositions."

As such, in mid-May 1941, the Japanese offering was analyzed minutely by the State Department. Hull and his experts were again disappointed. They concluded that "very few rays of hope shone from the document. What Japan was proposing was mostly to her own advantage. In effect, it called for a species of joint overlordship of the Pacific area by Japan and the United States, with Japan the baron of the part that embraced nine-tenths of the population and the wealth, and with little consideration for the rights and interests of other nations." The question facing the American government

[32]*FR: Japan, 1931-1941,* II, 411-12; *FR: Diplomatic Papers, 1941,* IV, 172-73, 179, 185; references cited in n. 30.

was "whether to begin the conversations with the Japanese. As the document stood," in Hull's view, "it offered little basis for an agreement, unless we were willing to sacrifice some of our most basic principles, which we were not. Nevertheless, it was a formal and detailed proposal from Japan. To have rejected it outright would have meant throwing away the only real chance we had had in many months to enter with Japan into a fundamental discussion of all the questions outstanding between us. . . . Consequently, we decided to go forward on the basis of the Japanese proposals and seek to argue Japan into modifying here, eliminating there, and inserting elsewhere, until we might reach an accord we both could sign with mutual good will."[33]

But it was not to be that simple. The trouble for the future lay in the erroneous conception of the American negotiating position that inevitably resulted from the assignment of a false value to the "Draft Understanding" by the decision makers in Tokyo. From April on, Japanese cabinet and supreme command leaders regularly used that document as a yardstick against which to measure the various proposals that subsequently emanated from the United States government. From incorrectly asssuming in the spring of 1941 that the American attitude was more favorable than it was, Japan's leaders moved toward the argument some two months later that the American mood was stiffening and that the terms then being offered by Washington were far harsher than those "originally proposed."

This alleged "change in the American attitude," which was confirmed in Japanese eyes by the content of an American draft plan dated June 21 and by the President's oral statement of early September, proved more and more disappointing as time passed. The initial Japanese hope of being able to retain the essence by compromising on the form gradually waned, and, as it did so, Japan's own position in the negotiations hardened. Those who had been suspicious of Washington's motives from the outset, or who were opposed to even the slightest diplomatic concession, began finding it easier to interfere. A typical method was to attack the sincerity of the United States by pointing to the marked differences between the "American" offer of mid-April [Iwakuro's "Draft

---

[33]On the May 12 proposal and the American reaction thereto, see Hull, *Memoirs*, II, 999-1001 (the source of the quotations in the text); *FR: Japan, 1931-1941*, II, 332-33, 415-26; IMTFE "Transcript," 10748-51 (Ballantine affidavit).

Understanding"] and the "second" proposal of June 21 [actually the first American statement of a basis on which conversations might be conducted].[34]

Although Nomura's key role in this entire matter is apparent, the primary responsibility of the government in Tokyo should not be overlooked. At a time of crisis in its relations with the United States that government elected to send to Washington a man of only limited practical experience in foreign affairs. Nomura himself had no illusions about his qualifications for the post. The wisdom of his reluctance to accept such an assignment was borne out by the misgivings that assailed him once the conversations were well under way. He even considered resigning and on more than one occasion expressed himself in favor of that course. But he was encouraged to stay on. And when he later asked that a career man such as Saburō Kurusu be sent to assist him, the request was not given favorable consideration until a change in cabinets had occurred, a new Foreign Minister had taken over, and the situation had so far deteriorated that Kurusu, no matter how expert, would indeed have accomplished the extraordinary had he been able to arrest the trend toward war.[35]

The crux of the matter, the explanation behind Nomura's failure to report fully and accurately, lies perhaps not so much in any language difficulty as in Nomura's lack of diplomatic experience and in his conception of his role as ambassador. There is no doubt that he was eager to see negotiations begun. He hoped that they would succeed in restoring friendly relations between Japan and the United States. Nomura knew, however, that there were men in Tokyo and on the continent of Asia who would react against any program envisaging fundamental concessions on Japan's part. He may therefore have felt that the risk inherent in not forwarding Hull's remarks was less than the danger that might have resulted from a thorough and factual report. Other evidence of Nomura's method of

[34]The text draws on statements in Tōgō, *Jidai no Ichimen,* 152, 160; Satō, "Dai-Tōa Sensō wo Maneita Shōwa no Dōran," 125; Shigemitsu, *Shōwa no Dōran,* II, 69; *Sokki-roku,* 343: 9 (Tōjō affidavit). Individual evaluation can generally provide the necessary safeguards against the element of calculated self-interest occasionally encountered in some postwar testimony. Although the time references are later, see also *FR: Diplomatic Papers, 1941,* IV, 527-28, and Shinichi Tanaka, *Taisen Totsunyū no Shinsō* [The Truth behind the Plunge into War] (Tokyo, 1955), 50-51.

[35]See Tōgō, *Jidai no Ichimen,* 222-25; *Sokki-roku,* 337: 7 (Tōgō affidavit), 251: 9-10 (Yamamoto affidavit and related documents); Nomura, "Kafu Kaisō," 25.

operation suggests that he may also have hoped to entice Tokyo into launching serious negotiations by giving an encouraging and optimistic impression from the start.[36] Despite Hull's insistence to the contrary, Nomura may even have assumed from "inside" information supplied by Iwakuro and Ikawa that the United States was more favorably disposed than was actually the case. Whatever the reason or reasons, Nomura did not report to his government all that he knew; Tokyo consequently remained in the dark concerning matters of vital importance.

Later developments, such as the outbreak of the German-Soviet war, Japan's occupation of southern French Indochina, and the freezing of Japanese assets in the United States and elsewhere, were obviously of great significance in influencing governmental attitudes on both sides of the Pacific during the final months before Pearl Harbor, but the chronically disruptive effect of the initial misconception under which the leaders in Tokyo continued to labor should not be minimized. The Hull-Nomura conversations dragged on through 1941 without the facts of the situation ever coming to light, until, in the end, what had once been a promising effort for peace suddenly terminated in failure with Japan's abrupt and decisive resort to war.

---

[36]See, for instance, Tōgō, *Jidai no Ichimen*, 160-62; *Sokki-roku*, 337: 7 (Tōgō affidavit); Shigemitsu, *Shōwa no Dōran*, II, 62-63, 74-75; Hull, *Memoirs*, II, 1003-1004.

PAUL SCHROEDER

The Axis Alliance and Japanese-American Relations, 1941

Paul W. Schroeder (born 1927) is Professor of History at the University of Illinois. He has written *Metternich's Diplomacy at Its Zenith, 1820-1823* (1962).

THE JAPANESE-AMERICAN negotiations and the policy pursued therein by the United States have been investigated and interpreted a number of times. It is neither possible nor necessary to review those interpretations here. Only three major points in this study are to be injected into the controversy. The first of these has already been made, namely, that the Tripartite Pact was initially a major issue in dispute but soon declined in importance and was used only for propaganda purposes at the end. The other two points are more general. The first is that there was a real change in the positions and the policies of both Japan and the United States in the course of the negotiations, a change which was ultimately of decisive significance. The second point is that this change, particularly in American policy, was a development so natural as to appear inevitable and so popular as to be virtually irreversible.

The first of the two points still to be discussed is controversial. The prevailing interpretation of the Japanese-American negotiations is that no change of any importance occurred throughout the talks. In its original and most extreme form, this argument stems from the State Department. Hull and his associates have always maintained flatly that there was no change in the respective positions of the two powers throughout the negotiations. The United States never altered her fundamental policy, which was one of insisting upon Hull's Four Points, the sanctity of treaties, and the principle of being a good neighbor in international relations. "The principles set forth in our November 26 proposal," insisted Hull, "were in all important respects essentially the same principles we had been proposing to the Japanese right along."[1] Japan, on the other hand (so the

---

[1] *Pearl Harbor Attack. Hearings Before the Joint Committee on the Investigation of the Pearl Harbor Attack,* 79th Congress, 2nd Session, 39 Parts (Washington, 1946), XI, 5369.

---

argument runs), was from first to last bent on a ruthless policy of military expansion.[2] Her sole purpose in the negotiations was to persuade or compel the United States to yield to Japan control of the entire Pacific, from Hawaii to India and beyond.[3] There was nothing the United States could have done which would have deterred Japan from her course of aggression. "It was not within the power of this Government otherwise than by abject submission to Japan's terms, to halt Japan in her course," claimed Hull.[4] "Japan [in August 1941] . . . was on a steady and fixed course of conquest which would reach us in Japan's own chosen time."[5] Her aggression, moreover, was totally senseless and irrational, for the United States was offering Japan everything a peaceful nation could desire. "There was nothing in there [the Ten Points Plan]," maintained the Secretary, "that any peaceful nation pursuing a peaceful course would not have been delighted to accept."[6] Japan's incurable militarism, however, rendered of no avail all American generosity and patience. The negotiations did nothing more than to reveal the irreconcilable character of the positions of the two governments.

The clash between Japan and the United States, the argument continues, was molded by decades of history. Japan had become inherently belligerent; the United States was inherently peace-loving. The policies of peace which Hull espoused embodied, as he saw it, the practices of historic Americanism. "We have," he asserted, "from over an indefinite period in the past stood for all the doctrines that you see set out [in the Ten Points Plan]."[7] They were, in fact, universal principles, subscribed to by all peaceful men the world over. Nothing in American history resembled Japan's actions in the Pacific. In her own sphere, the Western Hemisphere, the United States had always acted solely in self-defense. The Monroe Doctrine, "as we interpret and apply it uniformly since 1823," said Hull, presumably including thereby also the Roosevelt Corollary, "only contemplates steps for our physical safety." The Japanese New Order, in contrast, was a mere cover-up for aggression.[8] In the

[2]Hull's statement, Nov. 23, 1945, *ibid.*, II, 409-410.
[3]Testimony by Hull, Nov. 27, 1945, *ibid.*, 606.
[4]Testimony, May 16, 1946, *ibid.*, XI, 5384.
[5]*Ibid.*, 5395.
[6]*Ibid.*; testimony, Nov. 26, 1945, *ibid.*, II, 555.
[7]*Ibid.*, II, 613.
[8]Memo by Hull, April 20, 1940, U.S. Department of State, *Foreign Relations of the United States: Japan, 1931-1941,* 2 vols. (Washington, 1943), II, 284.

same manner, self-defense, equal opportunity, and peace had always been the keynotes of American foreign policy in the Far East. Hull's political adviser, Stanley K. Hornbeck, who yields to no one in defense of historic American Far Easten policy, writes:

> Our people and our Government have, from the very beginning of our national life, asserted that in the commercial relations of sovereign states there should *not* be a "closed door" *anywhere.*

Again:

> The intentions of the United States in regard to the Western Pacific and Eastern Asia have always been peaceful intentions. Our procedures have been procedures of peace.

The American acquisitions of Hawaii, Guam, and even of the Philippines, Mr. Hornbeck is careful to point out, are also in reality clear evidences of a peaceful, liberal attitude.[9]

In contrast stood the record of Japanese aggression in the past. Japan had always intended to go to war with the United States. The negotiations in 1941 were merely a sham; Kurusu's mission was simply one of stalling the United States along until Japan was ready to attack, while Nomura served as a blind.[10] The efforts of the so-called "peace party" in Tokyo also were meaningless, the argument runs. For since 1937, according to Hull, Tojo at the head of the military was in "supreme control" of everything Japan possessed, including her Navy and the Emperor.[11] The course of Japanese aggression, moreover, had been determined long before the outbreak at the Marco Polo bridge. Following the advent of the Tanaka cabinet in 1927, Hull maintained, "Japan had consistently been pursuing only one fixed policy—that of expansion by aggression."[12] Part and parcel of this policy was an eventual attack upon the United States. Modern Japan had trained herself well in the execution of such a policy. Her whole history from 1895 to the present was one of international duplicity and military aggrandizement. The Sino-Japanese War of 1894-1895, the Russo-

[9]Stanley K. Hornbeck, *The United States and the Far East: Certain Fundamentals of Policy* (Boston: World Peace Foundation, 1942), 10, 14-16.

[10]Sumner Welles, *The Time for Decision* (New York: Harper, 1944), 295; testimony by Welles, Nov. 23, 1945, *Pearl Harbor Attack*, II, 471.

[11]Testimony by Hull, Nov. 26, 1945, *Pearl Harbor Attack*, II, 553; Nov. 27, 1945, *ibid.*, 612.

[12]Testimony by Hull, May 16, 1946, *ibid.*, XI, 5379.

Japanese War of 1904-1905, the Twenty-one Demands of 1915, the Anti-Comintern Pact of 1936—these and many other events formed the pattern sinister.[13]

It is not to be supposed that this extravagant theory still finds many defenders. Most of it is plainly the product of wartime passions and postwar politics. One is tempted to remark, paraphrasing George Bernard Shaw, that even in Washington it is possible to say very foolish things about one's enemies simply because one is at war with them. The underlying idea that no change was possible throughout the negotiations because of Japan's intransigence, however, remains current. Basil Rauch, for example, has this to say of the fixed Japanese intent:

> *Japan in the spring and summer of 1941 would accept no diplomatic arrangement which did not give it everything that it might win in the Far East by aggression, without the trouble and expense of military campaigns.*[14]

The careful scholar Herbert Feis, who does not by any means accept the State Department's thesis uncritically, nevertheless contends that the gap between Japan and the United States never really lessened and that neither side fundamentally altered its original stand. The only two changes in their positions, Mr. Feis says, were, first, the Japanese offer to renounce further southwestern advances and to accept less than full victory in China and, second, the attempt by both governments toward the end to seek a *modus vivendi*.[15]

Other authorities could be cited with the same general intent, namely, that there was never any serious prospect of Japanese-American agreement, that the two nations' positions were fundamentally irreconcilable, and that both of them were too committed to opposite goals to change. One hesitates to disagree in the face of their more or less unanimous testimony. Yet it would seem that the basic question is not whether Japan and the United States ever approached agreement or whether they were always at odds. It is true that they never came close to a real settlement. The more

[13]Statement by Hull, Nov. 23, 1945, *ibid.,* II, 407-410. It is ironical to note that one of the American arguments during the negotiations was that Japan, who had been so peaceful and progressive prior to 1931, should return to her old ways. See memo by Welles, Washington, Aug. 4, 1941, *Foreign Relations, Japan, II, 541-544.*

[14]Basil Rauch, *Roosevelt, from Munich to Pearl Harbor* (New York: Creative Age Press, 1950), 396. Italics in original.

[15]Herbert Feis, *The Road to Pearl Harbor* (Princeton, 1950), 171-172.

important question, however, is whether Japan and the United States were at odds over the same things throughout the conversations—whether the issues that separated them were the same at the end as at the beginning.

Here, it is contended, a real change took place. That some shifts in diplomatic position occurred during the negotiations no one will seriously deny. One needs only to compare the Japanese proposal of May 12 with those of November 7 and 20 and the American plan of May 16 with that of November 26 to see that there was unquestionably a change. Japan was clearly asking for less, and the United States was demanding more, in November than in May. It is also plain that there was a decisive change in regard to one of the major issues in dispute, the Tripartite Pact. These, it is here claimed, were only parts of a greater development. In the summer of 1941, the basic aims of both Japanese and American foreign policy underwent an important transformation. The result was that their basic quarrel in November was no longer the same as it had been in May.

Until approximately the middle of July 1941 the policy of Japan was unmistakably aggressive in nature. Her goals were expansionistic, although she was becoming more and more apprehensive and doubtful about attaining them. She was still committed to ending the China conflict on her own terms. She still hoped to have her puppet government headed by Wang Ching-wei coalesced into the Chinese government, with Japan preserving a very large measure of military and economic control within China. Furthermore, she had definite plans for southward expansion as far as possible—certainly into French Indo-China and Thailand and if circumstances allowed also into the Netherlands East Indies. The diplomatic methods she used to implement her program showed similarly a policy of offense. Her browbeating of the Vichy French and high-pressure negotiation with the Dutch over the East Indies testify to this. She still expected a German victory, counting on it and the Tripartite Pact to isolate the United States and persuade America not to interfere in the Pacific. The last, rather desperate expressions of this policy of offense are the resolutions of the Imperial Conference of July 2. Here Japan resolved, in spite of the danger of war with the United States and Great Britain, to press on with her previously prepared plans for expansion southward. The final overt act in the Japanese campaign was the occupation of southern Indo-China in late July, a move already determined over a month before as part of the old expansionist policy.

The American position in the Far East in this same period was definitely defensive. As has been shown, the United States policy was one of holding the line in Asia, while building up her home defenses and concentrating on aid to Great Britain in Europe. The United States had thus two essential and immediate objectives in Asia: first, stopping Japan from any further advance southward that would menace the British supply line and, second, keeping Japan out of the European war.[16] To help accomplish these objectives, a major aim of American diplomacy was to persuade Japan to withdraw from the Tripartite Pact, even if only by degrees.[17] The remaining American goal, the liberation of China, was of necessity a distinctly subsidiary and remote one. As Ambassador Grew wrote in November 1940:

> We need not aim to drive Japan out of China now. That can be taken care of, perhaps, if and after Britain wins the war with Germany. But stopping Japan's proposed far-flung southward advance and driving her out of China are two different matters. We can tolerate her occupation of China for the time being, just as we have tolerated it for the past three years. I doubt if we should tolerate any great extension of the southward advance.[18]

Throughout the first half of 1941 the American position was plainly that, although she would aid China within limits to keep Japan occupied there, she did not intend to go to war for the sake of China. She would, however, go to war to defend American territory and probably also that of the British and the Dutch in Asia. Even the crucial freezing orders, strong measures though they were, were entirely consistent with the defensive nature of the American policy. They were imposed because the Japanese, having moved into southern Indo-China, were in a position gravely menacing all of southeastern Asia. The freezing orders were to teach Japan that she had gone far enough—indeed, too far—and that she must now begin to retreat.

The embargo produced precisely the result intended. Japan, faced with the consequences of her move, began to recoil. The struggle within Japan for the control of policy took a decided turn for the better (from the American point of view), with the initiative passing into the hands of moderates such as Konoye and Toyoda. The brave

---

[16]Grew cites Roosevelt's letter of Jan. 21, 1941, as evidence of this strategy (Joseph C. Grew, *Turbulent Era*, 2 vols., Boston, 1952, II, 1259-1260).

[17]Memo, May 19, 1942, *Foreign Relations, Japan,* II, 335.

[18]Grew, *Turbulent Era*, II, 1232-1233.

promises and boastful programs of Japanese expansionism, like those of the resolutions of July 2, were for the moment ignored or forgotten, as Japan went clearly on the defensive.[19] Her main objective now was somehow to extricate herself from the desperate position in which she was entangled, to get relief from the inexorable economic pressure of the embargo, and to avoid what seemed to be inevitable war. She was not concerned for the time with expanding her empire; the problem was now one of salvaging as much as she could. To gain peace or at least a breathing spell, she was willing to make what seemed to her to be two major concessions. She was ready to take a course independent of Germany and indifferent to the Tripartite Pact. She was also willing to stop her southward advance and even, at the end, to withdraw from her latest acquisition, southern Indo-China. The one thing she would not do to evacuate China and to renounce her aims there. This in her eyes was impossible. She could modify her terms somewhat, but the retention of a considerable economic and military hold, particularly on North China, was considered by her military leaders absolutely indispensable, for political reasons if for none other. There are a number of moves in this period which indicate the defensive character of Japanese policy—the rift with Germany, Konoye's

[19]This point, that Japan went on the defensive after July 26, lies of course at the very center of the controversy over Japanese-American relations in 1941. It clashes with the opinion of Langer and Gleason, among others, who believe that the best opportunity for Japanese-American agreement existed in May and that, after the German assault on Russia, Japan was driven by her military extremists irretrievably into a course of aggression and war *(Undeclared War, 477, 493, 625).* The work just cited is an outstanding one, written by eminent scholars whose judgment must be given great weight. Nevertheless, the clear impression gained by the writer, especially from the International Military Tribunal for the Far East, "Record of Proceedings of the International Military Tribunal for the Far East," (hereafter *IMTFE*), materials, is that Japan, after the freezing orders, was hesitant, worried, and in retreat, so that the final decision for war could be taken only after considerable delay and genuine internal struggle and as a last resort. (One notes, for example, a definite progressive change in tone between the decisions of the Imperial Conferences held on July 2, September 6, and November 5 [IMTFE, Doc. No. 1652].)

This impression coincides with the contemporary observations of Ambassador Ott, who on this point may be more readily believed because he records facts and feelings distasteful to him and to his government. His report of Oct. 4, 1941 (IMTFE, Doc. no. 4065A), based, he says, on his own observations and on "a careful sounding of the Army leaders," including Tojo, paints a gloomy picture of the state of feeling in Japanese official circles. Widespread hesitancy and indecision, lack of unity in the

invitation to Roosevelt to attend the Leaders' Conference, the postponement of the decision for war even after the fall of Konoye, and the last-minute proposals of November 20. The fall of Konoye and the accession of Tojo did not really change Japanese policy but merely presaged its ultimate failure. The real difference between Konoye and Tojo was not that the one wanted peace and the other war. It was rather that, when each was faced with a choice between war and humiliating terms, Konoye would waver indefinitely, while Tojo would choose war.

The policy of the United States, meanwhile, underwent a corresponding change: America went on the diplomatic offensive after July 1941. Her aims were no longer simply those of holding the line against Japanese advances and of inducing Japan to draw away from an alliance which the United States considered menacing. The chief objective of American policy now was to push Japan back, to compel her to withdraw from her conquests. The United States was determined to see that Japan assumed such a peaceful attitude in Asia that she could never again threaten the security of her neighbors. She was to renounce her dream of hegemony in Asia, to give up her plans for expansion, and to accept defeat in China.[20] The objective that had previously been the least important and pressing in

---

national leadership, a recognition of the evidently hopeless stalemate in the Japanese-American negotiations and the ultimate futility of a wait-and-see policy, combined with an inability to find and decide upon any alternative course—these were the salient conditions Ott noted. Nor was opinion more hopeful in the nation as a whole. Japanese morale, Ott judged, was low. The people were oppressed by a sense of isolation and encirclement, by the futility and hopelessness of the China Affair, and by an awareness of Japan's "numerous economic and material deficiencies."

Noting a strong reluctance on the part of the Army leaders to discuss possible American participation in the war, Ott concluded that this was not simply due to the desire to preserve secrecy in the negotiations. "Even stronger," he maintained, "is the often reported atavistic fear of getting entangled in a conflict with the United States. . . . The Japanese Government . . . wants to embark on such a conflict only if worst comes to worst and wants to decide the time itself; at least help in deciding upon it."

Evidently Tojo and his associates succeeded in concealing from the German Ambassador the very considerable extent of Japanese preparation for war, and apparently Ott also underestimated the military's determination to fight if worst came to worst. Nevertheless, Ott's comments on the general climate of Japanese morale and opinion remain of interest.

[20]Feis, *Road to Pearl Harbor,* 273.

American policy, the liberation of China, now became the crucial consideration. American diplomats made a prompt and total evacuation of Japanese troops the *sine qua non* for agreement. The weapon of severe economic pressure on Japan which had been forged and used by the United States, up to and including the time of the freezing orders, to hold the line against Japanese expansion, now was employed to enforce the American demands for the evacuation of China. The Japanese were given to understand that there would be no relaxation of the embargo until Japan gave up her gains by aggression there.

The old defensive goals were not forgotten. They remained uppermost especially in the minds of American military planners. The military strategists continued to insist to the end that the primary objectives of American policy should remain the defeat of Germany and the exclusion of Japan from the war. Brigadier General Leonard T. Gerow, acting Assistant Chief of Staff, maintained that even the impending defeat of China would not warrant involvement of the United States in a war with Japan. Chief of Staff General George Marshall and Admiral Harold R. Stark agreed with Gerow.[21] The reports prepared by the Army Intelligence Service from July to December 1941 all display a single consistent point of view, along with a number of important insights. First was the belief that the European war remained uppermost and that the previous essentially defensive objectives pursued by the United States in the Far East should be maintained.[22] Second was a recognition of the estrangement between Japan and Germany and of the completely altered Japanese attitude toward the Tripartite Pact.[23] Third was a belief that the Konoye government was really trying to extricate Japan from her difficulties without war. Brigadier General Miles, in charge of Army Intelligence, believed that the United States might gain her essential objectives through the use of "strong diplomacy," provided that she made sure that Konoye could carry the Japanese Army and Navy with him in his policy.[24] Fourth and most important was the conviction that it was unnecessary, and probably even harmful, for the United States to insist on an immediate evacuation of China.

[21]Memos, Gerow to Marshall, Nov. 3 and 21, 1941, *Pearl Harbor Attack,* XIV, 1066-1067, 1106-1107; memo, Marshall and Stark to Roosevelt, Nov. 27, 1941, *ibid.,* 1083.

[22]*Ibid.,* 1334-1384.

[23]Memo by Brigadier General Sherman Miles, Sept. 5, 1941, *ibid.,* 1352-1353.

[24]*Ibid.;* also memo by Miles, Aug. 16, 1941, *ibid.,* 1347.

This last point, of course, touches the very heart of the whole Japanese-American controversy. The argument of the Army Intelligence Service with regard to it is important enough to be given close attention. Colonel Hayes A. Kroner, acting Assistant Chief of Staff of the Service, supplies this in a memorandum of October 2. The first reason why the United States should not insist on the evacuation of China was that such a move would be impossible for Japan for political reasons:

> This division is of the belief that the present Cabinet in Tokyo [Konoye's third cabinet] does not yet feel strong enough to enforce any order for withdrawal of Japanese troops from China, even though under pressure from the United States, it might be inclined to do so.

The move, Kroner maintained, would thus be disastrous for the Konoye regime. Worse, it also "would be highly detrimental to our interests." The removal of so many troops from China back to the Japanese homeland would create grave internal problems for Japan. The civilian government might well be unable to prevent a military explosion leading directly to war with the United States. In addition, with Japanese troops freed from China the threat to Siberia and the southwest Pacific would be gravely increased. "In other words," Kroner concluded, "we must cease at once our attempts to bring about the withdrawal of Japanese armed forces from China."[25]

Ironically enough, at the same time that Kroner was issuing this warning the very events which he feared were taking place. On this same day, October 2, Hull delivered to the Japanese an Oral Statement rejecting the Konoye proposals. It killed the chances for a Leaders' Conference and made certain the downfall of the Konoye government in Japan. The main reason for the American refusal to deal with Konoye, as already seen, was Japan's unwillingness to evacuate China. Thus, at this very time, the Konoye government was tottering to its fall and carrying its hope for peace in the Pacific with it because it could not budge the American diplomats from their insistence that Japanese troops had to get out of China forthwith. And all the while, American military planners were urging that the United States ought by all means to let the Japanese stay. The clash between the United States strategic interests and her diplomatic policy cannot be seen more plainly.

Other men outside the military remembered the old defensive goals. Ambassador Grew, as shown, repeatedly urged that the

---

[25]Memo by Kroner, Oct. 2, 1941, *ibid.*, 1357-1358.

President should make an attempt to meet Konoye halfway. His main argument was that the strong American action in the embargo had created the opportunity for the United States to gain her essential aims, if only she did not insist on getting everything at once. "History will determine," he wrote later, "whether this opportunity was missed by an attempt to achieve at once our long-range objectives, an utter impossibility under the circumstances then obtaining, at the expense of the immediately vital and essential interests of our country."[26] As for the President, his actions up to the very eve of Pearl Harbor indicate that his interest was primarily centered on Europe. He was particularly concerned with the Far East only as it affected the European war, and the China question for him was secondary.

What happened, then, was not that the original defensive goals were forgotten, but that they were submerged. As Japan began to retreat and as the United States grew steadily stronger, the original problems lost their former urgency. Once the rift between Germany and Japan became plain and the American naval activities in the Atlantic went unnoticed by Japan, there was no longer any real need to worry about the Tripartite Pact. Objectionable it might still be, but hardly dangerous. Moreover, the failure of the Japanese, after the occupation of south Indo-China, to carry farther the program of southward expansion as determined on July 2 diminished at least for the moment the imminent danger of a move to the south. At the same time, Japan's repeated pledges not to extend her advance any farther south and to withdraw from Indo-China upon reaching peace with China, backed up at the end by an offer of immediate evacuation of south Indo-China, indicated that the southward drive was not an immutable part of Japanese policy. Any concessions the Japanese made, however, did them no good. In the wave of reaction against Japan's move into south Indo-China, the initiative in American policy had passed into the hands of those leaders who had long advocated a strong, no-compromise, no-appeasement stand against Japan. These men—Morgenthau, Knox, Stimson, and others—backed up Hull in his uncompromising principles in order to carry through a modern policy of "thorough." Japan was not merely to be contained and held back, but to be squeezed and harried until she conformed, that is, until she disgorged her gains and abandoned her evil ways.

26Grew, *Turbulent Era,* II, 1262.

In one way, the policy thus conceived and executed was indeed a development of historic American policy in the Far East. The United States had long upheld, at least on paper, the cause of China's integrity and independence. For an equally long period she had, for reasons of democratic idealism and commercial self-interest, stood for the Open Door in China.[27] The lively interest felt by Americans over the fate of China was always an important factor in Japanese-American relations and could easily grow, as it did, into the paramount consideration. But in another sense the change in policy was a reversal of a historic American position. For it was also a long-standing American policy, equally as traditional as the Open Door and far more consistently observed in practice, that the United States would not go to war for the sake of China. This policy was now in effect overthrown. American diplomats made it clear that the United States would accept war with Japan in preference to any settlement between Japan and China which did not restore intact China's territorial and administrative integrity. It is commonly agreed that this was the one real cause of the war. Had the China issue been solved or left to one side, the other two problems could surely have been adjusted without open conflict. In insisting that the Japanese withdraw immediately and completely from China and in employing the weapons of extreme economic pressure to compel Japanese agreement, the United States was carrying out a new offensive policy which made the crucial difference between peace and war.

It would be entirely wrong to suppose that this change in policy was simply the reasoned decision of policy makers. It would be still worse to charge that it represents the underhanded maneuverings of an administration leading the nation by a back road into war. The shift in policy, decisive though it was in its effects, was a very natural development. In a sense, it was truly and tragically inevitable. For years the United States had been exerting a gradually growing pressure on Japan in an effort to hold her at bay, a pressure conceived as a countermeasure to the outward thrust of Japanese expansion and reaching its climax in the joint freezing orders. American foreign policy would have had to be extraordinarily sensitive to the changed situation and unusually flexible to have prevented the United States from going on the offensive too

[27]Paul H. Clyde, "Our Concern for the Integrity of China," *Annals of the American Academy of Political and Social Science*, CCXV (May 1941), 72.

strongly. The moment that Japan began to draw back, the very force being exerted against her, unless relaxed, would automatically carry the United States to the offense. The measures designed to restrain Japan would serve equally well to force her back.

Moreover, even had the administration wanted to relax the pressure on Japan, this would have been very difficult to do. Chief among the reasons was public opinion. Over the course of a decade, the American people had built up a profound hatred and distrust of Japan. When the time came that the United States could put heavy pressure on the Japanese, it was the moment the public had long awaited. Virtually no one wanted the pressure relaxed. The most influential writers, politicians, and newspapers called for even more, and when at the very end there arose some concern over the probable consequences of this uncompromising policy, it was already too late.

V The Axis and Aggression, 1941

Politicians and diplomats usually think they control events, and people usually hold their government officials to a standard of "strict accountability." While men, especially government officials, must of course be held responsible for their actions and their results, the fact is that the web of intentions and causality is extremely complex and tangled. Historians have often found that events moved faster than men assumed and in ways that were not understood at the time. This is demonstrated in Part V, which consists of excerpts from three chapters ("America and the World Triangle," "Germany, the United States and Japanese Expansion," and "Germany and Pearl Harbor") in James V. Compton's *The Swastika and the Eagle* (1967), Louis Morton's "Japan's Decision for War" (1959), and Raymond Esthus' "President Roosevelt's Commitment to Britain to Intervene in a Pacific War" (1963). Compton shows in fascinating detail how Hitler sought to use the September 1940 Tripartite Pact with Japan as a means to prevent American intervention in the European war, while the Japanese used the pact for their own purposes in the Far East, and how German policy, designed to "bluff" the United States into acquiescence, served only to confirm "Axis aggression" in American eyes and encourage Japan to be reckless in its policy toward the United States. In ways that German geopoliticians did not understand, they achieved results opposite those they thought they were pursuing, and shared responsibility for bringing about the Pearl Harbor assault. Morton explains how the Japanese Army and Navy from 1936 on were able to make their ambitions, objectives, and policies those of the national government, and why the Japanese took the gamble of attacking American territory in the Pacific. By 1941, Morton concludes, the Japanese tragically believed that the alternative to war was internal collapse, and that they and their opponent, the United States, would or could fight a limited war. Finally, Esthus deals with the American side of the dilemma over war in the Pacific: what would be the American commitment if Japan attacked only British or Dutch territory or Thailand? Esthus shows that Roosevelt never answered the question, but that he apparently did promise the British armed support if they were attacked and the United States was not. Ironically, to the very end Roosevelt was clutching at straws to forestall war when events overtook his timetable.

JAMES V. COMPTON
The Swastika and the Eagle

James V. Compton (born 1928) is Associate Professor of History at San Francisco State College. He has studied in Germany and England, and taught at the University of Edinburgh.

IN THE MONTHS following the outbreak of the war, the Germans, while persistently disclaiming any Far Eastern interests, renewed their pressure upon Tokyo for an alliance. The drive for a military arrangement varied in intensity according to events in Europe and especially according to the attitude of England. When Hitler finally recognized that the war with England might be a protracted one after all, he ordered preparations for Sea Lion and stepped up the efforts for an arrangement with Japan which were to culminate in the Triangle Pact. The lengthening of the struggle with Britain had yet another effect on German policy; it moved the United States to the center of German-Japanese relations. Hitler's assumptions expressed in July and again in November 1939 that isolationist sentiment had rendered America "not dangerous"[1] were shaken in 1940 as American policies made it manifestly clear that war with Britain in the long run meant involvement with the United States.

* * *

The decisive document setting out the German position was sent to Tokyo in September.[2] This consisted of Ribbentrop's ideas "covering the cooperation of Germany, Italy and Japan for the purpose of neutralizing America" as well as the necessity for a quick

[1]Attolico to Ciano, 3/7/39, Italian Foreign Ministry, *I Documenti Diplomatici Italiani,* series 8 (Rome, 1952—) XII, p. 34. Hitler statement in International Military Tribunal, *Trial of the Major War Criminals Before the International Military Tribunal,* 42 vols. (Nuremberg, 1947-49), XXVI, p. 331 (789 - PS). (hereafter *IMT.)*

[2]This document has not been found. However, Stahmer recapitulated the contents as he had given them to Matsuoka in a conference of September 9 and 10, at which they were reported to have been "well received." Stahmer and Ott to Foreign Ministry 10/9/40, U.S. Department of State, *Documents on German Foreign Policy, 1919-1945,* Series D, 13 vols. (Washington, 1949-64), XI, p. 57.

From James V. Compton, *The Swastika and the Eagle: Hitler, the United States, and the Origins of World War II* (Boston: Houghton Mifflin Company, 1967).

decision in the matter. This document contained some fifteen points, the most relevant of which may be summarized as follows:

1. Germany had no desire for a world war and was especially interested in the exclusion of the United States.

2. Germany sought no Japanese military assistance against England.

3. The proper role of Japan was "restraining and preventing the United States from entering the war by all means."

4. There was little chance of a German-American war in the near future, but that a Japanese-American war "cannot ultimately be avoided."[3]

5. A strong and determined Axis attitude would be "a powerful and effective deterrent on the United States."

For Germany, then, as for Japan, America was manifestly the object of the Pact. The only thing that Germany seemed to demand of Japan in exchange for recognition of her Far Eastern hegemony was not, as the Japanese must have feared, a military commitment in Europe, but rather a stiff line toward America. And firmness in policy, as the Japanese well knew, was a matter of interpretation.

The negotiations of the following days revealed Japanese pressure for more general and consultative measures, while the Germans strove for specific, military clauses. Ribbentrop was especially anxious to exempt an attack by the U.S.S.R. from the operation of the Pact in order to leave no doubt whatever that it was aimed at the United States. He also (unsuccessfully) sought to include a pledge to go to war at once in order to convince the Americans that if she entered the conflict "she would find herself at war with three great powers."[4] These efforts seemed the more justified by German reports of vigorous American efforts to prevent the Japanese from signing any pact at all. Furthermore, Matsuoka was under very considerable pressure from naval, business and court circles for a moderate policy toward America and freedom of action in military matters.[5] It is evident from these negotiations that the unity on the

[3]Ott had been taking this line in Tokyo right along. Ott to Foreign Ministry 21/5/40, 12/6/40, IX, pp. 654, 551.

[4]Many of the documents during the negotiations may be found in the so-called Matsumoto Compendium, *IMTFE*/LXIV, pp. 27987-28018. Also, Foreign Ministry to Tokyo Embassy 20/9/40, *DGFP*/D/XI, p. 133.

[5]Ott to Foreign Ministry 23/9/40, *DGFP*/D/XI, p. 156. IMTFE/LXIV, p. 27987. Cabinet sitting and protocol, 16/9/40, *ibid.*, XV, pp. 6345-6378.

object of the Pact (the U.S.A.) did not extend to the method to be employed. The now familiar divergence of purpose persisted. The Pact was signed on September 27 in Berlin.[6] It consisted of a preamble in which cooperation was pledged to maintain a new order in Asia and Europe, followed by six articles. The first two of these recognized the leadership of Germany and Italy in Europe and that of Japan in the Far East. The third article pledged cooperation and assistance "with all political, economic and military means when one of the three contracting parties is attacked by a power not at present involved in the European war or in the Sino-Japanese conflict." The fourth article established a joint technical commission, while the fifth left the present "political standing" of the parties with the U.S.S.R. unaltered. The final article provided a ten-year duration for the arrangement.

The operational clause (article 3) was clearly a compromise between the German demand for a war pledge and the Japanese desire to limit the obligation to consultation. Furthermore, there was no specific mention of the object of the Pact: the United States. However, the exception of the U.S.S.R from the operation of the Pact made the target self-evident. As we have seen, the German instructions for negotiating the agreement indicated beyond doubt that intimidation of America was the objective. Moreover, both Hitler and Ribbentrop made the point repeatedly to the Italians during the negotiations that the Pact would be "the best way either to keep America entirely out or render her entry into the war ineffective." The Foreign Minister admitted to Ciano that the Pact might also be useful sometime against Russia, but it was clearly aimed "before all else to cripple America" and cause her to hesitate "one hundred times" before entering the European war.[7]

Ribbentrop at the signature ceremony did not mention America specifically (perhaps at a Japanese suggestion), confining himself to a general warning that any state attacking a Pact member would "have to contend with the combined power of three nations of two hundred and fifty million people."[8] Two days earlier, however, he

[6]For description of the ceremony, see William L. Shirer, *Berlin Diary: The Journal of a Foreign Correspondent, 1934-1941* (New York, 1941), p. 536. For text see *DGFP/D/XI*, p. 204.

[7]Hitler to Mussolini, 17/9/40, 4/10/40, *DGFP/D/XI*, pp. 104, 248. Malcolm Muggeridge, ed., *Ciano's Diary, 1939-1943* (London, 1947), 19/9/40, p. 291.

[8]Oshima testimony, International Military Tribunal for the Far East, "Record of Proceedings," XIII, p. 6054 (hereafter *IMTFE*). Quoted in Theo Sommer, *Deutschland und Japan zwischen den Mächten, 1935-1940* (Tübingen, 1962), p. 428.

had been more specific in a letter to Count Schulenberg, the German envoy in Moscow.

This alliance is exclusively directed aganst the American warmongers. Its exclusive purpose is to bring the element pressing for America's entry into the war to their senses. This is not to be expressly mentioned in the treaty, but it is unmistakably to be deduced from the context.[9]

At least three Japanese statesmen agreed with this judgment, although one reversed himself after the war.[10] Grew, Hull and Roosevelt accepted the view that their country was the object of the Pact, and post-war German testimony has also generally confirmed this, although stressing the defensive nature of the arrangement.[11]

That the Pact was, by its own terms, defensive and preventative was perfectly true. It was not aimed at the United States in the sense of seeking to provoke that country into the war, but rather the opposite. This cannot, however, alter the fact that the United States was to be rendered inactive so that aggression could proceed unchecked. The specific and repeated mention of the new order in the text made it unmistakably clear that it was an arrangement which sanctioned the ruthless expansion which was the hallmark of that new order. Moreover, as we shall see in the next chapters, the defensive tone of the Pact was no obstacle to its use by Germany in urging a course on her partner which ran the gravest risk of war with the United States. Japan was to put it to similar use in the weeks immediately prior to Pearl Harbor. Finally, it cannot be doubted that the "defensive" Pact might easily have become offensive in the hands of a victorious Axis bloc.

* * *

[9]Ribbentrop to Schulenberg, 25/9/40, U.S. Department of State, *Nazi-Soviet Relations, 1939-1941* (Washington, 1948), pp. 195-196.

[10]For Oshima's statement, Grew to Hull. 2/10/41 U.S., U.S. Department of State, *Foreign Relations of the United States: Japan, 1931-1941*, 2 vols. (Washington, 1943), II, pp. 171-173. For Konoye's statement 4/10/41, Microfilm records of the German Foreign Ministry, State Secretary's File, Japan, V, frame 60672. For Matsuoka's statement, Grew to Hull 5/10/40, *FRUS/Japan*/II, pp. 171-173. Oshima's denial, *IMTFE*, LXXVI, p. 34012.

[11]Grew to Hull, 29/9/40, *FRUS/Japan*/II, p. 170. *The Memoirs of Cordell Hull,* 2 vols. (New York, 1948), I, 429. Roosevelt speech 12/10/40, Samuel I. Rosenman, comp. *The Public Papers and Addresses of Franklin D. Roosevelt,* 13 vols. (New York, 1938-50), IX, 466. Ribbentrop Testimony, *IMT*/X, p. 188. At his trial, Weizsaeker termed the Pact "a warning poster for the United States." Weizsaeker testimony, *Nuremberg Military Tribunal: Trial of the Former German Diplomats,* vol. XVI, pp. 7898-7995 (hereafter *Case 11*).

We must now turn against this background of a deteriorating but still useful alliance, to the German image of Japanese foreign policy and the pressures exerted upon Tokyo in the light of this information, first in a general way and then in regard to three particular problems. The more general picture of Japanese foreign policy in Berlin was summarized in the instructions for the German delegation prepared by the Foreign Ministry for talks with Foreign Minister Matsuoka in March and April [1941].[12] Japan was described as a country committed to an expansionist policy. This expansion was guided by the vision of a "greater East Asia sphere" consisting of Japan (as the dominating power), Manchuria, China, Indo-China, Thailand, the Dutch East Indies, the Philippines and possibly Malaya, Singapore and Burma. In addition to this, a broader field, "Oceana," which included the island world between the American and Asian continents, except for Australia and New Zealand, would be thrown open for settlement of surplus population, Japanese and other.[13] The motives for this expansion were held to be economic, although political-ideological elements centering around visions of Japanese destiny were important in some circles.

The execution of Japanese plans was contingent on two sets of factors: the actions and policies of other powers concerned with the area on the one hand and the flux of Japanese domestic politics on the other.[14] Happily the countries Japan had to cross did not include Germany, at least politically or territorially, and Germany had thus far supported Japanese policy.[15] However, it was necessary, according to the instructions, for Japan to liquidate the Chinese question, to free her back from any Soviet threat and prepare herself for conflict with Britain in case of a "military undertaking which could

[12]These instructions were a series of memoranda dated 18/3/41, and contained in a special section of *Staatssekretaer* file, Japan/II, entitled *Matsuoka Besuch* (136708). The more general observations on Japanese goals were prepared by Woermann. See also F. C. Jones, *Japan's New Order in East Asia: Its Rise and Fall, 1937-1945* (London, 1954), chap. I.

[13]The Oceana concept had been mentioned by Matsuoka on February 24. Woermann memorandum in *Matsuoka Besuch.*

[14]Jones emphasizes this latter feature in his analyses. He is convinced that there was in fact no master plan of conquest from 1937 to 1941 and describes Japanese foreign policy as "the shuttlecock of domestic politics." Jones, *op. cit.,* p. 450.

[15]Hitler repeated this fact yet again to Kurusu 3/2/41, *DGFP/D/*XII,p. 9. Possible German-Japanese colonial conflict is dismissed in "Memo Regarding Former German Colonies" 18/3/41, *Matsuoka Besuch StS/*Japan/II /136713.

have as its goal a thrust south in the direction of Hong Kong, the Philippines and Singapore."[16]

The relationship to the United States, the report continued, was a special one because of the American Pacific fleet, the threat from Hawaii and the Philippines to the greater East Asia sphere and the fact of Japanese economic dependence on that country. Since the United States had proceeded with rearmament in the Pacific and a policy of economic pressure as well as support of independent states in Southeast Asia, the Imperial Government was faced with a difficult problem: how to obtain alternative sources of raw materials without in the process provoking the United States into war.[17]

There were, the instructions concluded, a number of possibilities open to Japan in her policies toward these countries by which she might attempt to achieve the conditions required for expansion. The choice of tactics was largely a function of the second set of factors: the rise and fall of cabinets and especially the fate of Foreign Minister Matsuoka. All of this gave Japanese policy "a certain indecisiveness" *(Ratlosigkeit)* in the German view and led to that "fundamental incoherence of policy which caused Japan to be distrusted and condemned everywhere."[18]

This fluidity of Japanese policy, frustrating as it was to her partners, did however at least allow room for maneuver and pressure on Tokyo. The problem was that Berlin had really very little to offer the Japanese except European victories as a reward for acquiescing in German demands. Nevertheless, German pressure on Japan was persistent. Against this general picture of Japanese policy, the line which Germany urged on Japan throughout 1941 was clear and consistent. In brief, the Japanese were encouraged to expand. Pressure on the Indies and Indo-China, an attack on Singapore and later, as Barbarossa bogged down, on Vladivostok as well, a general drive to the south, seizure of raw material sources

[16]"Memorandum Regarding Japanese Foreign Policy" 18/3/41, *ibid.*/136704.

[17]*Ibid.*, subsection: Japan-USA. See also memorandum of Ott 22/1/41, *StS/ Japan*/II/136526, which detailed the threat of the United States to Japan. On United States support of Indo–China see Memorandum (Weizsaecker) 18/1/41, *DGFP/D*/XI, p. 1125. Also Memo (Dooman) 14/2/41, *FRUS*/Japan/II, p. 137.

[18]Ott to Foreign Ministry 13/10/41, *StS/Japan*/V/60703. The Germans followed Japanese domestic politics with the greatest interest. Ribbentrop-Mussolini conference 14/5/41, *DGFP/D*/XII, p. 797. Comment on cabinet change in Ott to Foreign Ministry 17/7/41, 20/7/41, *StS/Japan*/IV/60348, 60380.

and naval activity, particularly that which would tie up the American fleet, were all welcomed. Moreover, the Japanese were urged to be firm and unyielding toward the United States. Japanese-American agreements were discouraged.

Japanese anxieties regarding American reaction to all of this were allayed by assurances that Germany also sought to block American entry into the war, that American policy was largely bluff, that even if she should come in it would not alter the course of the struggle due to American military weakness and tripartite strength. Tokyo was given to understand that although direct provocation of America was to be avoided, if war did come with the United States, Germany would immediately recognize her Pact obligations. As the year progressed, the tone of German advice showed that Hitler's desire to keep America out was becoming outweighed by the need for an Asian stroke to relieve the pressure in Europe. If he did not seek a Japanese-American war by his Far Eastern policy, he did urge a course of action on his allies which, in the light of what was well known about Japanese intentions, ran the most serious risk of this occurring.

* * *

The second aspect of Japanese policy which interested the Germans during this fateful year was the expansion to the south, a project with more direct implications for the United States.[19] By March the Japanese had gone far toward gaining the influence they sought in Indo-China, and Thailand, although the Dutch Indies still eluded them due partially to pressure from Great Britain and the United States.[20] Regarding Singapore, the Germans were told that although "the will to attack" was present, worries about the Anglo-American military reaction as well as the need to liquidate the Chinese "incident" all tended to restrain this operation.[21] By late June and July, the Japanese were reportedly attempting to re-

[19]For general discussion of this aspect of Japanese policy, Jones, *op cit.,* chap. VIII. American observations on various phases of this are found in *FRUS*/1941/VI, chap. 1-4.

[20]The general picture in Jones, *op cit.,* p. 238. For Anglo-American influence see Ott to Foreign Ministry 20/1/41, 21/1/41, *StS/Japan*/II/136511, 136513.

[21]Memo (Ott) 25/3/41, *DGFP/D*/XXI, p. 361. Ott to Foreign Ministry 6/6/41, *DGFP/D*/XII,p. 967. Memo (Weizsaecker) 23/1/41, *StS/Japan*/II/136524. Matsuoka told American Ambassador Steinhardt that "under no circumstances would Japan attack Singapore." Moscow Embassy to Washington 24/3/41,*FRUS*/Japan/II, p. 143.

establish their expansionist momentum, and Matsuoka told Ott that the tension in the Dutch East Indies was "unbearable" and that Singapore would be occupied in the not too distant future.[22] During the autumn, Ott reported that a drive south was possible "anytime." Faced with the inevitability of a clash with the Anglo-Saxon powers and seriously concerned about oil supplies, the armed forces, Ott reported, were now ready for acts which would involve blockade of Singapore, occupation of Thailand and the Philippines and an attack on Borneo and Sumatra. From the Washington Embassy, Berlin was also informed that the raw material problem was pushing the Japanese southward "and the Philippines must be included in this."[23] In November, Japanese naval movements in a southwestern direction were reported by the German consulate in Saigon, and Ambassador Oshima told Ribbentrop that while a full operation against Singapore was out until the following spring, a move to the south was now "unavoidable" and that the Japanese must prepare even to attack the Philippines. On November 21, Ott cabled Berlin that the time of decision was at hand on these projects, possibly including "a surprise attack on the Philippines."[24]

In all of this, the Germans were left in no doubt at all that the largest factor in Japanese calculations was the United States and that Japanese actions were bound inevitably to involve the United States, possibly militarily. In January, Ott wrote that Japanese plans were entirely in the German interest except for "the nearly certain entry of the U.S.A." The Americans were pictured as seeking to "sabotage" the new order in Asia and American concern about Japanese imperialism had been made very clear in Tokyo.[25] Matsuoka explained this state of affairs personally to Hitler and predicted a five-year guerrilla war with America as a distinct possibility.[26]

[22]Ott to Foreign Ministry 21/6/41, 4/7/41, *IMTFE/*XIX, p. 7009, 7030. In fact an imperial conference of July 2 had decided to move against Indo-China and Thailand even at the risk of war with the Anglo-Saxons. *IMTFE/*XV, pp. 6557-6559.

[23]Ott to Foreign Ministry 4/10/41,*StS/Japan/*V/60672. Ott to Foreign Ministry 11/10/41, *StS/Japan/V/60693*. Thomsen to Foreign Ministry 31/10/41, *StS/Japan/* V/60802.

[24]Saigon Consulate to Foreign Ministry 13/11/41,*StS/Japan/*V/60838. Memo (Ribbentrop) 17/11/41,*StS/Japan/*V/60868. Ott to Foreign Ministry 21/11/41, 23/11/41,*StS/Japan/*V/60885, 60897.

[25]Ott to Foreign Ministry 31/1/41, *DGFP/D/*XI, p. 1231. Ott to Foreign Ministry 4/2/41,*StS/Japan/*II/136550.

[26]Hitler-Matsuoka conference 4/4/41, *DGFP/D/*XII, p. 453.

Berlin was warned repeatedly throughout the summer of the imminent risks of American Far Eastern intervention in response to Japanese expansionist moves.[27] The German Naval Attaché in Tokyo pointed specifically to the danger of an American military reply to any operation against the Philippines, while Thomsen came forward with the flat prediction that any such move would lead "beyond doubt to an American declaration of war against Japan."[28] From Washington and Rome came further reports in September and October about American resolution to defend Singapore as well.[29] Ott, commenting on Japanese plans, warned that in the long run Japan might not be able to hold out against continuous American pressure, and might need armaments from Germany to use against the United States.[30] In November, Ott reported that military preparations for an expedition to the south had now been taken up by the armed forces "with all seriousness" and a peaceful solution no longer regarded as possible. The Ambassador was entirely convinced that the forthcoming Japanese military moves would draw the United States in since the Japanese could not avoid attacking the Philippines "on military grounds." Germany must take this fact into account and be prepared to sign a pledge of support. Ominously, Ott warned that there was now talk not only of attacking Thailand and Singapore but also of eliminating the threat posed to Japanese plans from American military forces at Guam, the Philippines *and Hawaii.*[31]

Well informed, then, of Japanese expansionist tendencies and of the inherent risk of American involvement, what advice did the German leaders tender to their allies in this matter? The essence of the line Germany was to take throughout 1941 was given on January 8 by Adolf Hitler. He told his admirals that Japan should be encouraged to expand "even if the U.S.A. is then forced to take

---

[27]Memorandum (Weizsaeker) 10/7/41, *StS/Japan/*IV/60285. Informationsstelle III 12/7/41, 2/9/41, *ibid.*, 60389, 60553. Ott to Foreign Ministry 15/7/41, 22/7/41, *ibid.*, 60325, 60395. Bangkok Embassy to Foreign Ministry 18/7/41, *ibid.*, 66369.

[28]Tokyo (Naval Attaché) to OKM 22/8/41, *ibid.*, 60518. Thomsen to Foreign Ministry 27/8/41, *ibid.*, 60529. Thomsen added that the United States might not object to a more cautious Japanese expansion in certain areas, however.

[29]Rome Embassy to Foreign Ministry 16/10/41,*StS/Japan/*V/60736. Thomsen to Foreign Ministry 26/9/41, *StS/Japan/*IV/60654. Ott had cabled the same warning about Singapore earlier. Ott to Foreign Ministry 6/6/41, *DGFP/D/*XII, p. 967.

[30]Ott to Foreign Ministry 11/10/41,*StS/Japan/*V/60713.

[31]Ott to Foreign Ministry 18/11/41, 20/11/41, *ibid.*, 60875, 60883. (Emphasis mine.)

drastic steps." Ten days later, he added in this regard that he "did not see a great danger from America even if she did come in."[32] At the *Wilhelmstrasse,* as we know, this indifference to an American entry was not fully shared although there is no record of objections from this quarter to the risky policy urged on Japan.[33]

In February Ribbentrop began to exert pressure to attack Singapore, a continuous theme of German policy toward Japan notwithstanding the equally continuous warnings that such an event might well evoke an American military response. A stroke against Singapore by Japan would, according to Ribbentrop, serve three purposes: it would be the final blow against England, it would enable Japan to secure now what she wanted after the war and it would keep America out (providing Japan did not directly attack an American position and thereby give Roosevelt a pretext). Even if the United States entered, Ribbentrop went on, it could have no effect since the Japanese fleet could easily handle a weak and divided American navy.[34]

In any event the Japanese ought to talk plainly to the Americans and give them to understand that if America should interfere in the construction of the new order in Asia they faced "an iron front."[35] Ten days later the Foreign Minister pursued these topics with Oshima with even greater urgency. It would be "a crime against the spirit of the future" for Japan to evade her responsibilities at this time. American strategic disadvantages were quite overwhelming, he emphasized, and this fact should preclude Japanese anxieties on this score. The quality and quantity of the German armament would take care of the American threat in Europe, but the Japanese ought to make a lightning attack on Singapore to present the United States with a *fait accompli* in the Pacific as well. Oshima assured the Foreign Minister that Japan was preparing to attack Singapore and

[32]*FCNA*/1941, 8-9/1/41, p. 13. Raeder testimony, *IMT/*XIV, p. 117. Ribbentrop testimony, *IMT/*X,p.297. Hitler-Mussolini conversation 20/1/41, *IMT/*XXXIV,p. 462.

[33]Weizsaeker testimony, *Case 11/*XVI, pp. 7907, 8066. Ott's concern in Memorandum (Ott) 31/1/41, *DGFP/D/*XI, pp. 1232-1233.

[34]However, naval circles were less optimistic about the outcome of a Japanese-American naval conflict. See memorandum, "Considerations on the Question of Japan in the Tripartite Pact." *OKM—KTB/*C/VII-Memo 11/2/41.

[35]Ribbentrop-Oshima conference 13/2/41, *NCA/*IV, pp. 471-475. German pressure on the Japanese was noted by Hull, *op cit.,* p. 1034.

the Philippines as well if need be. Ribbentrop sounded a note of caution on the latter point. Would it not, he asked, be better tactics for the Japanese to concentrate on Singapore, thus depriving Roosevelt of the excuse of provocation for coming in? If America then entered anyway, it would only prove that she intended to do so all along. In any case, whatever the Japanese decided to do they need not worry about the Americans, for if they were so foolish as to send their fleet beyond Hawaii, the Japanese navy would, Ribbentrop was sure, "do a complete job," and thus bring the war to a rapid conclusion.[36]

More comprehensive general directives for activating Japanese policy in the Far East were contained in basic order number 24 of March 5. "The aim of the cooperation initiated by the Tripartite Pact must be to bring Japan into active operations in the Far East as soon as possible." The purpose of this was to harass the English and thereby "precisely to keep America out of the war" since that country was in no position to fight Japan. Hitler three weeks later told his admirals that Japan should attack Singapore "as soon as possible" and should do so without fear since the Americans could not possibly cope with Japanese naval power.[37]

The arrival in Berlin of Matsuoka in March gave the Germans an opportunity to press their views in person. At the first meeting on March 29, Ribbentrop spent most of the time explaining American weaknesses to his Japanese colleague. American submarines, for example, were described as so bad "that Japan need not bother at all about them."[38] In meetings on the following two days, Matsuoka expressed Japanese anxieties regarding America and drew a picture of the dangers of a five- or ten-year guerrilla war with the United States. Ribbentrop would have none of it. America, he assured his visitor, undermining a caution he expressed on other occasions, would not fight, even for the Philippines. The Americans would never venture beyond Hawaii and therefore the Japanese should go

---

[36]Oshima-Ribbentrop conference 23/2/41, *DGFP/D/*XII, p. 143. See also Memo (Weizsaeker) 22/2/41, *StS/Japan/*II/136576.

[37]Basic order 24, 5/3/41, U.S. Department of State *Nazi Conspiracy and Aggression,* 8 vols. plus Supps. A and B (Washington, 1946-48), VI, pp. 906, 907. Fuehrer conference 18/3/41, U.S. Navy Department, *Fuehrer Conferences on Matters Dealing with the German Navy, 1939-1945,* 7 vols. (Washington, 1947), III, p. 37. See also Ribbentrop to Tokyo embassy 27/3/41, *DGFP/D/*XII, p. 183.

[38]Ribbentrop-Matsuoka conference 29/3/41, *NCA/*IV, p. 521.

right ahead and not squander "this unique moment of history."[39] (History for Ribbentrop was filled with "unique moments.")

On April 1, Hitler himself reiterated these points to the Foreign Minister. "Never in human imagination could there be better conditions for a joint effort of the Tripartite Pact countries . . . seldom has a risk been smaller." With England preoccupied, the United States unarmed, the U.S.S.R. facing one hundred and eighty divisions and German disinterest in the Far East, what more could Japan desire? Turning to America, there were, he explained, three courses of action open to that country: to arm herself, to aid England or to face a two-front war. The first two were long-range propositions and in any event mutually exclusive, while the third was strategically unthinkable. Therefore, America was no factor at all. Matsuoka agreed with everything, but unfortunately he had to admit that not everyone in Japan was of this persuasion. "Certain circles" in Tokyo made life very difficult for him, he explained, and thus he could not really make any pledge at this time regarding Singapore. All he could say was that a Japanese attack would occur "someday." Hitler's disappointment at this letdown may have been visible, for Matsuoka hastened to add that the whole problem was that the Japanese "had not yet found their Fuehrer."[40]

On April 4, there was another meeting between Hitler and Matsuoka which is of the greatest interest. Matsuoka raised again the likelihood of an American military reaction to an attack on Singapore. Hitler admitted that this was undesirable but assured the Foreign Minister that provision had already been made for this contingency. Adding now a significant new inducement to the arguments already employed, Hitler explained that "Germany on her part would immediately take the consequences if Japan should get involved with the United States." The exact circumstances and origins of the involvement were not important. "It does not matter with whom the United States first gets involved, Germany or Japan. Germany would strike without delay." Matsuoka then informed Hitler that Japan was in fact already preparing for war with America and, since the conflict was inevitable anyway, was considering the wisdom of striking the first blow. Hitler entirely subscribed to these comments.[41] In spite of a post-war denial that at this meeting Hitler

[39]Ribbentrop-Matsuoka conference 31/3/41, 1/4/41, *DGFP/D/*XII, pp. 381, 389.
[40]Hitler-Matsuoka conference 1/4/41, *DGFP/D/*XII, p. 386.
[41]Hitler-Matsuoka conference 4/4/41, *DGFP/D/*XII, p. 453.

had presented Japan with a blank check to attack the United States,[42] it is obvious at the very least that Hitler was perfectly aware of the risk that Japanese expansion would involve American intervention and that he was at this point quite prepared to take this risk and underwrite the Japanese effort to the point of going to war with America.

* * *

With the opening of conversations between Secretary Hull and Ambassador Nomura in February [1941], which were to last with interruptions down to the final days before Pearl Harbor, German anxieties were sharply aroused. The Nazi leaders were especially worried that the talks would weaken the image of the Pact in American eyes.[43]

As the talks between Hull and Nomura got underway, both Hitler and Ribbentrop urged that if the Japanese really had to go on with them, they should at least use them as an instrument of tripartite solidarity by taking a stiff line with the Roosevelt administration.[44] "The United States," Ribbentrop informed Oshima, "had to understand that any aggressive ambitions would find themselves up against an iron wall of determined nations, one which comprised virtually the whole world." [45]

This initial hope that Japan would use the negotiations to intimidate America received a rude shock with the report of an interview Nomura had given American journalists in Washington. In

[42]Meissner testimony, *Case 11/X*, p. 4545. This view does receive some support from the comment Matsuoka made to U.S. Ambassador Steinhardt in Moscow on his return voyage. Matsuoka had the impression, or so he told the American, that Hitler and Mussolini wanted to avoid war with America. Steinhardt to Hull 11/4/41, *FRUS*/Japan/II,p.184.

[43]Opening of the Hull-Nomura talks, Memo (Hull) 8/3/41, *FRUS*/Japan/II, p. 389. Kordt testified after the war that the German Embassy in Tokyo tried to heighten German anxieties on the subject in order to make Berlin more aware of the dangers of an American intervention. Kordt testimony, *Case 11/XV*, p. 7426. See also Ott testimony, *Case 11/XXI*, pp. 10175, 10176. The Pact issue was in fact raised by Hull early in the proceedings. Memo (Hull) 14/3/41, *FRUS*/Japan/II, p. 396. Hull, *op. cit.*, p. 1061.

[44]Hitler-Kurusu meeting 3/2/41, *DGFP/D/XII*, p. 9. Ribbentrop-Oshima conference 23/2/41, *ibid.*, p. 139. Wakamatsu affidavit, *IMTFE/LXXV*, p. 33702.

[45]Ribbentrop-Oshima conference 23/2/41, *DGFP/D/XII*, p. 139. The text of this conference was sent to Ott with instructions to continue pressure along these lines in Tokyo. Foreign Ministry to Tokyo Embassy 28/2/41, *StS/Japan/II/136587*.

this, he had characterized the issue of whether an American war with Germany meant one with Japan as well as "a question of treaty interpretation which I do not want to go into."[46] Ribbentrop immediately fired off an angry cable to Ott demanding explanations. The issue was, Ott was to tell the Japanese, "unequivocally clarified by the text of the Pact." It would have been more expedient if Nomura had simply referred to that text.[47]

The Matsuoka visit to Berlin late in March provided renewed opportunities for pressure to be firm with the Americans, as well as, as we have seen, encouragement to expand regardless of the United States. The Foreign Minister reminded his Japanese colleague that the goal of the Pact was "to frighten America into abandoning the course she has chosen." In accomplishing this purpose, the Japanese had their vital role to play by being unyielding and by refusing to sign any agreement with the United States.[48] Hitler made the same point to the Japanese diplomat on March 4. In the latter meeting, he assured Japan that regardless of which country became involved first in war against America, Germany or Japan, Germany would "take the necessary steps at once." He warned that the Americans "would always be interested in disposing of one country first, not with the idea of coming to an agreement with the other, but with the idea of disposing of it next." Therefore, a bold and united front must be shown or the Pact partners might be defeated separately.[49]

On May 11, Ribbentrop instructed Ott to tell the Japanese that the war in which the Axis was now engaged was in fact "a death struggle" for Japan as well. The defeat of Germany and Italy would leave the Japanese to face an overpowering Anglo-Saxon coalition which might also include the Soviet Union. It was essential to make Roosevelt's decisions as difficult as possible. Japan simply could not allow the President to inject an element of uncertainty into this proposition through Japanese equivocation. Ribbentrop then got more specific. The Japanese, he wrote, must surely be aware that Roosevelt was waging a *de facto* war against Germany through a continuous series of unneutral acts. Under these circumstances, the

[46]Thomsen to Foreign Ministry 21/2/41, *ibid.,* 136573.

[47]Ribbentrop to Tokyo 24/2/41, *DGFP/D*/XII, p. 154. Ott to Foreign Ministry 25/2/41, 27/2/41,*StS/Japan*/II/13653, 136585. Ott to Foreign Ministry 6/3/41, *ibid.,* 136615.

[48]Ribbentrop-Matsuoka conference 31/3/41, *DGFP/D*/XII, p. 376.

[49]Hitler-Matsuoka conference 1/4/41, 4/4/41, *DGFP/D*/XII, pp. 386, 453.

Japanese ought to tell the Americans flatly that in their view American policy had been unneutral and that a continuation of this policy by such means as patrol activity or convoys would "be considered as a deliberate step toward war" and consequently would unfailingly compel Japan also to enter the war immediately. Finally, Ribbentrop ordered Ott to request to see a text of any reply Japan should make to American proposals.[50]

However in spite of "vigorous initiatives on my part," Ott was not able to prevent the dispatch of instructions to Nomura prior to German inspection.[51] When he did see them, after the fact, he was appalled. "This instruction," he informed Matsuoka, "breathes an atmosphere from which even the mildest criticism of America's unneutral conduct is excluded." It amounted in Ott's view in fact to "a legitimation of America's intimidation policy," since it suggested a renunciation of the new order envisioned by the Triangle Pact and in addition went "very far in relieving America in the Pacific." Matsuoka's only response was to dismiss the contents of the message as "figures of speech" and to ask the Germans to have confidence in him. Ott was not impressed by these explanations, although considering the bellicose tone Matsuoka adopted that same day with U.S. Ambassador Grew, the plea for confidence was not entirely unjustified. To Ribbentrop the Japanese action was "inexplicable" and Tokyo, he feared, was already "on the downward path."[52]

During the summer Ribbentrop kept up a steady stream of reminders to Tokyo. The Japanese, if they thought for a moment of coming to an agreement with the Anglo-Saxons, were pursuing "an extraordinarily short-sighted policy" and ought to be told this.[53] The

---

[50]Ribbentrop to Ott 11/5/41, *ibid.,* p. 777. Ott to Foreign Ministry 11/5/41, *ibid.,* p. 753. Langer and Gleason believe that mid-May offered the best hope for a Japanese-American settlement and that German pressure was paramount in preventing it. *The Undeclared War,* p. 477.

[51]Ott to Foreign Ministry 13/5/41, *DGFP/D/*XIII, p. 794.

[52]Ott to Foreign Ministry 14/5/41, *ibid.,* p. 806. The text of the instructions is found in *FRUS/*Japan/II, pp. 420-425. Matsuoka was not entirely unjustified in requesting German confidence. He had told Grew that Hitler had shown "patience and generosity" toward American provocation and that an American attack on German submarines would be regarded by Japan as "an act of American aggression." Grew to Roosevelt 14/5/41, *ibid.,* p. 145. Ribbentrop to Tokyo Embassy 15/5/41, *DGFPff/*XII, pp. 820-821.

[53]Ribbentrop to Tokyo Embassy 10/7/41,*StS/Japan/*IV/60285. Ribbentrop to Tokyo Embassy 19/7/41, *ibid.,* 60372. Ott to Foreign Ministry 21/7/41, *ibid.,* 60395.

problem, as he saw it, was that the Japanese were not aware of their own strength and of the weakness of the United States and Great Britain. Ott was requested to make the following points absolutely clear to the Japanese: Germany had triumphed in Russia ("the core of the red army has been destroyed"); the failure of the United States to carry through reprisals against the Japanese for the occupation of Indo-China, coupled with the verbal emptiness which resulted from the Atlantic conference, gave the real picture of the American situation. It was now clear that American threats to Japan were an "obvious sign of weakness and proof that America does not dare militarily to undertake anything serious against Japan." It was equally well known that the American people opposed war, except for "articles in Jewish newspapers." Thus there was every reason for the Japanese to call this bluff without delay.[54]

Roosevelt's "shoot at sight" speech in September, which had so alarmed German naval circles, offered a new opportunity of reminding the Japanese of their proper role regarding the United States. Ribbentrop described the speech as an attempt by Roosevelt to picture Germany as the aggressor, thus relieving Japan of her obligations in the event of a German-American war. The President wanted to "explode the triangle" and remove the prospect of a two-front war, than which "there is nothing the American people fear so much." Germany would not yield to these provocations in the Atlantic, Ribbentrop went on, but the Japanese must certainly recognize by now that under the circumstances negotiations with America were "hopeless." The Japanese had now at long last to make clear to the Americans by "an unmistakable declaration" that a further step by Roosevelt on the road to aggression against the Axis would lead necessarily to war "against the triumphant alliance." Foreign Minister Toyoda could only ask once again that Germany "trust Japan that the negotiations with America are being conducted in the spirit of the alliance."[55]

In October, Japanese diplomats in Washington and Tokyo com-

---

[54]Ribbentrop to Tokyo Embassy 25/8/41, *ibid.* Ott got the usual vague reply to this polemic. Ott to Foreign Ministry 28/7/41, Microfilm records of the German Foreign Ministry, Under Secretary's File, Japan-America, frame 24984. See also Ott to Foreign Ministry 5/9/41, 12/9/41,*StS/Japan*/IV/60581, 60602, in which Ott demanded "something authoritative" about the Japanese reponses to America.

[55]Ribbentrop to Tokyo Embassy 13/9/41,*StS/Japan*/IV/60606. Ott to Foreign Ministry 13/9/41, *ibid.* Toyoda replied in general terms but again refused to let the German Ambassador see the texts of the Japanese replies to Washington.

plained to their American counterparts that German representations to be firm with America had become "exceedingly powerful"; that the Germans were "insatiably pressing" the Japanese for a flat statement that Japan would declare war on America in the event of a German-American conflict.[56] The Germans seemed especially anxious during this month to counteract any tendency of American policy moves to intimidate the Japanese or weaken their resolve. Repeal of the Neutrality Acts and the arming of merchant ships simply made it all the more urgent to adopt, in the triangle spirit, a firm line for, as Ribbentrop put it early in November, the weaker the Japanese appeared, "the stronger the threat of Mr. Roosevelt."[57]

The final hectic weeks were now at hand. The pressures within the triangle dramatically shifted their direction and German Far Eastern policy was overtaken by the preparation and execution of the attack on Pearl Harbor. This basic train of events was set in motion at a cabinet meeting in Tokyo on November 5. At this meeting the Japanese government decided to continue negotiations until November 25 while proceeding with war preparations in case the talks should break down. Meanwhile, if the outlook for the discussions grew dim, the Japanese were to sound out their triangle partners on support in the event of a Japanese-American war, the decision for which, however, was to be taken independently and regardless of Axis support.[58]

Carrying forward these directives, proposals were submitted to Washington "as a last possible bargain."[59] This was followed a week later by the dispatch of the former Japanese Ambassador at Berlin, Kurusu, to assist Admiral Nomura in these efforts. The Germans did not know of the specific cabinet decisions but Ott's dispatches during this time warned repeatedly that government and public opinion alike were being steeled for conflict, that pro-American sentiment had dried up and that military preparations were being accelerated.[60] Foreign Minister Togo personally assured Ott that

[56]Welles-Wakasugi conference 13/10/41, *FRUS*/Japan/II, p. 680. Memo (Grew) 15/10/41, *ibid.,* p. 686.

[57]Ott to Foreign Ministry 28/10/41, 31/10/41, *StS/Japan/*V/60796, 60798. Ribbentrop to Tokyo Embassy 9/11/41, *ibid.,* 60829.

[58]Cabinet meeting 5/11/41, *IMTFE*/XXX, pp. 10333-10338.

[59]These were the so-called "A" and "B" proposals. *FRUS*/Japan/II, pp. 709, 755. Grew had warned that Japanese military action might come with "dramatic and dangerous suddenness." Grew to Roosevelt 3/11/41, *ibid.,* p. 704.

[60]Ott to Foreign Ministry 5/11/41,*StS/Japan/*V/60810.

Kurusu would negotiate only "within the firm bound ties of the Pact which cannot now be overstepped" while Ambassador Oshima in Berlin confirmed that the Kurusu mission would be an almost certain failure, after which foreign policy with America would have to be "activated."[61] A public speech by Prime Minister Tojo, which was sent on to Germany, seemed to confirm all of this: the Pact was eulogized, the Anglo-Saxons termed "a vital threat" and Japanese-American relations pictured as so bad that "catastrophe" threatened.[62]

Still more ominous in the days following the November 5 meeting was the noticeable reversal of the flow of diplomatic pressure between Berlin and Tokyo. The *Japanese* now began to press the *Germans* regarding Pact obligations in the event of a Japanese-American war. The soundings were begun by diplomatic and military representatives to try and ensure triangle solidarity in the forthcoming conflict.[63] On November 21, Ribbentrop replied to these overtures unequivocally. He instructed Ott to tell the Japanese that in the event of a war with the United States, Germany's involvement was *"selbstverstaendlich"* (automatic), that there could be no separate peace "in the event of a war between Germany or Japan and the United States for any reason whatsoever" and that Germany would be quite prepared to lay down a specific agreement in writing to this effect.[64] The Japanese War Minister expressed gratification to Ott that in the event of such a war Japan "would not be left in the lurch." However, he wanted to be quite certain on one point: did the Japanese understand it correctly that Germany would stand by Japan *"even in the event of Japan opening the war against the U.S.A.?"* (my italics). Ott's reply was definite: "I referred him to the [Ribbentrop] statement and to our readiness to sign a mutual agreement on the subject."[65]

This was the situation two weeks before Pearl Harbor. The final decision to fight was taken by the Japanese on November 27. Again, the German diplomats did not know of this specifically but the

---

[61]Ott to Foreign Ministry 6/11/41, *ibid.,* 60819. Memorandum (Erdmannsdorf) 13/11/41, *ibid.,* 60846. Thomsen to Foreign Ministry 15/11/41, *ibid.,* 60856.

[62]Ott to Foreign Ministry 17/11/41, *ibid.,* 60859.

[63]Ott to Foreign Ministry 5/11/41, 6/11/41, *ibid.,* 60810, 60819. Memorandum (Weizsaeker) 7/11/41, *StS/USA/IX/422316.* Ott to Foreign Ministry 18ff1/41, *StS/Japan/V/60873.* Kretschmar testimony, *IMTFE/LIX,* p. 24643.

[64]Ribbentrop to Tokyo Embassy 21/11/41,*StS/Japan/V/60879.*

[65]Ott to Foreign Ministry 23/11/41, *ibid.,* 60897.

reports reaching Berlin in these final two weeks were somber in the extreme regarding a Japanese-American conflict. The struggle within the Tokyo government had now reached "the decisive stage," Berlin was told. If the United States did not yield now, "the most extreme consequences for which America alone carries the responsibility are unavoidable." The Japanese reaction to the American "comprehensive settlement" (which had proposed, *inter alia,* a virtual nullification of Japan's role in the Triangle Pact) had been met by a mood of "grim resistance," and intensified military preparations, according to Ott.[66]

The only question in the Ambassador's mind was whether at this late stage the Americans could still think that the Japanese were bluffing.[67] On November 30, the Japanese Ambassador at Berlin was instructed by Foreign Minister Togo to transmit the news officially to Hitler and Ribbentrop that the Washington talks had collapsed, that Japan would have to resort to military measures to curtail the American threat and that there was "an extreme danger of war" between the two countries which "may come quicker than anyone dreams."[68] On December 3, Ott cabled Berlin that "the critical point is at hand," that the rudeness *(Schoffheit)* of the American ultimatum had extinguished all hope of peace and that military operations could now be expected "in the nearest future."[69] On December 5, in the final notes before Pearl Harbor, Ott spoke of the destruction of "the last rays of hope" and "the unavoidable conflict with the United States."[70]

Meanwhile, with full knowledge of the extremely perilous state of

[66]Ott to Foreign Ministry 20/11/41, 21/11/41, *ibid.,* 60883, 60885. The American proposals of 26/11/41, in *FRUS*/Japan/II, pp. 768-770. Japanese reaction in Ott to Foreign Ministry, *StS/Japan*/V/60901.

[67]Liaison conference 27/11/41, IMTFE/LXXX, p. 35706. Ott to Foreign Ministry 29/11/41,*StS/Japan*/V/60995. Thomsen to Foreign Ministry 29/11/41, 3/12/41, *ibid.,* 60099, 60920.

[68]Tokyo to Embassy in Berlin 30/11/41, *NCA*/VI, p. 308.

[69]Ott to Foreign Ministry 3/12/41,*StS/Japan*/V/80924. On the same day, the Japanese Ambassador at Rome told Mussolini that "the outlook for a conflict between Japan and the United States . . . must now be regarded as possible and due to start immediately." Ciano, *Diary* 3/12/41, p. 461.

[70]Ott to Foreign Ministry 5/12/41, *UStS/Japan-Amerika*/25043. Ott to Foreign Ministry 5/12/41, *StS/USA*/X/44731. The German Naval Attaché at Tokyo cabled on December 6 that the Japanese armed forces had decided on war with the United States three weeks previously. An attack was expected before Christmas. *NCA,* sup. A, pp. 991, 992. However it is doubtful if this reached the Foreign Ministry prior to the news of Pearl Harbor.

Japanese-American relations, including a cable from Ott the previous week specifically mentioning Hawaii as a possible target, Ribbentrop continued to give the Japanese all the assurances they could wish at a crucial interview with Ambassador Oshima at the *Wilhelmstrasse* on November 29. He summoned the Ambassador to tell him that it was "essential for Japan to effect the new order in East Asia without losing this opportunity." Oshima first reminded the Foreign Minister that there was no hope of peace between America and Japan and then sought to pin him down by asking him point blank if war between Japan and America under any circumstances would mean an automatic German-American war as well. Ribbentrop seemed to draw back for the moment and merely replied that "Roosevelt is a fanatic and it is impossible to tell what he would do." However, later in the conference, Ribbentrop asserted that "Germany would of course join the war immediately." And once having joined it, she would sign no separate peace. "The Fuehrer," he added, "is determined on that point."[71]

Ribbentrop after the war accused Oshima of misinterpreting his words and Oshima himself at the Tokyo trial disclaimed any recollection of Ribbentrop's assurances, adding that even if he (Ribbentrop) had said such things, "it was just for effect."[72] If true, it is difficult to see what "effect" the Reich Foreign Minister could have been seeking in this case. In addition, we have Ribbentrop's earlier statement on the matter given by Ott in Tokyo and Oshima's own cable on the conversation in which he expressed the conviction that on the basis of what Ribbentrop had said, "Germany would not refuse to fight."[73] To make the position even clearer, when Ott was summoned to the Japanese Foreign Ministry on November 30 and told that "the Japanese did not fear the rupture of relations and hoped that for their part Germany and Italy would stand by Japan in accordance with the Pact," Ott replied that of Germany's position in the event of a Japanese-American war "there could be no doubt." When Togo asked if he could assume that Germany in this case "viewed its relationship to Japan as a complete community of fate," Ott replied affirmatively and reiterated German willingness to sign an agreement in the matter.[74]

[71]Ribbentrop-Oshima conference 29/11/41, *NCA*/VII, pp. 160-162. Ott to Foreign Ministry 20/11/41, 21/11/41, *StS/Japan*/V/60883, 00885.
[72]Ribbentrop testimony, *IMT/X*, p. 38. Oshima affidavit, *IMTFE/LXXVI*, pp. 34030-34033.
[73]Oshima to Tokyo 29/11/41, *NCA*/VII, p. 160.
[74]Ott to Foreign Ministry 30/11/41,*StS/Japan/V*/60917.

This is precisely what the Japanese now set about to arrange. Instructions were sent from Tokyo on December 2 to start negotiations on a "no separate peace" pact. Although it will be recalled that the Germans had by this time been warned of "an extreme danger of war" which might come "quicker than anyone dreams," Berlin encouraged the project.[75] Ribbentrop accepted in principle on December 5 an agreement providing for complete mutuality of obligation covering all aspects of a war between the United States and any tripartite member, including full military support.[76] On the same day Ott cabled the news that war with America was now "unavoidable" and that Japan assumed that its outbreak under any circumstances would be a *casus foederis.* Events had now overtaken diplomacy (there had been some delay in contacting Hitler at the front) and before the pact could be signed a cable from Tokyo dated December 7 explained why this formality was no longer needed.[77]

* * *

The attack on Pearl Harbor was unilateral in the sense that the Germans had not been informed of the specific target. Thus, the surprise in Berlin was undoubtedly genuine. Yet this surprise did not occasion any hesitation about going to war with America although, since Japan was the aggressor, there was no legal obligation to do so.[78] Hitler's reasons for declaring war so quickly and before America had done so are not entirely clear. According to Ribbentrop, Hitler by December had decided that the American policy in the Atlantic had "practically created a state of war" and that, therefore, the declaration was merely a formality. In addition, Ribbentrop quoted Hitler as saying that the Japanese would "never forget if we do not take the consequences."[79] Moreover, national and personal prestige probably entered in. Erich Kordt quotes Hitler

[75]Togo to Oshima 2/12/41, *IMTFE/LVIII*, p. 24031. Tokyo to Oshima 30/11/41, *NCA/VI*, p. 308. Oshima to Tokyo 2/12/41, *IMTFE/LXXVI*, p. 34031.

[76]Oshima to Tokyo 5/12/41, in Jones, *op cit.,* p. 327. Mussolini had assured the Japanese on December 3 on the same point. Ciano quotes the Duce as follows: "Thus we arrive at a war between continents, which I have foreseen since 1939." Ciano, *Diary* 3/12/41, pp. 405-406.

[77]Ott to Foreign Ministry 5/12/41, *UStS/Japan-Amerika/25043*. Tokyo to Oshima 7/12/41, in Jones, *op. cit.,* p. 328.

[78]Weizsaeker described the German declaration as "a judicial error and a political mistake." Weizsaeker, *op. cit.,* p. 328. Ribbentrop agreed on the legal point, *IMT/X*, p. 297.

[79]*Ibid.,* p. 298. Ribbentrop, *op cit.,* p. 170. See reference to Hitler statement in *NYT* 2/11/41.

as remarking that "a great power like Germany declares war itself and does not wait for war to be declared on it," while the interpreter, Dr. Schmidt, had the impression that Hitler wanted to precede Roosevelt with the war declaration for reasons of personal prestige.[80]

We must above all remember Hitler's state of mind in those early December days. Slowed by rain in October and encountering unexpected Russian resistance, Barbarossa had not been going well as the winter set in. On November 24, General von Kleist's armored group had been defeated, and during the first week in December the German drive ground to a halt and was even thrown into reverse in the snows around Moscow. For the first time Hitler was experiencing defeat—and that in a theater where victory was to have brought all other successes in its train. The frosty recollection of Napoleon's Grand Army was no doubt present as Hitler mused upon this situation. In these circumstances, the sudden attack at Pearl Harbor must have seemed to the destiny-conscious mind of the Fuehrer one of those fateful strokes to which a "world historical figure" must respond.[81]

In any event there is testimony that surprise in Berlin soon turned to "an ecstasy of rejoicing" and the entry of the Japanese into the war was viewed then as "a deliverance" and "a new lease on life." Hitler's speech to the Reichstag on December 11 consisted, as we have seen in an earlier chapter, largely of violent personal abuse of Roosevelt coupled with distinct expressions of relief that German-American relations had finally come to a head. The declaration was duly dispatched to Washington,[82] and Hitler evidently came to feel a

---

[80] *Wahn und Wirklichkeit* (Stuttgart, 1948), p. 325. Paul Schmidt, *Statist auf diplomatischer Bühne, 1923-1945* (Bonn, 1949), p. 554.

[81] This was quite ironic, for precisely at the moment of Hitler's exultant war declaration on the United States, the Russians, informed in advance (possibly by the German comintern agent Richard Sorge) that the Japanese did not intend to strike northwards, had been able to throw against the Germans crucial reinforcements withdrawn from the Far East. From this moment, Barbarossa was probably doomed. J. Erickson, *The Soviet High Command,* pp. 599, 631, 662. (London, 1962). For Hitler's mood see also General Warlimont's statement that Hitler was "literally mesmerized by his concept of the political situation" and unable to grasp its ultimate implications. Warlimont, *op. cit.,* p. 50.

[82] *Wahn und Wirklichkeit,* pp. 311, 325. Franz von Papen, *Memoirs* (London, 1281-1952), 484. Ribbentrop sounded "joyful" to Ciano on the telephone. "He was so happy in fact that I congratulated him even though I am not so sure of the advantages." *Diary,* 8/12/41, p. 407. Hitler's Reichstag speech of December 11, in Gordon W. Prange, ed., *Hitler's Words* (Washington, 1944), pp. 367-377. Walter

certain pride in the Pearl Harbor attack as a proper method of conducting international relations. "You gave the right declaration of war," he told Oshima.[83] This was the way Germany handled things. . . . When Ribbentrop gave his opinion that "the alliance thus brought about what we had wanted to avoid at all costs: a war between Germany and America,"[84] he attributed far too much substance to the Tripartite Pact. All of the weaknesses so glaringly apparent in German-Japanese relations from the signing of the Anti-Comintern Pact down to the establishment of the "world triangle" were manifest during 1941. There had still been no agreement on a proper picture for the frame. Even the common goal of intimidating America was viewed from quite different perspectives. There was no real community of interest, for the Japanese were receptive to German suggestions according to the needs of national policy and the state of balance between pro- and anti-Axis elements in the government. Yet the evidence does not support the view that German pressure was without weight in Japanese decisions or that the fate of Germany was irrelevant. In the question of how the Germans used such influence as they had, the matter of intention as well as tendency naturally arises.

According to the Nuremberg prosecutor, "Japan was given every encouragement to adopt a policy which would almost certainly bring the United States into the war."[85] Not surprisingly, this allegation was disputed at the trial and in other post-war testimony. Ribbentrop told the tribunal that Germany had done everything right down to Pearl Harbor to keep America out, and several of the diplomats, expressing rare agreement with their former chief, upheld this view. Weizsaeker added that Germany had been anxious for Japan to enter the war against Great Britain and the Soviet Union but not against America.[86] General Jodl declared that "we should have

---

Warlimont, *Inside Hitler's Headquarters* (London, 1964), p. 207. Ribbentrop to Washington Embassy 11/12/41, *FRUS/1941/I*, p. 588. Japan requested Germany to declare war at once. Tokyo to Foreign Ministry 8/12/41, *StS/ USA*/44742. Louis Lochner has recorded his impression that most Berliners thought Hitler too clever to declare war on America after Pearl Harbor, Lochner, *What About Germany?* (New York, 1942), 199-200.

[83]Hitler-Oshima conference 14/12/41, *NCA*/V, p. 603.

[84]Ribbentrop, *op cit.,* p. 159.

[85]*IMT*/XXII, p. 458.

[86]Ribbentrop testimony, *IMT*/X, p. 379. Kordt testimony, *Case 11*/XV, p. 7430. Woermann testimony, *ibid.,* pp. 11251, 11257. Ernst von Weizsaeker, *Erinnerungen* (Munich, 1950), p. 325.

much preferred a new and powerful ally without a new and powerful enemy" in speaking of the circumstances of the Japanese entry into the war. The only dissenting post-war testimony on the German side comes from Captain Reinecke, formerly of the operations staff of the *Oberkommando der Marine*. Testifying at the diplomats' trial, he recalled hearing plans for pushing the Japanese into the war against "the enemies and potential enemies of Germany, including the United States."[87]

The evidence generally supports the view that Germany would have preferred a Japanese attack elsewhere. The immediate intention was not to goad Tokyo into a direct attack on the United States.[88] In urging triangle unity the Germans may well have believed sincerely that America could have been sidetracked. Moreover, a certain indifference to American involvement based on belief in her military weakness as well as the denial of any real basis for entry through rapid Japanese action undoubtedly played a role. However, this does not undermine the assertion of the Nuremberg prosecutor as to the tendency of German pressure nor acquit the Berlin regime of the knowledge that what they were urging the Japanese to do ran at least the gravest risk of provoking America into the war. That risk was plainly there, as it had been in the Atlantic. But in the Pacific Hitler was prepared to take it, especially as his dream of Eastern *Lebensraum* began to go sour.

By pressing upon Tokyo the virtual inevitability of a Japanese-American war, by stressing American military weakness and bluff, by urging an attack on Russia and on American supplies to that country, by encouraging a southward expansion in the full knowledge that this must involve vital American interests, by advocating that the Japanese adopt a completely uncompromising attitude in their relations with America and finally in the face of continuous and dire warnings of imminent hostilities by promising the Japanese full military and political support even if Japan were the aggressor, Berlin made itself a party to the course of events which culminated in the attack of December 7. The German surprise at Pearl Harbor was genuine, but this is merely a sad reflection on the inability of the German leadership to grasp the implications of their own deliberate and increasingly reckless policy in the Far East.

---

[87]Jodl testimony, *IMT*/XV, p. 398. Reinecke testimony, *Case 11*/IV, p. 1904.

[88]As late as December 5, Ott requested that the Japanese avoid a direct attack on American territory. Ott to Foreign Ministry 5/12/41, *UStS/Japan-Amerika*/25043.

This policy, in spite of disclaimers of the intention of doing so, in fact played a substantial role in converting the European conflict into the Second World War.

LOUIS MORTON
Japan's Decision for War (1941)

Louis Morton (born 1913) is Professor of History at Dartmouth College. He was Chief, Pacific Section, of the Office of Military History in the United States Army during 1946-1960, and has authored numerous articles and books, including *War in the Pacific* and *Strategy and Command* (1963).

FEW IF ANY of the fateful decisions of history are as well documented as the one Japan made on December 1, 1941, to go to war with the United States and Great Britain. The sequence of events that led to this decision has been described in rich detail and at first hand by those who played the leading roles in this drama of national suicide, and, with somewhat more detachment, by the students of diplomacy and Far Eastern affairs. The rise and fall of cabinets in prewar Japan, the confidential deliberations of its highest political bodies, the tortuous path of its diplomacy, and the views of its most influential leaders have been analyzed and illuminated by jurists and scholars alike. For those who wish to retrace the road to Pearl Harbor, the signposts are indeed numerous and the way well lighted.

Not so well charted is the course taken by the Japanese Army and Navy to gain by force what the politicians and diplomats could not win by negotiation. The path is a faint one, but the journey along it rewards the traveler with an understanding of the strange mixture of reality and illusion which led Japan to attack the most powerful nations in the Pacific. It confirms and clarifies, too, the role of the military in Japan's political life and makes clear how the needs and

From Kent Roberts Greenfield (ed.), *Command Decisions* (New York: Harcourt, Brace and Co., 1959). Reprinted from *Proceedings* by permission; Copyright © 1954 U.S. Naval Institute.

capacities of the Army and Navy at once established and limited national objectives and ambitions. And along this path lies the explanation for Japan's dramatic blow against Pearl Harbor and its choice of time, place, and method of attack.[1]

The Army in Japan traditionally stood for a course of expansion which would make Japan the unchallenged leader of Asia. In 1936 the Army gained a predominant position in the political life of the nation and its program became the official policy of the government, and since then it had been preparing for war. The program adopted in that year called for, among other things, the establishment of a "firm position" on the Asiatic Continent—a euphemistic way of saying that China must be conquered; expansion into southeast Asia to secure the bases and raw materials needed to make Japan economically strong and self-sufficient; strengthening the military forces of the nation; development of critical war industries; and the improvement of air and sea transportation.[2]

Though this program was to be achieved gradually and peacefully, if possible, it clearly implied military action both in China and in southeast Asia. And to prepare for that contingency, the Japanese Government turned all its efforts into military channels. In 1936, appropriations for military expenditures rose sharply and continued to rise thereafter. The entire economy of the nation was placed under rigid controls and oriented toward war; heavy industries were expanded, the production of aircraft and munitions was increased,

---

[1]The substance of the present essay is contained in the author's article entitled "The Japanese Decision for War," published in *U.S. Naval Institute Proceedings,* LXXX (December, 1954), 1325-34. Other published accounts in English of the event leading to Japan's decision may be found in Herbert Feis, *The Road to Pearl Harbor* (Princeton: Princeton University Press, 1950); Samuel Eliot Morison, *History of United States Naval Operations in World War II,* Vol. III: *The Rising Sun in the Pacific, 1931-April 1942* (Boston: Little, Brown, 1948); the two volumes of William L. Langer and S. Everett Gleason, *Challenge to Isolation* (New York: Harper, 1952), and *The Undeclared War, 1940-1941* (New York: Harper, 1953); U.S. Department of State, *Foreign Relations of the United States, Japan: 1931-1941* (Washington, 1943). A number of other works dealing in part with this subject will be found in the present author's critical essay on the bibliography of the Pearl Harbor attack published in *U.S. Naval Institute Proceedings,* Vol. 81, No. 4 (April, 1955), 462-69.

[2]International Military Tribunal of the Far East (IMTFE), Exhibit 216; Political Strategy Prior to the Outbreak of War, Part I, App. I, Japanese Studies in World War II, No. 147. These Japanese studies were written by Japanese Army and Navy officers at the direction of G-2, Far East Command. Mimeographed translations are on file at OCMH.

and every effort was made to stockpile weapons, equipment, and strategic raw materials.[3]

The shortage of oil was the key to Japan's military situation. It was the main problem for those preparing for war, and, at the same time, the reason why the nation was moving toward war. For the Navy the supply of oil was critical; for the Army it was always a limiting factor. And none of the measures taken to curtail civilian consumption or to manufacture substitutes ever gave Japan enough of this precious commodity to free it from the restraint exercised by the Dutch, the British, and the Americans, who controlled the sources of supply. Without oil, Japan's pretensions to empire were empty shadows.[4]

Japan's move into China in July 1937, eight months after it had signed the Anti-Comintern Pact with Germany, produced further difficulties. The vigor of the Chinese reaction soon led to full-scale war, an eventuality the Japanese military neither expected nor desired. Moreover, the United States, like other nations with interests in China, refused to acquiesce in this fresh assault on the *status quo* in Asia. In unmistakable terms, it made clear to Japan that it still stood by the open-door policy and the territorial integrity of China. Japan's action in China was in violation of all existing treaties, and, in the American view, the only solution to the "China incident" was the complete withdrawal of Japanese forces from China. This was a price the military leaders of Japan would never pay for the good will of the United States.

The war in China, from which Japan could extract neither honor nor victory, proved a continuing drain on the resources of the nation, requiring ever more stringent controls, higher appropriations, and further expansion of war industries. By the end of 1941, Japan's industry and manpower had been so completely mobilized that the transition to total war was scarcely noticed.

The growth of Japan's military forces matched its industrial growth. Between 1936 and 1941 the size of the Army more than

---

[3]Jerome B. Cohen, *Japan's Economy in War and Reconstruction* (Minneapolis: University of Minnesota Press, 1949), Chap. I; United States Strategic Bombing Survey (USSBS), *The Effect of Strategic Bombing on Japan's War Economy* (Washington, 1946), p. 12; IMTFE, Judgment, Part B, pp. 114-353; History of the Army Section, Imperial General Headquarters, 1941-1945, Japanese Studies in World War II, n. 72, p. 5.

[4]USSBS, *Oil in Japan's War* (Washington, 1946), p. 1; IMTFE, Judgment, p. 902.

doubled. The number of divisions rose from 20 to 50; air squadrons, from 50 to 150. And China provided the testing ground for doctrine and a reservoir of combat-trained veterans. Naval forces grew rapidly also after 1936 when Japan withdrew from the international naval conference of that year. By 1940 combat tonnage had jumped to over one million tons, giving Japan a navy more powerful than the combined American and British Fleets in the Pacific.[5]

Despite these preparations for war, neither the Army nor the Navy developed during the decade of the thirties any specific plans for the use of this formidable military machine against a coalition of Western Powers. In the files of the High Command were general statements of policy and annual operations plans, but, except for those that concerned China, they were defensive in concept and dealt only with the United States and Soviet Russia. In no case, it was emphasized, should Japan fight more than one enemy at a time. The plans were, in the words of one Japanese officer, "outdated writings" and "utterly nonsensical."[6]

The absence, during this period, of specific plans reflecting national objectives and government policy is remarkable. The preparation of such plans is the major function of a general staff and was routine in the United States and other democratic countries where the military was much more closely controlled than in Japan. The fact that the Japanese General Staff—which had studied in the best schools in Europe—had failed to prepare such plans as late as 1940 cannot be attributed either to peaceful intentions or to a supreme confidence in diplomacy. It was based solely on a realistic appreciation of Japan's economic weakness and lack of the strategic resources required for modern warfare.

Toward the end of 1940, after Germany had conquered most of Western Europe, Japan set out to remedy its basic weaknesses by a program of expansion in southeast Asia. There, in the crumbling British, Dutch, and French empires, lay the oil, rubber, bauxite, and other vital resources Japan needed so badly. Only the United States and Soviet Russia stood in the way, and their interference, the Japanese believed, could be checkmated by political alliance. Thus, in the months that followed, Japan sought to immobilize the United States with the Tripartite Pact (between Germany, Italy, and Japan,

[5]Hist Army Sec, Imperial GHQ, pp. 2-3; USSBS, *Japanese Air Power* (Washington, 1946), pp. 4-5; USSBS, Japanese Naval Shipbuilding (Washington, 1946), App. A.

[6]Political Strategy Prior to Outbreak of War, Part IV, Japanese Studies in World War II, No. 150, pp. 1-2; IMTFE, Deposition of Shinichi Tanaka, Exhibit 3027.

signed on September 1940) and to gain the friendship of Russia with a five-year pact of nonaggression and neutrality.

Simultaneously with these diplomatic and political measures, the Japanese Army and Navy began to prepare more actively for a general war while laying the basis for military action in the south. Renewed efforts were made to stockpile vital resources, and in late October the Total War Research Institute was established. In December 1940 the Army ordered three divisions, then in South China, to begin training for operations in tropical areas. During the next few weeks special studies were made of the geography, terrain, and climate of Malaya, Indochina, the Netherlands Indies, Thailand, and Burma, and of the problems involved in military operations there. By January 1941 Japanese pilots were flying reconnaissance and taking aerial photographs over the Malayan coast and the Philippines, and the War Ministry and Foreign Office were printing military currency for use in the southern area. It was at this time, too, that Admiral Isoroku Yamamoto, commander of the Combined Fleet, conceived the idea of a carrier-based air attack on Pearl Harbor and ordered his staff to work out the problems posed by such an operation. The Japanese Army and Navy were unmistakably moving away from the defensive concepts which had guided their planning during the preceding decade.[7]

The summer of 1941 was the critical season for the diplomats as well as the soldiers of Japan. The war in China was still on, draining the meager oil reserves of the nation and creating an insoluble barrier to agreement with the United States. The Tripartite Pact had produced an effect opposite from that intended and erected another obstacle to an understanding between the two countries. And finally, the Dutch, backed by the Americans and British, had successfully resisted Japanese efforts to secure economic concessions in the Indies.

The German invasion of Russia in June 1941 forced the Japanese to review their program for the conquest of southeast Asia. For over a week they debated the question of the effect of Germany's action on Japan. Some thought it better to move north now rather than south, others that the time had come to make concessions and reach

[7]IMTFE, Tanaka Deposition; Imperial GHQ Army Dept. Directive No. 791, 6 Dec 40, No. 810, 16 Jan 41, No. 812, 18 Jan 41, all in Imperial GHQ Army Directives, Vol. I; IMTFE, Judgment, pp. 878-81; Robert E. Ward, "The Inside Story of the Pearl Harbor Plan," *U.S. Naval Institute Proceedings* LXXVII (December, 1951), pp. 1272-75.

agreement with the United States, whose hand in the Pacific had been strengthened by the Russo-German war. President Roosevelt, who listened in on the debate through the medium of MAGIC—the code name applied to intercepted and decoded Japanese messages—characterized it as "a real drag-down and knock-out fight . . . to decide which way they were going to jump—attack Russia, attack the South Seas, [or] sit on the fence and be more friendly with us."[8] The Foreign Minister, Yosuke Matsuoka, favored the first course; the Army, the second; the Premier, Prince Fumimaro Konoye, the third.

On July 2, 1941, at a conference in the Imperial Presence, the leaders of Japan made their decision. It was a clear-cut defeat for the pro-Axis Foreign Minister and those who believed with him that Japan should attack Russia. For the others it was a compromise of sorts. Negotiations with the United States, begun in February 1941, would be continued in an effort to settle the issues between the two countries. At the same time, the plans already made for the domination of Thailand and Indochina, the first objectives in the southern area, would be put into effect immediately. "We will not be deterred," the Imperial Conference decreed, "by the possibility of becoming involved in a war with England and America."[9] In short, Japan would attempt the difficult feat of sitting on the fence and advancing south at the same time.

The problems posed by Germany's attack on Russia were hardly settled and the decision made to abide by the Tripartite Pact and the drive southward when a new crisis arose. On June 21 U.S. Secretary of State Cordell Hull had handed the Japanese Ambassador, Admiral Kichisaburo Nomura, a note asking for some clear indication of a genuine desire for peace and making allusions to the pro-German attitude of certain members of the Japanese Government. This communication was still unanswered; and now Matsuoka insisted on outright rejection of the note and the termination of the talks. The Premier, Prince Konoye, wished instead to reply with counter-proposals already prepared by the Army and Navy. Matsuoka would not budge from his position, and Konoye, given the nod by War

[8]Ltr, Roosevelt to Ickes, 1 Jul 41, cited in Langer and Gleason, *The Undeclared War, 1940-1941,* p. 646. The July 2 decision is included among the IMTFE Exhibits as No. 588; Ltr, Grew to author, 19 Jun 41, OCMH.

[9]IMTFE, Exhibit 585. The events leading to the decision are covered in Political Strategy Prior to Outbreak of War, Part IV, and Feis, *Road to Pearl Harbor,* pp. 209-19.

Minister General Hideki Tojo and after consultation with the Emperor, submitted the resignation of the entire Cabinet on July 16. Two days later he received the Imperial mandate to form a new Cabinet which, except for Matsuoka who was replaced by Admiral Soemu Toyoda, was the same as the old one. The Japanese could now go ahead with the program outlined at the Imperial Conference of July 2.[10]

The first move of the new government was the virtual occupation of French Indochina. Protesting that Indochina was being encircled, Japan issued what was in effect an ultimatum to the Vichy Government on July 19. On July 24 Roosevelt offered to guarantee to the Japanese equal access to the raw materials and food of Indochina in return for the neutralization of that country, but nothing came of the proposal. The following day Japanese troops moved into the southern portion of Indochina. Japan now possessed strategically located air and naval bases from which to launch attacks on Singapore, the Philippines, and the Netherlands Indies.

Although the French acquiesced in this raid on their empire, the United States was not so obliging. In the view of the State Department, this fresh Japanese aggression constituted a threat to American interests in the Far East and justified the imposition of additional economic restrictions, then being considered by the President, as a warning to Japan.[11] These restrictions were finally put into effect on July 26 when the President, against the advice of his Chief of Naval Operations, Admiral Harold R. Stark, issued an order freezing Japanese assets in the United States. Since Japan no longer had the dollars with which to purchase the urgently needed materials of war, the effect of this measure, which the British and

[10]IMTFE, Judgment, pp. 928-30; Feis, *Road to Pearl Harbor*, pp. 223-26.

The American position, which remained virtually unchanged throughout the negotiations was outlined by Cordell Hull in four points:

1. Respect for the territorial integrity and the sovereignty of each and all nations;

2. Support of the principle of noninterference in the internal affairs of other countries;

3. Support of the principle of equality, including equality of commercial opportunity;

4. Nondisturbance of the *status quo* in Pacific except as the *status quo* may be altered by peaceful means.

Report of the Joint Committee on the Investigation of the Pearl Harbor Attack, 79th Cong., 2nd Sess., Doc. 244 (Washington, 1946), p. 294.

[11]*Foreign Relations of the United States, Japan*, Vol. II, p. 342.

Dutch supported, was to create an economic blockade of Japan. So seriously did Admiral Stark regard this move that he warned Admiral Thomas C. Hart, commander of the Asiatic Fleet, to take "appropriate precautionary measures against possible eventualities."[12]

The sharp American reaction to their move into Indochina came as a surprise to the Japanese and precipitated an intensive review of the nation's readiness to wage war. The picture was not encouraging. The powerful Planning Board which coordinated the vast, complex structure of Japan's war economy found the country's resources meager and only enough, in view of the recent action of the United States, for a quick, decisive war to gain the riches of the Indies. "If the present condition is left unchecked," asserted Teiichi Suzuki, President of the Board, "Japan will find herself totally exhausted and unable to rise in the future." The blockade, he believed, would bring about Japan's collapse within two years, and he urged that a final decision on war or peace be made "without hesitation."[13] The Navy's view was equally gloomy. There was only enough oil, Admiral Osami Nagano told the Emperor, to maintain the fleet under war conditions for one and a half years and he was doubtful that Japan could win a "sweeping victory" in that time. His advice, therefore, was to drop the Tripartite Pact and reach agreement with the United States.

The Army and other powerful forces in the Japanese Government did not share these views. They thought there was enough oil on hand to wage war and that renunciation of the Tripartite Pact would not necessarily bring about a change in U.S.-Japanese relations. Marquis Koichi Kido, the Emperor's chief adviser, discussed the problem with Prince Konoye and agreed that before a decision on war or peace could be made, the Army and Navy would have to reach agreement.

By the middle of August the two services had agreed on a broad line of strategy. The impetus came from a series of studies presented by the Total War Research Institute, a subordinate body of the Planning Board. Forecasting the course of events during the next six months, the Institute called for the invasion of the Netherlands

---

[12]Rad, CNO to CINCAF, 25 Jul 41, in *Pearl Harbor Attack, Hearings Before the Joint Committee on the Investigation of the Pearl Harbor Attack* (Washington, 1946), Part 14, pp. 1400-01.

[13]Political Strategy Prior to Outbreak of War, Part IV, pp. 9, 73-77.

Indies in November, followed the next month by surprise attacks on British and American possessions in the Far East. Anticipating that the United States and Great Britain would utilize Soviet bases in a war against Japan, the Institute's studies dealt with the problems of economic mobilization; military planning, except in the most general sense, was left to the services.[14] These studies, as well as others, were discussed heatedly during the tense days that followed the U.S. embargo. From these discussions emerged four alternative lines of strategy, all of them designed to accomplish the swift destruction of Allied forces in the Far East and the early seizure of the Netherlands Indies. The first was based on the Institute's studies and provided for the seizure of the Indies and then the Philippines and Malaya. The second called for a step-by-step advance from the Philippines to Borneo, Java, Sumatra, and Malaya. The reverse, from Malaya to the Philippines, constituted a third line of action and one which would have the advantage of delaying attack against American territory. The fourth plan proposed at this time consisted of simultaneous attacks against the Philippines and Malaya followed by a raid advance along both axes to the Indies. Admiral Yamamoto's plan for an attack against Pearl Harbor, work on which had begun in January, did not enter into the calculations of the planners at this time.

Army and Navy planners agreed that the first plan was too risky for it would leave Japanese forces exposed to attack from the Philippines and Malaya. The Navy preferred the second plan; it was safe, provided for a step-by-step advance, and created no serious problems. The Army objected to it, however, on the ground that by the time the main objectives in the Netherlands Indies and Malaya were reached the Allies would have had time to strengthen their defenses. The third plan, with its early seizure of Malaya and bypassing of the Philippines, appealed greatly to the Army planners who hoped in this way to gain southeast Asia and delay American entry into the war. But this course, as the Navy pointed out, also placed American naval and air forces in the Philippines in a strategic position athwart Japan's line of communication and constituted a risk of the utmost magnitude. The fourth course, simultaneous attacks and advance along two axes, created serious problems of coordination and timing and a dangerous dispersion of forces. But because it was the only course which compromised the views of

[14]IMTFE, Exhibits 870, 870-A, and 871.

both groups, it was finally adopted. For the first time the Japanese had a strategic plan for offensive operations designed to achieve the goals of national policy against a coalition of enemies.[15] Operational plans for each objective were still to be made, forces organized, trained, and rehearsed.

Though the Army and Navy had agreed on strategy, the Japanese Government was still reluctant to take the final step. Contributing to this lack of resolution was the slowing down of Germany's advance in Russia and the Japanese Navy's concern over the shortage of oil reserves. From the end of July until his resignation in October, Premier Konoye sought to persuade his cabinet colleagues to adopt a less aggressive policy in an effort to reach agreement with the United States.

The first sign of this new policy was a proposal, delivered by Admiral Nomura in Washington on August 6, for a personal meeting—a "leaders' conference"—between the Japanese Premier and President Roosevelt. General Tojo had agreed to this proposal only on the understanding that Konoye would use the occasion to press the program for expansion to the south. The American reply on August 17 that a prerequisite to such a meeting was the settlement of the issues between the two countries confirmed Tojo and the Army leaders in their view that the United States would never yield to the Japanese demands and that war should begin as soon as the Army and Navy were ready.[16]

The difference between the two Japanese points of view was temporarily resolved early in September and formalized at an Imperial Conference held on September 6. The agreement, characteristically Japanese, was expressed in language which both sides could accept and interpret in their own way. The negotiations with the United States, it was agreed, would be continued, as Konoye wished. But at the same time military preparations would be pushed to completion so that the nation would be ready for war by the end of October, that is, in six weeks. "If by the early part of October," the conferees decided, "there is no reasonable hope of having our demands agreed to in the diplomatic negotiations . . . we will immediately make up our minds to get ready for war. . . ."[17]

---

[15]Political Strategy Prior to Outbreak of War, Part IV, pp. 9-10.

[16]Konoye Memoirs, *Pearl Harbor Attack Hearings,* Part 20, pp. 3998-4000, 4009-10; *Pearl Harbor Attack Report,* pp. 298, 302-07, 310; *Foreign Relations of the United States, Japan,* Vol. II, pp. 549-55.

[17]Konoye Memoirs, *Pearl Harbor Attack Hearings,* Part 20, pp. 4022-23. The wording of this important statement varies in different documents. IMTFE Defense

The Imperial Conference also fixed the minimum demands Japan would make and maximum concessions it would grant in the negotiations with the United States and Great Britain. The former were hardly likely to gain acceptance. First, both the Western Powers would have to promise to discontinue aid to China, close the Burma Road, and "neither meddle in nor interrupt" a settlement between Japan and China. Second, America and Britain would have to recognize Japan's special position in French Indochina and agree not to establish or reinforce their bases in the Far East or take any action which might threaten Japan. Finally, both nations would have to resume commercial relations with Japan, supply the materials "indispensable for her self-existence," and "gladly cooperate" in Japan's economic program in Thailand and Indochina. In return for these "minimum demands," the Japanese were willing to agree not to use Indochina as a base for further military advance, except in China, to withdraw from Indochina "after an impartial peace" had been established in the Far East, and, finally, to guarantee the neutrality of the Philippine Islands.[18]

While the negotiations with the U.S. went forward, the Army and Navy General Staffs continued their preparations for war and the troops earmarked for operations in the south intensified their training, usually under conditions approximating those of the areas in which they would fight. Since agreement had already been reached on the strategy for war, General Hajime Sugiyama, Army Chief of Staff, was able shortly after the September 6 Imperial Conference to direct that detailed operational plans for the seizure of Malaya, Java, Borneo, the Bismarck Archipelago, the Netherlands Indies, and the Philippines be prepared.[19] The Army planners immediately went to work and the next two months witnessed feverish activity in the General Staff.

By the end of August the Navy planners had worked out their plans for seizing bases in the western Pacific and had from Admiral Yamamoto a separate plan for an attack on Pearl Harbor. "Table-top maneuvers" at Tokyo Naval War College between September 10 and 13 resulted in agreement on operations for the seizure of the

---

Document 1579 gives a slightly different wording as does Judgment, Chapter VII, page 939. The Japanese phrase "Kaiseno Ketsui su" may be translated literally "decide to open hostilities." Konoye apparently did not interpret the phrase as meaning that it was a decision for war; Tojo did.

[18]Konoye Memoirs, *Pearl Harbor Attack Hearings,* Part 20, pp. 4022-23; IMTFE, Doc. 1652, Exhibit 588.

[19]IMTFE, Tanaka Deposition, Exhibit 2244.

Philippines, Malaya, the Netherlands Indies, Burma, and islands in the South Pacific, but there was still some doubt about Yamamoto's plan. The exercise had demonstrated that a Pearl Harbor strike was practicable, but many felt that it was too risky, that the U.S. Pacific Fleet might not be in port on the day of the attack, and that the danger of discovery during the long voyage to Hawaii was too great. But Admiral Yamamoto refused to give up his plan and finally, when he failed to convert his colleagues, offered to resign from the Navy. The combination of his strong argument that the success of the southward drive depended on the destruction of the American Fleet, his enormous prestige, and his threat to resign were too much for opponents of the plan. In mid-October, a month after the maneuvers, the Navy General Staff finally adopted his concept of a surprise carrier-based attack on Pearl Harbor and incorporated it into the larger plan for war.[20]

This larger plan, which was virtually complete by October 20 and was the one followed by the Japanese when war came, had as its immediate objective the capture of the rich Dutch and British possessions in southeast Asia. The greatest single threat to its success was the U.S. Pacific Fleet at Pearl Harbor, and this threat the Japanese now hoped to eliminate by the destruction or neutralization of the fleet at the start of the war. U.S. air and naval forces in the Philippines, which stood in position along the flank of their advance southward, the Japanese expected to destroy quickly also, seizing the islands later at their leisure. Finally, America's line of communications across the Pacific was to be cut by the capture of Wake Island and Guam. Once these threats had been removed and the coveted area to the south secured, Japanese military forces would occupy strategic positions in Asia and in the Pacific and fortify them immediately. These bases would form a powerful defensive perimeter around the newly acquired empire in the south, the home islands, and the vital shipping lanes connecting Japan with its new sources of supply. With these supplies the Japanese thought they could wage defensive war indefinitely.[21]

[20]For a full account of the evolution of the Pearl Harbor plan, see Ward, "The Inside Story of the Pearl Harbor Plan," *U.S. Naval Institute Proceedings,* LXXVII, 1272-81.

[21]Japanese Army-Navy Central Agreement, Nov 41, copy in USSBS, *The Campaigns of the Pacific War, pp. 43-46; Combined Fleet,* Top Secret Order No. 1, copy in *Pearl Harbor Attack Hearings,* Part 13, pp. 431-84; Political Strategy Prior to Outbreak of War, Part IV, pp. 47-123; Hist Army Sec, Imperial GHQ, rev. ed., pp.

The area marked for conquest formed a vast triangle whose east arm stretched from the Kuril Islands in the north, through Wake Island, to the Marshall Islands. The base of the triangle was formed by a line connecting the Marshall Islands, the Bismarck Archipelago, Java, and Sumatra. The western arm extended from Malaya and southern Burma, through Indochina, and thence along the China coast.

The acquisition of this area would give to Japan control of the resources of southeast Asia and would satisfy the national objectives in going to war. Perhaps later, if all went well, the area of conquest could be extended. But there is no evidence in the Japanese plans of an intention to invade the United States or to seek the total defeat of that nation. Japan planned to fight a war of limited objectives and, having gained what it wanted, expected to negotiate for a favorable settlement.

Japanese planners anticipated that certain events might require an alteration in their strategy and outlined alternative courses of action to be followed in each contingency. The first possibility was that the negotiations then in progress in Washington would prove successful. If this unexpected success was achieved, all operations were to be suspended even if the final orders to attack had been issued. The second possibility was that the United States might take hostile action before the attack on Pearl Harbor by sending elements of the Pacific Fleet to the Far East. In that event, the Japanese Combined Fleet would be deployed to intercept Amercan naval forces while the attacks against the Philippines and Malaya proceeded according to schedule.

The possibility of a Soviet attack, or of a joint U.S.-Soviet invasion from the north, was a specter that haunted the Japanese. To meet such a contingency, Japanese ground forces in Manchuria were to be strengthened, while air units from the home islands and China were to be transferred to meet the new threat. Thereafter, the attack to the south would proceed on schedule.

The forces required to execute this vast plan for conquest were very carefully calculated by Imperial General Headquarters. A large force had to be left in Manchuria, and an even larger one in China. Garrisons for Korea, Formosa, the home islands, and other positions required additional forces. Thus, only a small fraction of the Japanese Army was available for operations in the south. Of the total strength of the Army's 51 divisions, 59 mixed brigades, and 1,500 first-line planes, Imperial General Headquarters could allocate only 11 divisions and 2 air groups (700 planes) to the operations in the south.

In the execution of this complicated and intricate plan, the Japanese planners realized, success would depend on careful timing and on the closest cooperation between ground, naval, and air forces. No provision was made for unified command of all services, then or later. Instead, separate agreements were made between Army and Fleet commanders for each operation. These agreements provided simply for cooperation at the time of landing and for the distribution of forces.

In addition to supporting the Army's operations in the south, the Combined Fleet had other important missions. Perhaps the most important, and certainly the most spectacular, was that assigned the Pearl Harbor Striking Force. Later, this force was to support operations of the 4th Fleet in the capture of Guam and the Bismarck Archipelago, and then assist in the southern operations. The 6th Fleet (submarines) was to operate in Hawaiian waters and along the West Coast of the United States to observe the movement of the U.S. Pacific Fleet and make surprise attacks on shipping. The 5th Fleet was to patrol the waters east of Japan, in readiness for enemy surprise attacks, and, above all, keep on the alert against Russia.

The Japanese plan for war was complete in all respects but one—the date when it would go into effect. That decision awaited the outcome of the negotiations then in progress and of the struggle in the Cabinet between those who advocated caution and those who pressed for immediate action. "Time had become the meter of strategy" and Japan "was crazed by the tick of the clock."[22]

The six-weeks' reprieve Konoye had won on September 6 to settle the outstanding issues by diplomacy went by quickly without producing a settlement. A new proposal, which Nomura delivered to Hull on September 27, was rejected by the Americans, who were unwavering in their position on China. Nomura renewed the request for a meeting between Roosevelt and Konoye but on October 10 was constrained to tell Foreign Minister Toyoda that there was not "the slightest chance on earth" of a "leaders' conference" so long as Japan refused to compromise. The negotiations, in the words of

[22]Feis, *Road to Pearl Harbor,* p. 270.

Toyoda, had "slowly but surely . . . reached the decisive stage."[23]
There was apparently no way of reconciling the basic differences
over China. The domestic situation was no better. The demands of the Army
and Navy for a decision on the question of war were becoming ever
more insistent. Oil stocks were steadily diminishing, the most
favorable season of the year for operations was approaching, and
failure to act soon might force a delay of many months and expose
the Japanese to a Soviet attack on Manchuria. Finally, on September
24, General Sugiyama and Admiral Nagano, the Army and Navy
Chiefs of Staff, submitted a joint letter calling attention to the
shortage of supplies, the effect of the weather on operations, and the
problems of mobilizing, staging, and deploying their forces. "With
all the force of their positions" they asked for a quick decision "by
October 15 at the latest," so that they could start operations by
mid-November.[24]

With no agreement in sight, Konoye sought to win an extension.
On October 12 he invited War Minister Tojo, the Navy and Foreign
Ministers, and the President of the Planning Board to his home for a
final conference on the question of war and peace. At the meeting
the Premier argued strongly for continuing the negotiations beyond
the deadline, then set at October 15. The Navy Minister would not
commit himself, but General Tojo, on the ground that success in the
negotiations would require concessions in China, refused to go along
with Konoye. The issue had now been narrowed to the withdrawal
of Japanese troops from China, and on the morning of October 14
the Premier again sought Tojo's consent. "On this occasion," he
urged the War Minister, "we ought to give in for a time . . . and save
ourselves from the crisis of a Japanese-American war." Tojo again
refused, and at a Cabinet meeting later in the day demanded that the
negotiations be terminated. Finally, late that night, he sent Konoye a
message stating that the Cabinet ought to resign, "declare insolvent
everything that has happened up to now, and reconsider our plans
once more."[25]

Without Tojo's support Konoye had no recourse but to resign.
The Army, seeking possibly to avoid responsibility for the decision
which must soon be made, suggested that his successor be a prince

---

[23]*Pearl Harbor Attack Report*, p. 322.
[24]Political Strategy Prior to Outbreak of War, Part IV, pp. 13-15.
[25]Konoye Memoirs, *Pearl Harbor Attack Hearings*, Part 20, p. 4010.

of the Imperial family. The suggestion was rejected as contrary to tradition and the Marquis Kido, together with the Council of Senior Statesmen (former premiers), recommended that Tojo himself be named Premier. The Emperor accepted this recommendation. On October 18 Tojo took office with an Imperial mandate to reconsider Japan's policy in relation to the world situation without regard for the September 6 decision. The fate of Japan was in the hands of its generals.

In Washington, where every Japanese move was carefully weighed and analyzed, the Japanese Cabinet crisis was cause for real concern and Ambassador Joseph C. Grew's cables from Tokyo did little to lessen it. On October 16, when Konoye resigned, Admiral Stark told Pacific and Asiatic Fleet commanders there was "a strong possibility" of war between Japan and Russia. Warning them that Japan might also attack the United States, Stark instructed the two commanders to take "due precautions." This message Admiral Hart and the commander of the Pacific Fleet at Pearl Harbor, Admiral Husband E. Kimmel, passed on to their Army colleagues, who, a few days later, received quite a different message from Washington informing them that they need not expect an "abrupt change in Japanese foreign policy."[26] Apparently the Army did not agree with the Navy's estimate of the international situation, and neither mentioned the possibility of an attack on Pearl Harbor.

The period from October 18 to November 5 was one of mounting tension and frantic preparations on both sides of the Pacific. In Tokyo the Tojo Cabinet and the High Command, meeting in an almost continuous series of "Liaison Conferences," considered every aspect of Japan's position and the possibilities of each line of action. Finally, on November 5, a decision was reached and confirmed by a conference in the Imperial Presence. This decision was substantially the same as that reached on September 6: to continue negotiations in an effort to reach an agreement with the United States, and, if no settlement was reached, to open hostilities. The deadline first set was November 25, later extended to November 29. The significance of this decision was revealed in a message the new Foreign Minister, Shigenori Togo, sent Admiral

---

[26]Memo, Gerow for CofS, 18 Oct 41, sub: Resignation of Japanese Cabinet; Rad, CNO to CINCPAC and CINCAF, 16 Oct 41, both in *Pearl Harbor Attack Hearings,* Part 14, pp. 1389, 1402. See also Ltr, Grew to author, 19 Jun 49, OCMH.

Nomura in Washington on November 4 telling him that relations between the two countries had "reached the edge." Next day he wrote that time was "exceedingly short" and the situation "very critical." "Absolutely no delays can be permitted. Please bear this in mind and do your best," Togo said. "I wish to stress this point over and over."[27]

The Imperial Conference agreed to make two more proposals to the United States. The first, Proposal A, was an amendment to the latest Japanese proposal and provided for a withdrawal from China and French Indochina, when and if a peace treaty was signed with Chiang Kai-shek. In certain areas in China, to be specified in the treaty, Japanese troops would remain for a "suitable period," vaguely and informally stated to be about twenty-five years. Further, the Japanese Government would interpret its obligations under the Tripartite Pact independently of the other Axis Powers. Lastly, Japan would agree not to discriminate in trade, provided all other nations did the same. In his instructions to Nomura, Foreign Minister Togo emphasized that while other matters could be compromised in his negotiations with the United States, Japan could not yield on the question of China.

In Proposal B, to be made if the first was rejected, no mention was made of the Tripartite Pact or the removal of Japanese troops from China. Japan would withdraw her troops from southern Indochina immediately and from the northern part of that country only after the negotiation of a peace treaty with Chiang Kai-shek, or after the conclusion of a "just peace" in the Pacific. In return, the United States was to agree not to interfere in the negotiations with China, and to cooperate with Japan in the acquisition and exploitation of natural resources in the Netherlands Indies. Finally, the United States was to resume commercial relations with Japan, and to provide that nation with oil.[28]

With the decision made and the deadline set, the Army and Navy drew up an agreement embodying the objectives of the war and an outline of operations. About the same time Admiral Nagano sent Yamamoto his final orders and told him to be ready to strike "by the first part of December." During the next few weeks the fleet was

[27]Dispatch, Togo to Nomura, 4 and 5 Nov 41, in *Pearl Harbor Attack Hearings,* Part 12, Exhibit 1, p. 92.
[28]The text of the two proposals is reproduced in IMTFE, Exhibit 770.

readied for action, and on November 26 the Pearl Harbor Striking Force left its lonely assembly area in the snowbound Kurils and sailed due east on its way to Hawaii.[29] The Army acted with similar dispatch. On November 6 General Sugiyama issued instructions to the Southern Army, which had the task of taking the southern area, to prepare detailed plans for operations. Four days later the ranking Army and Navy officers of the Southern Army and the Combined Fleet met in Tokyo to work out final arrangements for joint operations. On November 20 the actual order for the attack was issued, but with the proviso that operations would not begin until the results of the diplomatic negotiations were known.[30]

In Washington, the privileged few followed each move of the Japanese in the mirror of MAGIC while observing in reports from all parts of the Far East increasing evidence of Japanese military preparations. Japanese ship movements toward Malaya and the concentration of shipping at Formosa, staging area for the attack on the Philippines, were quickly detected by American observers. Ambassador Grew, who had reported as early as January 27, 1941, that there was talk in Tokyo of a surprise attack on Pearl Harbor, warned on November 3 that recent troop movements placed Japan in a position to start operations "in either Siberia or the Southwest Pacific or in both" and that war might come with "dramatic and dangerous suddenness." "Things seem to be moving steadily toward a crisis in the Pacific," wrote Admiral Stark to his Pacific Fleet commander, Admiral Kimmel, on November 7. "A month may see, literally, most anything. . . . It doesn't look good."[31]

The first proposal agreed upon at the Imperial Conference of November 5 was handed to Secretary of State Hull by Ambassador Nomura two days later. On the 12th the Secretary told the Japanese Ambassador that the proposal was being studied and that he hoped to have a reply ready wthin three days. When it came, it proved to be rejection of Proposal A on the ground that the offer to withdraw troops from China and Indochina was indefinite and uncertain and

[29]USSBS, *The Campaigns of the Pacific War*, App. 12, pp. 43-46; App. 14, p. 49. The Combined Fleet Top Secret Order Number 1 is printed in *Pearl Harbor Attack Hearings*, Part 13, pp. 431-84.

[30]Hist of *Southern Army, 1941-45*, pp. 4-8; Hist Army Sec, Imperial GHQ, pp. 29-39.

[31]Telgs, Grew to Hull, 27 Jan and 3 Nov 41, in *Pearl Harbor Attack Hearings,* Part 14, Exhibit 15, pp. 1042, 1045-60; Ltr, CNO to Kimmel, 7 Nov 41.

that the United States could not agree to the Japanese definition of nondiscrimination in trade.

On November 20 Admiral Nomura, who now had the benefit of the advice of his colleague Saburo Kurusu, sent from Japan as a special envoy, presented Proposal B, virtually a restatement of the "minimum demands" and "maximum concessions" of the September 6 Imperial Conference. Intercepted Japanese messages had already revealed to Hull that this was to be Japan's last offer for a settlement.[32] To the Secretary of State, the new Japanese offer "put conditions that would have assured Japan's domination of the Pacific, placing us in serious danger for decades to come." The commitments which the United States would have had to make were, in his opinion, "virtually a surrender."[33]

The problem faced by American political and military leaders was a serious one. An outright rejection of Proposal B might well provide Japan with the pretext for war. Full acceptance was out of the question. The only way out of this dilemma was to find a "reasonable counterproposal" or a basis for temporary agreement. In support of this view, Admiral Stark and Brigadier General Leonard T. Gerow, who as chief of the Army War Plans Division acted for the Chief of Staff during his absence, pointed out to the Secretary of State that a *modus vivendi* would "attain one of our present major objectives—the avoidance of war with Japan." "Even a temporary peace in the Pacific," Gerow urged, "would permit us to complete defensive preparations in the Philippines and at the same time insure continuance of material assistance to the British—both of which are highly important."[34]

During the next four days, various drafts of a *modus vivendi* were prepared, and on November 25 the entire matter was reviewed at a meeting of the service Secretaries and the Secretary of State. The general view was that the *modus vivendi* should be adopted, but Hull was pessimistic and expressed the view that the Japanese might "break out any time with new acts of conquest by force" and that national security now "lies in the hands of the Army and Navy."[35]

---

[32]Rad, Tokyo to Washington, No. 812, 22 Nov 41, IMTFE, Doc. 2593, Item 17.

[33]Cordell Hull, *The Memoirs of Cordell Hull,* 2 vols. (New York: Macmillan, 1948), Vol. II, p. 1069.

[34]Memos, Stark and Gerow for Secretary of State, 21 Nov 41, in *Pearl Harbor Attack Hearings,* Part 14, pp. 1104-07. General Marshall was attending the maneuvers in North Carolina.

[35]Hull, *Memoirs,* Vol. II, p. 1180.

Nor could the American Government ignore the unfavorable reaction of the Allied Powers to the *modus vivendi.* The Chinese reaction was especially sharp, and from Chiang came a bitter protest, supported by a cable from Churchill.

The President was faced with a fateful decision. The Army and Navy wanted time to prepare for war and were willing to buy it with minor concessions. But the slight prospect of Japanese acceptance of the *modus vivendi* was, in the view of the Secretary of State, hardly worth the risk of lowering Chinese morale and resistance and opening the way for appeasement. President Roosevelt agreed. Thus the American reply to Proposal B, handed to the Japanese Ambassador on the afternoon of November 26, omitted the *modus vivendi.*[36]

In view of the seriousness of the situation, the Army and Navy chiefs felt that commanders in the Pacific should be warned immediately. The Navy had already sent out word on November 24—to be passed on to the Army commanders—that prospects for an agreement with Japan were slight and that Japanese troop movements indicated that "a surprise aggressive movement in any direction, including attack on Philippines or Guam" was a possibility.[37] Now, on November 27, War Secretary Stimson asked General Gerow whether the Army should not send a warning. Gerow showed him the Navy message of November 24, but this failed to satisfy Stimson, who observed that the President wanted a warning message sent to the Philippines. As a result, a fresh warning, considered a "final alert," was sent to Hawaii, the Philippines, Panama, and San Francisco. The commander of each of these garrisons was told of the status of the negotiations with Japan, the imminence of hostilities, and the desirability of having Japan commit the "first overt act." Each was instructed to "undertake such reconnaissance and other measures" as he thought necessary and to carry out the tasks assigned in the war plan if hostilities occurred. With the exception of MacArthur, each of the commanders was also warned not to alarm the civilian population or to "disclose intent." At the same time G-2 (intelligence) of the War Department sent an additional and briefer message to Hawaii and

---

[36]*Foreign Relations of the United States, Japan,* Vol. II, pp. 766-70; Hull, *Memoirs,* Vol. II, pp. 1077-82; *Pearl Harbor Attack Report,* pp. 35-43.

[37]Rad, Op NAV to Comdrs Pacific and Asiatic Fleets, 242005 Nov 41, *Pearl Harbor Attack Hearings,* Part 14, p. 1405.

Panama, but not to the Philippines, warning against subversive activities.

The Navy warning of November 27, which was passed on to the Army commanders, was more strongly worded and definitely an alert for war. "This dispatch," it read, "is to be considered a war warning . . . and an aggressive move by Japan is expected within the next few days." Navy commanders were alerted to the likelihood of amphibious operations against either the Philippines, the Kra isthmus, or Borneo and instructed to "execute an appropriate defensive deployment preparatory to carrying out the tasks assigned in their war plans." The possibility of attack on Pearl Harbor was not mentioned in either message.[38]

Though the date November 26 marked the real end of negotiations, the Japanese were not yet ready to go to war. On November 27 a Liaison Conference summarily rejected the American note. But to gain a few days, the Japanese instructed Nomura and Kurusu November 28 to do their best to keep the conversation open. Now, on November 30, Tojo presented the Cabinet view for war, but even at this late date several of the senior statesmen expressed doubts about the wisdom of a war with the United States. Konoye asked why it was not possible to continue "with broken economic relations but without war," to which Tojo replied that the final consequence of such a course would be "gradual impoverishment."[39] Later that day the same group met with the Emperor and each man presented his views. Already the force scheduled to attack Pearl Harbor was on its way across the North Pacific and elements of the Southern Army were assembling for their various attacks.

Final details for the opening of hostilities were completed on November 30 at a meeting of the Liaison Conference. At that time the attack on Pearl Harbor was discussed and agreement reached on the form and substance of the note which would formally end the negotiations and sever the relations between the two countries.

---

[38]Memo, Gerow for Marshall, 27 Nov 41, sub: Far Eastern Situation; Rads, Marshall to CG USAFFE, Hawaiian Dept, Carib Def Comd, Nos. 624, 472, 451, 27 Nov 41, OCS 18136-118 and WPD 4544-16; Miles to G-2 Hawaiian Dept, No. 472, 27 Nov 41. Most of these are published in *Pearl Harbor Attack Hearings*, Part 3, p. 1021, Part 14, pp. 1328-30. Stimson's account of these events is in Part 39, p. 84. The Navy message is in Part 14, p. 1406. See also *Pearl Harbor Attack Report*, pp. 199-201.

[39]Konoye Memoirs, *Pearl Harbor Attack Hearings*, Part 20, p. 4012.

Hostilities would follow, but no declaration of war, it was decided, would be made in advance. The timing of the Japanese reply to Hull's note was discussed also and it was agreed that the Naval Staff would make the decision in order to gain the fullest advantage of surprise at Pearl Harbor and elsewhere.[40]

The decisions of the Liaison Conference were formalized and sanctioned by the council in the Imperial Presence on December 1. Tojo, who presided at the meeting, explained the purpose of the conference. Then the Ministers and the Chiefs of Staff discussed the question of war with the United States, Great Britain, and the Netherlands. The vote was unanimously for war. "Our negotiations with the United States regarding the execution of our national policy, adopted November 5, have finally failed," reads the record of the meeting. "Japan will open hostilities against the United States, Great Britain, and the Netherlands." The Emperor spoke not a single word during the meeting.[41]

All was in readiness; only the date for the start of war remained to be fixed and that was quickly decided. December 8 (Japanese Standard Time) was the date selected, and on December 2 the Army and Navy chiefs passed this information on to the forces moving into position for the attack. But on the slim chance that by a miracle the United States would agree to the Japanese terms, the Navy Chief of Staff added that should an amicable settlement be reached, "all forces of the Combined Fleet are to be ordered to reassemble and return to their bases." From Admiral Yamamoto's flagship at the Kure naval base went the message *Niitaka Yama Nobore* (Climb Mount Niitaka), the prearranged signal for the attack on Pearl Harbor.[42]

Various considerations underlay the choice of so early a date. Both the Army and Navy felt that delay would be disastrous. By March 1942 America's naval superiority as well as the reinforcements in the Philippines would make the plan extremely hazardous, if not impossible of execution. Moreover, by that time the Americans and British would have completed their preparations in the Philippines and Malaya. Weather, too, was a decisive consideration in the Japanese plan. The conquest of Malaya would

[40]IMTFE, Exhibits 2954 and 2955, Depositions of Tojo and Togo.

[41]IMTFE, Exhibit 588, Doc. 1652, Records of Imperial Conferences.

[42]These messages are reproduced in USSBS, *The Campaigns of the Pacific War*, p. 51, and elsewhere.

require five months and would have to be completed by spring, the best time for military operations in Manchuria in the event that Russia should decide to attack. Finally, December and January were favorable months for amphibious operations in the Philippines and elsewhere, with the tide and moon favoring the attacker.

In arriving at their decision for war, the Japanese gave little or no thought to the interests and desires of their Axis partners. Carefully, they kept their plans secret from Mussolini and Hitler, although Hitler at least would have greatly preferred a Japanese attack on Soviet Russia or on the British base at Singapore. Only on December 4, three days after the decision for war was made, did the Japanese Ambassador in Berlin hint at the possibility of early hostilities when he cautiously inquired whether the German Government would declare war on the United States if Japan moved first, a contingency that was not covered in the Tripartite Pact. Even then Hitler suspected nothing, and so little did the Japanese regard his wishes that they did not make an official request for a declaration of war until the afternoon of December 8.[43]

The first week of December 1941 was one of strain and nervous tension in Tokyo and of suspense and somber watchfulness in Washington. The signs of an early break were too clear to be missed by those who could read the intercepted Japanese messages and intelligence reports, but there was no realization of the danger to Pearl Harbor. Nomura and Kurusu saw Hull several times, but both sides knew nothing could come of these meetings. On December 4, Thursday, Congress adjourned for a long weekend. Next day the Japanese Embassy began to leave Washington and Nomura reported to his home office the partial destruction of codes.

On December 6 President Roosevelt composed a last-minute plea for peace to the Emperor. On the same day a Liaison Conference in Tokyo approved the decision to have Nomura deliver Japan's final note at 1 P.M. (Washington time) the next day, thirty minutes before the scheduled launching of the attack on Pearl Harbor. This note, in fourteen parts, began to arrive in Washington late on December 6. Thirteen of the fourteen parts of the message were in American

---

[43]Feis, *Road to Pearl Harbor*, p. 331; Langer and Gleason, *The Undeclared War*, pp. 910-11; *The Ciano Diaries, 1939-1943*, ed. by Hugh Gibson (Garden City, N.Y.: Doubleday, 1946), entries for 3 and 4 December 1941. On November 30, Foreign Minister Togo had told his Ambassador in Berlin that "war may suddenly break out between the Anglo-Saxon nations and Japan . . . quicker than anyone dreams." Quoted in Feis, *Road to Pearl Harbor*, p. 336.

hands that night, together with reports of two large Japanese convoys off Indochina, headed south. Unidentified aircraft, presumably Japanese, had been observed over Luzon, where by this time a full air alert was in effect and where the troops had already moved into defensive positions along the beaches. In Manila, Admiral Sir Tom Phillips, alarmed over Japanese movements, was just leaving for his flagship, *Prince of Wales,* after concluding arrangements with Hart and MacArthur for concerted naval action in the event of an attack.

That same day, December 6, the Japanese forces were rapidly approaching their destinations. The Pearl Harbor Striking Force, after a voyage across the Pacific, was heading southeast for the final run and at 11 P.M. (Washington time) was about 600 miles north of Oahu. On Formosa airfields were the Japanese planes for the attack on Clark Field in Manila, and the troops scheduled to seize advance airfields in the Philippines had already left staging areas in Formosa and the Pescadores. The invasion force for Guam was in position fifty miles north of the island and the Wake Island force stood ready at Kwajalein. Advance units of the Japanese 25th Army had left Hainan in two convoys on December 4 on their way to Malaya and on December 6 were nearing southern Thailand and Kota Bahru.

On the morning of December 7, Sunday, the fourteenth and last part of the final Japanese note was in American hands. Though it did not indicate when or where war would start, its intent was clear. A short time later two additional messages were intercepted. Taken with the fourteen-part note breaking off the negotiations, they were starkly revealing. One instructed the Japanese Ambassador to destroy the code machines and secret documents; the other, to deliver the fourteen-part message at 1 P.M. (Washington time). At 10:30 that morning Stimson and Knox went to Hull's office, where they were closeted for well over an hour, and at 12:30 the President received the Chinese Ambassador, to whom he read his note of the day before to the Emperor. "This is," he told Hu Shih, "my last effort for peace. I am afraid it may fail."[44]

General Marshall spent Sunday morning on the bridle path and reached his office about 11 o'clock. The intercepted message giving the deadline (1 P.M. Washington time) for delivery of the fourteen-part note struck him as significant and he suggested to Admiral Stark that an additional warning be sent to the Pacific. He then composed

---

[44]Feis, *Road to Pearl Harbor,* p. 340.

a message to the commanders in Hawaii, the Philippines, Panama, and San Francisco telling them that the Japanese were destroying their coding machines and would present at 1 P.M. Washington time "what amounts to an ultimatum." "Just what significance the hour set may have," he added, "we do not know, but be on alert accordingly." Declining an offer from Admiral Stark for the use of the Navy's radio, Marshall turned the message over to an officer for transmission over the Army's network and was assured shortly before noon that it would be delivered in thirty minutes. By a series of ironical circumstances and unexpected delays, the message to Hawaii was in turn entrusted to commercial telegraph and radio and then to a bicycle messenger who, on his way from Honolulu to Fort Shafter, was caught in the attack with his still encoded message.[45]

President Roosevelt's personal note to the Emperor reached Tokyo at noon of December 7 (Tokyo time) but was not delivered to Ambassador Grew until 11 o'clock that night. Shortly after midnight (about 11 A.M., December 7, Washington time), he called on the Foreign Minister to request an audience with the Emperor, but Togo said he would deliver the message himself. Meanwhile in Washington Ambassador Nomura had made an appointment to see Mr. Hull at 1:45 P.M. He and Kurusu arrived at the State Department a half hour late and were admitted to Hull's office at 2:20, only a few minutes after the Secretary had received a telephone call from the President telling him of the attack on Pearl Harbor. The Japanese emissaries handed the Secretary the fourteen-part note, which he already had on his desk. Hull, after pretending to read the note, turned to the two envoys. "In all my years of public service," he said with feeling, "I have never seen a document that was more crowded with infamous falsehoods and distortions—infamous falsehoods and distortions on a scale so huge that I never imagined until today that any Government on this planet was capable of uttering them."[46] The Japanese left without making any comment.

At approximately 8 A.M. Tokyo time, Ambassador Grew received from Foreign Minister Togo the Japanese fourteen-part note breaking off the negotiations. Later that morning, after Japanese bombs had fallen on Hawaii, Guam, and Wake, after Japanese forces had attacked the Philippines, Hong Kong, and Shanghai, and Japanese troops had landed in Malaya, Grew received an announce-

[45] *Pearl Harbor Attack Report*, pp. 219-28.
[46] *Pearl Harbor Attack Report*, p. 41.

ment that a state of war existed between Japan and the United States. Around noon General Tojo read to "a stunned and silent nation" the Imperial Rescript declaring war. The broadcast closed on the martial strains of "Umi Yukaba":

> Across the sea, corpses in the water;
> Across the mountain, corpses in the field
> I shall die only for the Emperor,
> I shall never look back.

From the vantage point of hindsight, Japan's decision to go to war appears as a supreme act of folly. By this decision the Japanese leaders appear to have deliberately committed their country to a hopeless struggle against a combination of powers vastly superior in potential industrial and military strength. This view has perhaps been most effectively presented by Rear Admiral Samuel Morison (USNR ret.), who characterized the Pearl Harbor attack which brought the United States into the war as a politically disastrous and strategically idiotic move. "One can search military history in vain," concluded Morison, "for an operation more fatal to the aggressor."[47]

But to the Japanese, their decision, though it involved risks, was not a reckless and foolhardy one. It was based, for one thing, on the expectation that the United States would prefer to negotiate rather than fight. The Japanese leaders fully appreciated the industrial potential of the United States and that nation's ability to fight a major war on two fronts. But they had to accept this risk, as General Tojo said, "in order to tide over the present crisis for self-existence and self-defense."[48]

The Japanese, it must be emphasized, did not seek the total defeat of the United States and had no intention of invading this country. They planned to fight a war of limited objectives and, having once secured these objectives, to set up a defense in such depth that the United States would find a settlement favorable to Japan an attractive alternative to a long and costly war. To the Japanese leaders this seemed an entirely reasonable view. But there were fallacies in this concept which Admiral Yamamoto had pointed out when he wrote that it would not be enough "to take Guam and the Philippines, not even Hawaii and San Francisco." To gain victory, he

---

[47]Morison, *The Rising Sun in the Pacific, 1931-April 1942*, p. 132.
[48]Political Strategy Prior to Outbreak of War, Part V, p. 37.

warned his countrymen, they would have "to march into Washington and sign the treaty in the White House."[49] Here was a lesson about limited wars that went unheeded then and is still often neglected. Perhaps the major Japanese error was the decision to attack the United States at all. The strategic objectives of the Japanese lay in southeast Asia and if they had limited their attacks to British and Dutch territory the United States might not have entered the war. Such a course would have involved risks but it would have forced the United States to act first. And there was, in 1941, strong opposition to a move that would have appeared to a large part of the American people as an effort to pull British and Dutch chestnuts out of the fire. As it was, the Japanese relieved the Roosevelt administration of the necessity of making a very difficult choice. The alternatives it faced on December 1941, when the Japanese were clearly moving southward, were either to seek from Congress a declaration of war if Japan attacked the British and the Dutch in southeast Asia or to stand by idly while the Japanese secured the rich resources of Malaya and the Indies which would enable them to prosecute the war in China vigorously to an early end. The Japanese attack on Pearl Harbor with one blow resolved all the problems and mobilized the American people as nothing else could have done.[50]

The Japanese based much of their hope for success on the situation in Europe. The war there favored their plans and they saw little possibility of an early peace. Germany, they believed, would defeat Russia, or at least gain military domination of the European Continent, but they doubted that the Germans would be able to

[49]Masuo Kato, *The Lost War* (New York: Knopf, 1946), p. 89.

[50]Henry L. Stimson and McGeorge Bundy, *On Active Service in Peace and War* (New York: Harper, 1948), p. 390. Evidence on public opinion is not conclusive. A Gallup poll reported in the New York *Times* for February 23, 1941, found that although 56 per cent of those polled were in favor of an effort "to keep Japan from seizing the Dutch East Indies and Singapore," only 39 per cent supported risking war in such an attempt. Again, in August 1941, a *Fortune* poll showed that 33.7 per cent of those polled were in favor of defending the Philippines, East Indies, and Australia, and only 22.3 per cent favored the defense of an unspecified portion of this area. The conclusion of John W. Masland, writing in 1941, was that "powerful commercial interests and articulate isolationist pressure groups" opposed American opposition to Japan; see John W. Masland, "American Attitudes Toward Japan," *Annals of the American Academy of Political and Social Science* (May, 1941), p. 165. See also *Public Opinion, 1935-1946*, prepared by Mildred Strunk under the editorial direction of Hadley Cantril (Princeton: Princeton University Press, 1951), p. 1077.

launch a successful invasion of England. At any rate, it was clear that both the British and Russians would be too preoccupied in Europe for some time to come to devote their attention to the Far East. The United States had an important stake in Europe, too, and would be unwilling to concentrate its forces in the Pacific, the Japanese estimated, so long as the outcome in Europe remained in doubt.

The possibility of avoiding war with the United States was seriously considered and discussed at length in Tokyo, but the Japanese were apparently convinced that if they moved south the United States would go to war. Their only hope lay in knocking out the American Fleet and removing the Philippine threat, so that the United States would be unable to take offensive action for from eighteen months to two years. By that time, the Japanese estimated, they would have secured the southern area and established themselves firmly behind a strong outer line of defense. With the resources thus won—such as oil, rubber, bauxite—they would be in a position to wage defensive warfare almost indefinitely. The United States, they reasoned, would be unable to sustain the major effort required to break through this defensive screen in the face of the losses imposed by a determined and well-trained foe. As a result, the Japanese leaders felt justified in their hopes that the United States would be forced to compromise and allow Japan to retain a substantial portion of her gains, thus leaving the nation in a dominant position in Asia.

This plan was not entirely unrealistic in 1941, but it completely overlooked the American reaction to Pearl Harbor and the refusal of the United States to fight a limited war—or Japan's ability to so limit it. The risks were recognized, but the alternatives were not estimated correctly. Yet, even had the Japanese appreciated fully the extent of the risks, they would probably have made the same decision. To them, correctly or incorrectly, the only choice was submission or war, and they chose the latter in the hope that their initial advantages and the rapid conquest of southern Asia would offset the enormous industrial and military potential of the enemy.

In the final analysis, the Japanese decision for war was the result of the conviction, supported by the economic measures imposed by the United States and America's policy in China, that the United States was determined to reduce Japan to a position of secondary importance. The nation, Tojo and his supporters felt, was doomed if it did not meet the challenge. In their view, Japan had no alternative but to go to war while she still had the power to do so. She might lose, but defeat was better than humiliation and submission. "Japan entered the war," wrote a prince of the Imperial family, "with a tragic determination and in desperate self-abandonment." If she lost, "there will be nothing to regret because she is doomed to collapse even without war."[51]

RAYMOND ESTHUS
President Roosevelt's Commitment to Britain To Intervene in a Pacific War

Raymond Esthus (born 1925) is Professor of History at Tulane University. He has written a number of articles and *From Enmity to Alliance: U.S.-Australian Relations, 1931-1941* (1964) and *Theodore Roosevelt and Japan* (1966).

SHORTLY BEFORE the Japanese attacked Pearl Harbor, the United States naval attaché in Singapore, John M. Creighton, sent the American naval commander at Manila a telegram stating that Britain had been assured of armed support by the United States if Japan launched an attack against British or Dutch possessions or against Thailand. The telegram, which reported British instructions to the Far East commander, Sir Robert Brooke-Popham, read in full:

Brooke-Popham received Saturday from War Department London: "We have now received assurance of American armed support in cases as follows: (a) we are obliged [to] execute our plans to forestall Japs landing Isthmus of Kra or take action in reply to Nips invasion any other part of Siam, (b) if Dutch Indies are attacked and we go to their defense, (c) if Japs attack us the British. Therefore without reference to London put plan in action if first you have good info Jap expedition advancing with the apparent intention of landing in Kra [or] if the Nips violate any part of Thailand. If NEI [Netherlands

[51]Statement of Prince Naruhiko Higashikuni, 9 Jun 49, ATIS, G-12 FEC, copy in OCMH.

Reprinted by permission from *The Mississippi Valley Historical Review*, L (June 1963), pp. 28-38.

East Indies] are attacked put into operation plans agreed upon between British and Dutch."[1]

Since the revelation of this telegram in the Pearl Harbor investigation, historians have differed about the truth of the facts which the telegram reported. At issue is the important question of whether Roosevelt gave assurances to the British government that the United States would come to the support of the British if Japan limited her attack to non-American territory. William L. Langer and S. Everett Gleason, after exhaustive research in United States and Japanese records, said that "the truth or falsity of this telegram is among the important problems relating to Pearl Harbor which have yet to be verified." Finding no confirmation in the available records and viewing the inconclusive evidence against the background of the repeated refusals of Roosevelt and Secretary of State Cordell Hull in 1941 to give such assurances, Langer and Gleason inclined to the view that no assurances were given. "Until further evidence to the contrary is forthcoming," they concluded, "it must be assumed that only the launching of Japanese attacks on American as well as on British and Dutch territory on December 7, 1941, finally resolved the dilemma which consistently plagued the Roosevelt administration in its efforts to reconcile the demands of national security with the limitations imposed by the Constitution, the Congress, and public opinion."[24] In the decade since Langer and Gleason wrote, enough information has been revealed from the British side, particularly with the publication in 1962 of Sir Llewellyn Woodward's *British Foreign Policy in the Second World War,* to warrant a re-examination of the question.

Throughout 1941 the British government had continually pressed the Roosevelt administration for assurance of armed support in the event of war with Japan. Before the Japanese move into southern Indochina in July, 1941, the British entreaties elicited little response in Washington. When Harry Hopkins went to London early in 1941 as Roosevelt's personal representative, British leaders attempted to gain assurances through him. "Eden asked me repeatedly," Hopkins wrote, "what our country would do if Japan attacked Singapore or

[1]John M. Creighton to Admiral Thomas C. Hart, December 6, 1941, United States, Congress, *Pearl Harbor Attack: Hearings before the Joint Committee on the Investigation of the Pearl Harbor Attack* (39 parts, Washington, 1946), X, 5082-83.

[2]William L. Langer and S. Everett Gleason, *The Undeclared War, 1940-1941* (New York, 1953), 921. See also Herbert Feis, *The Road to Pearl Harbor: The Coming of the War between the United States and Japan* (Princeton, 1950), 334-38.

the Dutch East Indies, saying it was essential to their policy to know."[3] Later, in April, the British Ambassador, Lord Halifax, and the Australian Minister, Richard G. Casey, urged Secretary Hull to approve a joint warning, threatening Japan with American intervention in the event of an attack on British or Dutch possessions in the Pacific.[4] To all the British and Australian pleas, Washington turned a deaf ear.

When the Japanese advanced into southern Indochina in July, in an obvious preparation for a southward attack, the Roosevelt administration began to move gradually, if hesitatingly, toward giving the British some assurance. As Japanese troops set up bases in southern Indochina, Roosevelt told Ambassador Kichisaburo Nomura that if Japan attacked the Dutch, Britain would assist the Dutch, and "in view of our own policy of assisting Great Britain, an exceedingly serious situation would immediately result."[5] But at this critical juncture Britain and the Dominions were seeking a firmer assurance. Drastic oil sanctions were then being invoked against Japan by the United States, Britain, the Dominions, and the Dutch, and the danger of war was greatly increased. Australia, anxious for a firmer statement of the American position, cabled the United Kingdom on July 25:

> It seems to us entirely feasible that in notifying the readiness of the British Commonwealth to concert with the United States in proposed economic action, the British Ambassador should intimate that we clearly realise the possible consequences of action, both for ourselves and the Netherlands, and that we assume that the United States Government also realises them. In a discussion which will arise on this basis, an indication of the United States' attitude will certainly appear. The nature of this in all probability will constitute the satisfactory understanding which we feel to be essential. We consider it vital, however, that the question should be raised in one form or another.[6]

[3]Robert S. Sherwood, *Roosevelt and Hopkins* (New York, 1948), 259, 428.

[4]British Embassy to the Department of State, April 21, 1941; Memorandum by Cordell Hull, April 22, 1941; Richard G. Casey to Hull, April 22, 1941, Department of State, *Foreign Relations of the United States: Diplomatic Papers, 1941* (7 vols., Washington, 1956-1961), V, 134-38.

[5]Memorandum by Sumner Welles, Acting Secretary of State, July 24, 1941, Department of State, *Papers Relating to the Foreign Relations of the United States: Japan, 1931-1941* (2 vols., Washington, 1943), II, 527-30.

[6]Paul Hasluck, *The Government and the People, 1939-1941 (Australia in the War of 1939-1945)* (Canberra, 1952), 526.

When it developed that sufficient time was not available to act on the Australian request prior to the implementation of sanctions, Australia made additional efforts to get a commitment from Washington. Australian Prime Minister Robert G. Menzies cabled the United Kingdom and the Dominion prime ministers on July 30: "If the Americans feel in their hearts that in the event of warlike retaliation by Japan they could not remain aloof from the conflict, surely they can be made to see that a plain indication by them to Japan at this stage would probably avoid war. I recognize the traditional reluctance of the United States to enter into outside commitments in advance, but where the commitment seems inevitable, there is everything to be gained by promptly accepting it, and everything to be lost by delay."[7]

A few days later in Washington Acting Secretary of State Sumner Welles made a statement to the British Ambassador and the Australian Minister which marked a substantial progression toward the sought-after commitment. Welles said that though no "definite" commitment could be made, the United States would probably come to the aid of the Commonwealth in a Pacific war. If Japan attacked Singapore and the East Indies, he said, a situation would be created which could not be tolerated by the United States. "By this I said I meant," Welles recorded in his memorandum of the conversation, "that such a situation as that in my judgment would sooner or later inevitably result in war with Japan. I said that Lord Halifax was fully familiar with our constitutional system and that consequently no definite commitments or threats to this effect could officially be made."[8]

At the Atlantic Conference, which convened on August 9, the British gained additional hope of American armed support, though the United States again refused to make a definite commitment. On the first day of the conference Welles went over the whole ground with Sir Alexander Cadogan of the Foreign Office. If Japan attacked, said Welles, public opinion in the United States would be the determining factor in any decision reached by the Congress and he personally believed that public opinion would support intervention if Japan attacked the Netherlands East Indies or British possessions. If this estimate was correct, he concluded, any prior commitment by the United States would have no practical effect. If a commitment

[7] *Ibid.*, 527.
[8] Memorandum by Welles, August 4, 1941, *Foreign Relations, 1941*, V, 254-56.

were made, though, and it became known, it would have a bad effect upon American public opinion.[9]

American spokesmen thus made clear that they could not give Britain what she most wanted, and British gains from the conference were limited. Churchill exacted a promise from Roosevelt to give a stiff warning to Japan, but when Hull got through watering it down it fell substantially short of what Britain desired. Whereas the original draft of the statement said that in the event of further Japanese aggression the United States would have to take measures which "might result in war," the warning given to Nomura merely said the United States would take steps necessary "toward insuring the safety and security of the United States."[10]

Despite the weakness of the American warning, there is nevertheless reason to believe that the British were greatly encouraged as a result of the talks at the Atlantic Conference. When in late August an Australian proposal for a joint warning to Japan was again raised and again set aside, London sent to Canberra a clear statement of its expectations of American support: "You should, however, be aware that the general impression derived by our representative at the Atlantic meeting was that, although the United States could not make any satisfactory declaration on the point, there was no doubt that in practice we could count on United States support if, as a result of Japanese aggression, we became involved in war with Japan."[11]

The British belief that they could count on American armed support "in practice" was soon reinforced when the United States requested the use of air bases on British territory in the Far East. According to War Department instructions to General Douglas MacArthur, who headed the new Far Eastern Command, the United States planned to integrate the defense of the Philippines, Australia, the Dutch East Indies, and Singapore through improvement of operating fields throughout the area and supplying them with fuel, bombs, and ammunition.[12] On October 15 the United States sent

[9]Memorandum by Welles, August 9, 1941, *ibid.,* I, 345-54.

[10]Memorandum by Welles, August 10 and 11, 1941, *ibid.,* I, 354-63; Winston S. Churchill, *The Grand Alliance* (Boston, 1950), 439-40, 448; Memorandum by Hull, August 17, 1941, and Oral Statements handed by Roosevelt to Nomura, August 17, 1941, *Foreign Relations: Japan, 1931-1941,* II, 554-59.

[11]Hasluck, *The Government and the People,* 534.

[12]Mark S. Watson, *Chief of Staff: Prewar Plans and Preparations (United States Army in World War II)* (Washington, 1950), 424-43.

formal requests to Britain, the Netherlands, Australia, and New Zealand, requesting co-operation in the development of bases at Singapore, Port Darwin, Rabaul, Port Moresby, and Rockhampton.[13] The ink was hardly dry on the American requests when favorable responses arrived in Washington. As it turned out, the war came before work was undertaken on the bases, but the American request for their use nevertheless underlined the expectations which Churchill had taken home from the Atlantic Conference.

In early November, when United States-Japanese negotiations were reaching a crucial stage, the Roosevelt administration edged a bit closer to the position that Britain wished it to take. Though a proposal by Churchill for a joint warning to Japan was turned down, the Joint Board of the Army and Navy, to which the warning proposal had been referred, marked out for the President a line beyond which Japan should not be allowed to proceed. Military action should be undertaken, the Board stated, if Japan attacked the territories of the British Commonwealth or the Netherlands East Indies or if Japanese forces moved into Thailand west of the hundredth meridian, or into Thailand's Kra Isthmus south of the tenth parallel, or into Portuguese Timor, New Caledonia, or the Loyalty Islands.[14]

By the end of November the showdown in the Far East was fast approaching and the issues dealt with in the Joint Board's recommendations ceased to be matters of speculation and became considerations of immediate practical concern. On November 26 Hull abandoned efforts to reach a *modus vivendi* with Japan, and in the subsequent days Washington and London, with much anxiety and soul-searching, awaited the Japanese attack. Reports poured into Washington and London of Japanese troop movements indicating an imminent attack on Thailand and possibly other areas. At Singapore, Brooke-Popham, the British commander in chief, agonized over whether to anticipate a Japanese movement into Thailand's Kra Isthmus, the area just north of Malaya. The British had developed plans for occupation of the Isthmus, Operation MATADOR, but hesitated to incur the responsibility for the first

[13]Hull to Ambassador John G. Winant (London), telegram, October 15, 1941, and Hull to Minister Nelson T. Johnson (Canberra), telegram October 15, 1941, *Foreign Relations, 1941*, I, 573-75; Hasluck, *The Government and the People*, 537-38.

[14]*Pearl Harbor Attack*, XIV, 1061-67.

violation of Thai territory. On November 28 Brooke-Popham urged upon the Chiefs of Staff in London the vital importance of being able to undertake MATADOR without delay if escorted Japanese convoys approached the coast of Thailand. On December 1 the Chiefs of Staff informed him that the United States government had been asked for an assurance of armed support if action were taken to forestall the Japanese on the Isthmus of Kra.[15]

In these last days before the outbreak of war, the Roosevelt administration, it is now known, finally succumbed to the British entreaties for assurance. Throughout 1941, until the end of November, Roosevelt, Hull, and Welles had consistently stated to the British that under the United States Constitution no commitment for armed support could be given. But despite the sound constitutional basis of this position, little by little the administration had moved toward giving the British the assurance they sought. Until December 1, the shift was slow, at times almost imperceptible, but nevertheless steadily in the direction of a commitment.

On December 1 the continuing erosion finally produced an avalanche. On the afternoon of that day Roosevelt told British Ambassador Halifax that if Japan attacked the Dutch or the British "we should obviously all be together." Two days later, in another conversation with the Ambassador, Roosevelt removed any possibility of ambiguity concerning the nature of American support. He said that when he talked of giving support to the British and the Dutch he meant "armed support." In these two conferences with Halifax, Roosevelt went even further. He made it clear that the promised aid would be forthcoming even if Britain went to war as a result of a Japanese attack on Thailand. Roosevelt told Halifax that he agreed with the British plan for operations in the Kra Isthmus if Japan attacked Thailand and that Britain could count on American support, though in this contingency support might not be forthcoming for a few days.[16]

On December 5 the Chiefs of Staff in London informed Brooke-Popham of the American commitment. The message stated that assurance of armed support from the United States had been received and that it covered three contingencies: (a) if Britain found

[15]S. Woodburn Kirby, *The War against Japan (History of the Second World War)* (3 vols. to date, London, 1957-), I, 76-78, 173-74.

[16]Sir Llewellyn Woodward, *British Foreign Policy in the Second World War (History of the Second World War)* (London, 1962), 186-87.

it necessary either to take action to forestall a Japanese landing in the Kra Isthmus or to occupy part of the Isthmus as a counter to the Japanese violation of any other part of Thailand; (b) if the Japanese attacked the Netherlands East Indies and Britain at once went to the support of the Netherlands; (c) if the Japanese attacked British territory. The message went on to authorize Brooke-Popham to order MATADOR without reference to Whitehall if reconnaissance showed that escorted Japanese ships were approaching the Isthmus or if the Japanese violated any other part of Thailand, and to put into effect the plans agreed to with the Dutch if the Japanese attacked the Netherlands East Indies.[17] On the same day the Dominions were also informed of the American commitment.[18]

The text of the message to Brooke-Popham brings us once again to the telegram sent from Singapore on December 6 by the American naval attaché, Captain Creighton. Its wording was identical with that of the message sent to Brooke-Popham. When Creighton was questioned by the joint congressional committee investigating the Pearl Harbor attack he was unable to recall the source of the information in his telegram of December 6; he characterized it as hearsay, nothing more than the report of a rumor.[19] It is now apparent, however, that he was transmitting a verbatim copy of the message that had been sent to Brooke-Popham and the Dominions.

The sum of this evidence from the United Kingdom and Dominion governments is sufficient to justify the conclusion that Roosevelt gave Britain a commitment of armed support in the case of a Japanese attack on British or Dutch territory or on Thailand. Several aspects of the question, however, are still not entirely clear. Whether Roosevelt's commitment extended to a move by Britain into the Kra Isthmus *prior* to a Japanese attack is in doubt. The British, as indicated by the messages sent to Brooke-Popham and the Dominions, took the commitment to cover a prior movement by

[17]Kirby, *The War against Japan,* I, 175.

[18]Hasluck, *The Government and the People,* 555-56; Lionel Wigmore, *The Japanese Thrust (Australia in the War of 1939-1945)* (Canberra, 1957), 109; F. L. W. Wood, *The New Zealand People at War: Political and External Affairs (Official History of New Zealand in the Second World War, 1939-1945)* (Wellington, 1958), 205-206.

[19]Creighton's testimony is in *Pearl Harbor Attack,* X, 5080-89; Admiral Hart's testimony concerning Creighton's telegram of December 6 is in *ibid.,* X, 4802-4809, 4818-19; the interrogatories and replies of Brigadier General Francis G. Brink, who was at Singapore with Creighton, are in *ibid.,* XI, 5514-16; Welles's testimony on the matter is in *ibid.,* II, 491-96, 502-504, 508.

Britain into the Isthmus. According to Woodward's account, however, Roosevelt told Halifax that he approved of Britain's plans regarding the Isthmus *if Japan attacked Thailand.* In practice it is virtually impossible to make a precise distinction between the two cases. The British planned to move into the area if Japan attacked another part of Thailand or if a Japanese expedition by sea was seen heading for the Isthmus. In this latter contingency it would be difficult to judge which side was taking prior action. It is likely that Roosevelt's commitment was sufficiently comprehensive to cover a British move into the Kra Isthmus following the sighting of a Japanese expedition approaching that area. It is doubtful, however, that the commitment extended to a British penetration of Thai territory prior to the sighting of such an expedition.[20] One point is clear from the available evidence. The British were not anxious to press the American commitment on prior action. When the critical moment of decision arrived, both Brooke-Popham and the British Minister to Thailand calculated the risks of prior action to be too great. MATADOR was never ordered into operation.[21]

An even more perplexing question which remains unanswered is whether, in the event no American territory were attacked, Roosevelt would have committed American armed forces to battle without a declaration of war by Congress. Critics of Roosevelt might conclude from the evidence now available that he would have done so. Such a conclusion is not necessarily valid. Roosevelt and his entire cabinet were convinced that the American public would support intervention to aid Britain.[22] It is possible, and indeed likely, that Roosevelt's commitment was based upon his confidence that Congress would immediately approve a proposal for a declaration of war if Britain went to war with Japan in defense of British or Dutch territory. In the case of war resulting from an attack on Thailand, his confidence was doubtless not so great. This probably accounts for

---

[20]Further clarification of this question may be possible when the full texts of Halifax's dispatches from Washington are opened to historians, but unless the British government modifies its fifty-year rule, those records will not be available until the year 1991. It is unlikely that records of the Roosevelt-Halifax conversations will ever be found on the American side, for it was Roosevelt's conscious policy not to record conversations.

[21]Kirby, *The War against Japan,* I, 177-86; Wigmore, *The Japanese Thrust,* 121-25. See also Denis Richards and Hilary St. George Saunders, *Royal Air Force, 1939-1945* (3 vols., London, 1953-1954), II, 14-17.

[22]Henry L. Stimson and McGeorge Bundy, *On Active Service in Peace and War* (New York, 1947), 390.

his remark to Halifax that in this case the armed support might be delayed for several days. Another indication that the constitutional problem was still with Roosevelt had been given when the question of a formal guarantee to Thailand was discussed on December 1. Roosevelt told Halifax that the United States Constitution did not allow him to give such a guarantee.

The events in Washington between December 1 and December 7 also make it highly probable that Roosevelt, despite his assurances to the British, intended to present the issue of peace or war to Congress. During those anxious days Roosevelt and his cabinet members were working over drafts of the message which would go to Congress. As Roberta Wohlstetter has observed in the most recent account of these happenings: "All the evidence would suggest that the attention of the President and his top advisers was centered on the most effective way to urge Congress that America should join with Great Britain in a war to stop further Japanese aggression."[23] Moreover, Harry Hopkins had a long conversation with Roosevelt six weeks after Pearl Harbor in which they talked about the constitutional problem they had faced. The manner in which it was discussed gives a strong indication that Roosevelt had not regarded his assurances to Britain as eliminating the need of congressional implementation of those assurances.[24]

The whole tenor of the discussions with Britain in 1941 supports the belief that both Roosevelt and the British were constantly aware of the constitutional problem and knew that it could not be ignored. Though some of the Dominions, particularly Australia, evidenced impatience with Roosevelt's "constitutional difficulties," the United Kingdom never took that position. Churchill even lectured the Dominions on occasion, telling them that it would be a mistake to push Roosevelt too far ahead of American public opinion.[25] The British were aware, therefore, that Roosevelt, in his conferences with Halifax on December 1 and 3, was promising more than he could guarantee.

The evidence also indicates that despite his commitment to the British, Roosevelt was not in a war-making mood in the last days before Pearl Harbor. Instead of welcoming a Pacific war as an occasion for intervention in the European war, Roosevelt was

[23]Roberta Wohlstetter, *Pearl Harbor: Warning and Decision* (Stanford, 1962), 275.
[24]Sherwood, *Roosevelt and Hopkins*, 427-29.
[25]Hasluck, *The Government and the People*, 547-48.

clutching at the straws of peace. When Halifax came to the White House on December 4 to express appreciation for Roosevelt's assurances, the President said that he had not given up all hopes of a temporary agreement with the Japanese. The Japanese envoy, Saburo Kurusu, had informed him indirectly that an approach to the Emperor might still secure a truce, and therefore, Roosevelt told Halifax, he wished to have warnings to Japan delayed until after his appeal to the Emperor. Roosevelt also said that the Japanese would require some economic relief. He did not have much hope that a truce could be arranged, he confided to Halifax, but he could not miss even the chance of a settlement.[26]

While Roosevelt was still hoping for peace, the march of events overtook his timetable for further diplomatic moves. As the fateful hour of the Japanese attack approached, the British faced the long-dreaded extension of the war with a new confidence. Roosevelt's commitment for armed support, whatever the implied qualifications, was an assurance of great value. The British now knew that Roosevelt believed the American public would accept war in the Pacific and that his leadership would be dedicated to bringing the country into the war if Japan attacked. By this assurance the British could see for the first time the vision of final victory in the World War.

[26]Woodward, *British Foreign Policy in the Second World War,* 187-88. Two days later Roosevelt still entertained a faint hope that his appeal to the Emperor might prevent the outbreak of war. When on December 6 the Australian Minister, Casey, urged him to send a strong warning to Japan, the President told him that he wished to await the outcome of his appeal to the Emperor before issuing a warning. *Pearl Harbor Attack,* XI, 5165-66.

Suggestions for Further Reading

The literature on the United States and the origins of the Second World War continues to grow as new records (especially those of the British and French governments) become available and as perspectives change and historians search out new problems. Literature published prior to 1957 has been succinctly reviewed in the first selection in this volume by Wayne S. Cole. The Franklin D. Roosevelt Library has published a valuable annotated compendium, *The Era of Franklin D. Roosevelt: A Selected Bibliography of Periodical and Dissertation Literature, 1945-1966* (Hyde Park, N.Y., 1967). The bibliography that follows includes some of the more important works on American, and related European and Far Eastern, foreign policy that have appeared between 1957 and 1969. (Works appearing in whole or in part in this volume are not listed below.)

General or survey works include Selig Adler, *The Uncertain Giant, 1921-1941: American Foreign Policy Between the Wars* (New York, 1965), Robert A. Divine, *The Reluctant Belligerent: American Entry into World War II* (New York, 1965), Jean-Baptiste Duroselle, *From Wilson to Roosevelt: Foreign Policy of the United States, 1913-1945* (Cambridge, Mass., 1963), Denna F. Fleming, *The Cold War and Its Origins, 1917-1960,* 2 vols. (London, 1961), André Fontaine, *A History of the Cold War: From the October Revolution to the Korean War, 1917-1960,* trans. D. D. Paige (London, 1968), James J. Martin, *American Liberalism and World Politics, 1931-1941,* 2 vols. (New York, 1964), William A. Williams, *The Tragedy of American Diplomacy* (Cleveland, 1959), and John E. Wiltz, *From Isolation to War, 1931-1941* (New York, 1968).

The varieties of political and economic attitudes that helped mold American foreign policy are dealt with in Selig Adler, *The Isolationist Impulse: Its Twentieth Century Reaction* (New York, 1957), Bernard J. Fensterwald, Jr., "The Anatomy of American 'Isolationism' and Expansionism," *Journal of Conflict Resolution,* II (June & Dec. 1958), Lloyd G. Gardner, *Economic Aspects of New Deal Diplomacy* (Madison, Wis., 1964), and Manfred Jonas, *Isolationism in America, 1935-1941* (Ithaca, N.Y., 1966), and "Pro-Axis Sentiment and American Isolationism," *The Historian,* XXIX (Feb. 1967). Neutrality and security are discussed in Wayne S. Cole, "Senator Key Pittman and American Neutrality Policies," *Mississippi Valley Historical Review,* XLVI (Mar. 1960), and Robert A. Divine, *The Illusion of Neutrality* (Chicago, 1962) and "Franklin D.
222

Roosevelt and Collective Security, 1933," *Mississippi Valley Historical Review*, XLVIII (June 1961). Pacifism, public participation in making foreign policy, refugee problems, and business interests are analyzed in John K. Nelson, *The Peace Prophets: American Pacifist Thought, 1919-1941* (Chapel Hill, N.C., 1967), Richard D. Burns and W. Addams Dixon, "Foreign Policy and the 'Democratic Myth': The Debate on the Ludlow Amendment," *Mid-America*, XLVII (Oct. 1968), Arthur D. Morse, *While Six Million Died: A Chronicle of American Apathy* (New York, 1968), David S. Wyman, *Paper Walls: America and the Refugee Crisis, 1938-1941* (Amherst, Mass., 1968), and Gabriel Kolko, "American Business and Germany, 1930-1941," *Western Political Quarterly*, XV (Dec. 1962), and John E. Wiltz, *In Search of Peace: The Senate Munitions Inquiry, 1934-36* (Baton Rouge, La., 1963).

General studies of the coming of war in Europe in 1939 include the controversial and significant A. J. P. Taylor, *The Origins of the Second World War* (London, 1961), the political science oriented work by William J. Newman, *The Balance of Power in the Interwar Years, 1919-1939* (New York, 1968), and Keith Eubank, *The Origins of World War II* (New York, 1969). Specific European crises, and assessment of American involvement in them, are analyzed in Henderson Braddick, "A New Look at American Policy during the Italo-Ethiopian Crisis," *Journal of Modern History*, XXXIV (Mar. 1962), Robert A. Friedlander, "New Light on the Anglo-American Reaction to the Ethiopian War, 1935-1936," *Mid-America*, XLV (Apr. 1963), and Brice Harris, Jr., *The United States and the Italo-Ethiopian Crisis* (Stanford, 1964). Two accounts of the struggles in Spain are Gabriel Jackson, *The Spanish Republic and the Civil War, 1931-1939* (Princeton, 1965), and Hugh Thomas, *The Spanish Civil War* (New York, 1961); the American dilemma is weighed in Allen Guttmann, *The Wound in the Heart: America and the Spanish Civil War* (New York, 1963), J. David Valaik, "Catholics, Neutrality, and the Spanish Embargo, 1937-1939," *Journal of American History*, LIV (June 1967), and Richard P. Traina, *American Diplomacy and the Spanish Civil War* (Bloomington, Ind., and London, 1968), while the crucial British role is assessed in Wm. Laird Kleine-Ahlbrandt, *The Policy of Simmering: A Study of British Policy During the Spanish Civil War, 1936-1939* (The Hague, 1962).

A general discussion of the Munich Conference is Keith Eubank, *Munich* (Norman, Okla., 1963); still indispensable, however, is the early but classic John W. Wheeler-Bennett, *Munich: Prologue to Tragedy* (London, 1948). Conflicting views of the American role appear in John McVickar Haight, Jr., "France, the United States, and the Munich Conference," *Journal of*

Modern History, XXXII (Dec. 1960), and two Marxist interpretations are, M. Baturin, "The United States and Munich," *International Affairs* [Moscow] V (Apr. 1959), and Andrew Rothstein, *The Munich Conspiracy* (London, 1958).

Biting critiques of British foreign policy are Margaret George, *The Warped Vision: British Foreign Policy, 1933-1938* (Pittsburgh, 1968), and Martin Gilbert and Richad Gott, *The Appeasers* (Boston, 1963).

Analyses of German foreign policy, with inevitable emphasis on Hitler's machinations, are Alan Bullock, *Hitler: A Study in Tyranny,* rev. ed. (New York, 1962), E. Robertson, *Hitler's Pre-War Policy and Military Plans, 1933-1939* (London, 1963), William L. Shirer, *The Rise and Fall of the Third Reich: A History of Nazi Germany* (New York, 1960), D. C. Watt, "The Rome-Berlin Axis: Myth and Reality," *Review of Politics,* XXII (Oct. 1960), and Elizabeth Wiskemann, *The Rome-Berlin Axis: A Study of the Relations Between Hitler and Mussolini,* rev. ed. (London, 1966). Two other careful works are Eugene Davidson, *The Trial of the Germans: An Account of the Twenty-two Defendants Before the International Military Tribunal at Nuremberg* (New York, 1966), and Ernst L. Presseisen, *Germany and Japan: A Study in Totalitarian Diplomacy, 1933-1941* (The Hague, 1958).

Analyses of the intricate and increasingly bad relations between the United States and Germany as seen from the German perspective are Saul Friedländer, *Prelude to Downfall: Hitler and the United States, 1939-1941,* trans. Aline B. and Alexander Werth (New York, 1967), Alton Frye, *Nazi Germany and the American Hemisphere, 1933-1941* (New Haven, 1967), Manfred Jonas, "Prophet Without Honor: Hans Heinrich Dieckhoff's Reports from Washington," *Mid-America,* XLVII (July, 1965), Warren F. Kimball, "Dieckhoff and America: A German's View of German-American Relations, 1937-1941," *The Historian,* XXVII (Feb. 1965), and Gerhard L. Weinberg, "Hitler's Image of the United States," *American Historical Review,* LXIX (July 1964).

Works that deal with America's increasing involvement in the "unde-clared war" in the Atlantic during 1939-1941 are Philip Goodhart, *Fifty Ships that Saved the World: The Foundations of the Anglo-American Alliance* (Garden City, 1965), Theodore A. Wilson, *The First Summit: Roosevelt and Churchill at Placentia Bay, 1941* (Boston, 1969), Andrew I. Schwartz, *America and the Russo-Finnish War* (Washington, D.C., 1960), Robert

Sobel, *The Origins of Interventionism: The United States and the Russo-Finnish War* (New York, 1960), Raymond H. Dawson, *The Decision to Aid Russia, 1941: Foreign Policy and Domestic Politics* (Chapel Hill, N.C., 1959), Warren F. Kimball, *'The Most Unsordid Act': Lend Lease, 1939-1941* (Baltimore, 1969), Mark Lincoln Chadwin, *The Hawks of World War II* (Chapel Hill, N.C., 1968), and T. R. Fehrenbach, *FDR's Undeclared War, 1939 to 1941* (New York, 1967).

American relations with Japan are surveyed in William L. Neumann, *America Encounters Japan: From Perry to MacArthur* (Baltimore, 1963). Roosevelt's famous "quarantine the aggressor" speech is assessed in three different ways in Dorothy Borg, "Notes on Roosevelt's 'Quarantine' Speech," *Political Science Quarterly,* LXXII (Sept. 1957), John McVickar Haight, Jr., "Roosevelt and the Aftermath of the Quarantine Speech," *Review of Politics,* XXIV (Apr. 1962), and Travis Beal Jacobs, "Roosevelt's Quarantine Speech," *The Historian,* XXIV (Aug. 1962). Other short studies of crucial matters include Gerald E. Wheeler, "Isolated Japan: Anglo-American Cooperation, 1927-1936," *Pacific Historical Review,* XXX (May 1961), James H. Herzog, "Influence of the United States Navy in the Embargo of Oil to Japan, 1940-1941," *Pacific Historical Review,* XXXV (August 1966), and John H. Boyle, "The Drought-Walsh Mission to Japan," *Pacific Historical Review,* XXXIV (May 1965). A public pressure group is measured in Donald J. Friedman, *The Road from Isolation: The Campaign of the American Committee for Non-Participation in Japanese Aggression, 1938-1941* (Cambridge, Mass., 1968). The fantastic web of intelligence and military intrigue is examined in Ladislas Farago, *The Broken Seal: "Operation Magic" and the Secret Road to Pearl Harbor* (New York, 1967), and in the brilliant work by Roberta Wohlstetter, *Pearl Harbor: Warning and Decision* (Stanford, 1962).

Crucial aspects of Japan's military diplomacy, which led ultimately to war against America, are studied in Ogata Sadako, *Defiance in Manchuria: The Making of Japanese Foreign Policy, 1931-1932* (Berkeley, 1964), David J. Lu, *From the Marco Polo Bridge to Pearl Harbor: Japan's Entry into World War II* (Washington, 1961), and Takehiko Yoshihashi, *Conspiracy at Mukden: The Rise of the Japanese Military* (New Haven, 1963). Preparation and execution of the plan to attack Pearl Harbor are discussed in John Dean Potter, *Yamomoto: The Man Who Menaced America* (New York, 1965).

Full-length studies of American officials who influenced foreign policy include the two-volume work by John Morton Blum, *From the*

Morgenthau Diaries: Years of Crisis, 1928-1938 and *Years of Urgency, 1939-1941* (Boston, 1959, 1965), Wayne S. Cole, *Senator Gerald P. Nye and American Foreign Relations* (Minneapolis, 1962), Robert Dallek, *Democrat and Diplomat: The Life of William E. Dodd* (New York, 1968), Beatrice Farnsworth, *William C. Bullitt and the Soviet Union* (Bloomington, Ind., 1967), Waldo Heinrichs, Jr., *American Ambassador: Joseph C. Grew and the Development of the United States Diplomatic Tradition* (Boston, 1966), Fred Israel, *Nevada's Key Pittman* (Lincoln, Neb., 1963), Marion McKenna, *Borah* (Ann Arbor, Mich., 1961), Elting E. Morison, *Turmoil and Tradition: A Study of the Life and Times of Henry L. Stimson* (Boston, 1960), and Julius W. Pratt, *Cordell Hull,* 2 vols. (New York, 1964). A good collection of penetrating essays is Norman A. Graebner (ed.), *An Uncertain Tradition: American Secretaries of State in the Twentieth Century* (New York, 1961). Willard Range, *Franklin D. Roosevelt's World Order* (Athens, Ga., 1959) tries to systematize Roosevelt's thinking; two studies that assess two of the more foresighted diplomats are Robert Dallek, "Beyond Tradition: The Diplomatic Careers of William E. Dodd and George S. Messersmith, 1933-1938," *South Atlantic Quarterly,* LXVI (Spring 1967), and Arnold A. Offner, "William E. Dodd; Romantic Historian and Diplomatic Cassandra," *The Historian,* XXIV (Aug. 1962).

List of Persons

(This list includes names of people not identified in the text.)

Austin, Warren, Republican Senator from Vermont, 1931-1946

Bailey, Josiah W., Democratic Senator from North Carolina, 1931-1943

Beck, General Ludwig, Chief of the General Staff of the German Army, 1935-1938

Beneš, Eduard, President of Czechoslovakia, 1935-1938

Bingham, Robert W., United States Ambassador to Great Britain, 1933-1937

Bridges, Styles, Republican Senator from New Hampshire, 1937-1961

Bullitt, William C., United States Ambassador to the Soviet Union, 1933-1936, and Ambassador to France, 1936-1940

Carr, Wilbur J., United States Minister to Czechoslovakia, 1938-1939

Chamberlain, Neville, British Chancellor of the Exchequer, 1931-1937, and Prime Minister, 1937-1940

Chang Chun, General, Chinese Foreign Minister, 1935-1937

Ciano, Count Galeazzo, Italian Foreign Minister, 1936-1943

Connally, Thomas, Democratic Senator from Texas, 1929-1953

Davis, Norman H., United States Ambassador-at-Large, 1933-1938

Dieckhoff, Hans, German Ambassador to the United States, 1937-1938

Dodd, William E., United States Ambassador to Germany, 1933-1938

Fish, Hamilton, Republican Representative from New York, 1919-1943

Grew, Joseph C., United States Ambassador to Japan, 1931-1941

Gurney, John C., Republican Senator from South Dakota, 1939-1945

Halifax, Viscount Edward, British Foreign Secretary, 1938-1940, and Ambassador to the United States, 1940-1946

Hassell, Ulrich von, German Ambassador to Italy, 1932-1938

Henlein, Konrad, leader of the Sudeten German Nazi Party, 1933-1938

Hirota, Koki, Japanese Foreign Minister, 1933-1936, 1937-1938, and Prime Minister, 1936-1937

Hornbeck, Stanley, Chief, Division of Far Eastern Affairs, United States Department of State, 1928-1937

Ickes, Harold L., United States Secretary of the Interior, 1933-1945

Johnson, Nelson T., United States Minister to China, 1929-1935, and Ambassador to China, 1935-1941

Kawagoe, Shigeru, Japanese Ambassador to China, 1935-1938

Kennedy, Joseph P., United States Ambassador to Great Britain, 1938-1940

Kordt, Erich, Counselor in the German Embassy, London, 1936-1938

Kordt, Theodor, Counselor in the German Embassy, London, 1938-1939

Kurusu, Saburo, Japanese Ambassador to Germany, 1939-1940

McKellar, Kenneth, Democratic Representative from Tennessee, 1916-1941

Marshall, General George C., Chief of Staff of the United States Army, 1939-1945

Matsuoka, Yosuke, Japanese Foreign Minister, 1940-1941

Messersmith, George S., United States Minister to Austria, 1934-1937, and Assistant Secretary of State, 1937-1940

Moffat, Jay Pierrepont, Chief, Division of Western European Affairs, United States Department of State, 1933-1935, 1937-1940

Morgenthau, Henry, Jr., United States Secretary of the Treasury, 1934-1945

Ott, General Eugen, German Ambassador to Japan, 1938-1942

Pittman, Key, Democratic Senator from Nevada, 1913-1941

Raeder, Admiral Erich, Commander in Chief of the German Navy, 1935-1943

Ribbentrop, Joachim von, German Ambassador to Great Britain, 1936-1937, and Foreign Minister, 1938-1945

Rosenman, Judge Samuel I., adviser and speech writer for President Franklin D. Roosevelt, 1933-1945

Schulenberg, Count Friedrich Werner von der, German Ambassador to the Soviet Union, 1934-1941

Stahmer, Heinrich, German Special Envoy to Japan, 1940

Stark, Admiral Harold R., Chief of United States Naval Operations, 1939-1942

Stimson, Henry L., United States Secretary of State, 1929-1933, and Secretary of War, 1940-1945

Weizsäcker, Ernst von, State Secretary in the German Foreign Ministry, 1938-1943

Welles, Sumner, United States Under Secretary of State, 1936-1943

Wheeler, Burton K., Republican Senator from Montana, 1923-1947

Willkie, Wendell, Republican candidate for President of the United States, 1940

Wilson, Sir Horace, Chief Industrial Adviser to the British Government, 1930-1939

Wilson, Hugh R., United States Minister to Switzerland, 1927-1937, Assistant Secretary of State, 1937, and Ambassador to Germany, 1938

Yoshida, Shigero, Japanese Ambassador to Great Britain, 1936-1939